THE ART OF RUNNING FASTER

Julian Goater

Don Melvin

Human Kinetics

Library of Congress Cataloging-in-Publication Data

Goater, Julian, 1953-
  The art of running faster / Julian Goater, Don Melvin.
     p. cm.
  Includes bibliographical references and index.
  ISBN-13: 978-0-7360-9550-1 (soft cover)
  ISBN-10: 0-7360-9550-0 (soft cover)
  1. Running. 2. Sprinting. 3. Speed. I. Melvin, Don, 1953- II. Title.
  GV1061.G6 2012
  796.42--dc23

                              2011041295

ISBN-10: 0-7360-9550-0 (print)
ISBN-13: 978-0-7360-9550-1 (print)

Acquisitions Editor: Peter Murphy; **Developmental Editor:** Anne Hall; **Assistant Editor:** Tyler Wolpert; **Copyeditor:** Annette Pierce; **Indexer:** Alisha Jeddeloh; **Graphic Designer:** Joe Buck; **Cover Designer:** Keith Blomberg; **Photographer (cover):** Sergio Ballivian/Aurora Photos/age fotostock; **Photographer (interior):** © Human Kinetics, unless otherwise noted. Photos on pages 62, 63, 64, 65, 66, and 68 © Gary Ford; **Photo Asset Manager:** Laura Fitch; **Visual Production Assistant:** Joyce Brumfield; **Photo Production Manager:** Jason Allen; **Printer:** Versa Press

Human Kinetics books are available at special discounts for bulk purchase. Special editions of book excerpts can also be created to specification. For details, contact the Special Sales Manager at Human Kinetics.

Printed in the United States of America.   10

The paper in this book is certified under a sustainable forestry program.

Human Kinetics
Web site: www.HumanKinetics.com

United States: Human Kinetics
P.O. Box 5076
Champaign, IL 61825-5076
800-747-4457
e-mail: info@hkusa.com

Canada: Human Kinetics
475 Devonshire Road, Unit 100
Windsor, ON N8Y 2L5
800-465-7301 (in Canada only)
e-mail: info@hkcanada.com

Europe: Human Kinetics
107 Bradford Road
Stanningley
Leeds LS28 6AT, United Kingdom
+44 (0)113 255 5665
e-mail: hk@hkeurope.com

Australia: Human Kinetics
57A Price Avenue
Lower Mitcham, South Australia 5062
08 8372 0999
e-mail: info@hkaustralia.com

New Zealand: Human Kinetics
P.O. Box 80
Mitcham Shopping Centre, South Australia 5062
0800 222 062
e-mail: info@hknewzealand.com

E5185

The 1970s and 1980s were indeed a 'Golden Age' of middle and long distance running throughout the world, with British athletes very much at the centre of the drama and excitement which surrounded the sport in those days. The current dominance of African runners can be traced back to this period, but other nations such as New Zealand, USA, Australia, and several European countries were also producing outstanding distance runners who could match, and often get the better of, their African rivals.

This book is based on the legends and 'running lore' which developed in these exciting times, and is dedicated to the numerous coaches, athletes, rivals, and training partners who helped, encouraged, inspired, and influenced me throughout my running career. Some of them are mentioned in these pages, many are not; but it was a privilege to know them, run with them, and briefly share experiences with them that have remained indelibly etched in my memory ever since.

This book is dedicated to all these unwitting contributors, most especially to Bob and Dave, Harry and Steve, and my team-mates and rivals from school, club, university, and RAF days.

Finally, and most importantly, this book is for my remarkable wife Sue who has lived through many of these events, suffered the trials and tribulations of the 'inside story' behind them, and yet has stood by me through thick and thin. She is indeed a saint.

—Julian Goater

And with love to Rodica, whose support was vital to this project, from beginning to end.

—Don Melvin

CONTENTS

PREFACE

I've been a fun runner most of my life. I have no particular talent, but I love running, and at various times I've worked hard to run the fastest times I could. And virtually all the runners I've met, including those working to break an hour for the 10K, take pride in their times. Ten seconds faster than last year. Yes!

A few years ago, I joined a running club. For the first time, I ran wearing a club vest and raced as a member of a team. My performance could affect the finishing position of the entire club. So I tried as hard as I could to get my 10K time back under 45 minutes, where it had been in my 30s. But I was stuck at 48 minutes, maybe 47-something on a good day.

Then I began to work in a small group with Julian Goater just once a week. The workouts were no more than an hour, including warm-up, stretching, cool-down and rests for recovery in the middle. Unlike the long runs I kept pounding out to get fitter, the sessions with Julian left me invigorated. Each workout taught me something new about running and about myself.

I became stronger, more supple, and better able to cope with being out of breath. And, miracle of miracles, at age 53 I broke a personal best for 10 miles I'd set 22 years earlier. My 10K time dropped from 48 minutes to 43-something. And I broke my personal best for the half marathon—by six minutes.

When a middle-aged runner breaks PBs he set in his 30s—and on less mileage, too—something's going on. The principles Julian has developed apply to all runners, young and old, talented and less so, novice and experienced. I know this firsthand, which is why I was eager to work with him on this book. These are principles runners everywhere need to know.

Don Melvin

INTRODUCTION

A State of Grace

This book is about something that many people don't realize exists: the art of running.

The way you move, how you structure your training, how you prepare for races, how you build confidence and determination, and how you develop your tactics—all of these elements are part of the runner's art.

Yet runners often feel their results depend on just two factors. One, of course, is talent. And it's taken for granted that the other is sheer, pig-headed determination, the will to churn out miles week after week. Nothing else, it is thought, will make a runner fitter. Nothing else will help a runner reach his or her potential: Just spend more time on the roads. Grit your teeth and grind it out. And if you don't have time enough to do that, you cannot improve your 10K time or achieve your goal in the marathon. You've reached your limit.

The thing is, that's not true.

Sometimes people, for reasons they cannot explain, achieve performances far superior to their previous bests—far better, even, than their most optimistic expectations.

How does this happen?

In running, as with most sports, craft and hard work can take you a long way. Planning, testing, and monitoring—the scientific approach—have their place. Sebastian Coe and his father, Peter, took a rigorously scientific approach to training, and it helped Seb set 11 world records and win two Olympic golds. Clearly, your training should be based on sound scientific principles.

But Seb's family also had an artistic bent: His mother was an actress; his sister danced with the Royal Ballet. And Seb managed to harness mind and body to achieve a state of grace where timing, balance, relaxation, and concentration worked in perfect harmony—and that was something more than science. Technique, intelligence and the ability to unleash the power of the mind can help take *you* there, as well.

The point is that human beings are individuals. What works for one might not work for another. Running is a thinking person's sport. Adherence to a rigid schedule might take one runner to great heights but lay another low with injuries. Each of us, from club runners to international competitors, needs to pay close attention to what works for us and what does not.

Sometimes, if we tune into our own successes and failures, if we think rather than stumble along by rote, we learn surprising lessons. Permit me one example from my own career.

It was March 1981. The English Cross Country Championships were approaching, and they were important to me. I'd run them ever since my days as a youth, when I'd finished second, and later as a junior, when I'd managed third. I had seen back then what a spectacle the senior men's race was. You'd see 1,800 runners set off in a great, competitive mass, all straining to escape the pack and shoot to the front as they set out on the nine-mile course. The earth would move as they thundered by. The course was three laps of three miles each, and usually by the third circuit the front-runners would lap those in the rear: The whole event was one continuous charge of spattered, heaving men.

The race was very important because it was the selection race for the World Cross Country Championships. The first nine people home would make up the England team. There was only one bite at the cherry, no other way to get to the World Championships. If I wanted to make the team, I needed a good performance that day.

I had been running well all winter, and besides that, I was propelled by a bit of anger. The previous year, 1980, I had not been selected for the British Olympic team despite having run the best 5,000-metre time in the country before the trials. I felt I'd been misled by the selectors, so I had something to prove.

Another factor was motivating me, too, as the National approached. I was a flight lieutenant in the Royal Air Force: Only two months before the race I'd been posted up to Harrogate, in North Yorkshire, nearly 200 miles from my home in North London and my coach, Harry Wilson. So I'd lost all the routine I'd developed down south. I had no complaints—that was part of being a serviceman. But at Harrogate I had been shocked by the bullying attitude of my boss, who told me virtually the day I arrived, 'I'm going to prove to you, you can't be an RAF officer and an international athlete. You've got to choose which you want to be.'

He regularly obstructed my training and racing, giving me extra tasks just as I was about to go on a lunchtime training session with other RAF runners. My mileage that winter was down. But my inner rage was up, so I was fuelled that year by a bit of bloody-mindedness: I'm going to show the bastard I *can* do both, I told myself.

I'd spent most of my life proving to various doubters it was possible to do A-levels *and* be a runner, and that I could get an Oxford degree *and* be an international athlete. But I'd never before experienced such a negative, obstructive attitude.

'You didn't believe all that stuff about the RAF encouraging sport—that was just a bit of propaganda', my boss told me. 'Now you're in the real Air Force. You've got to do your job just like everybody else! We can't have you swanning off all the time while your mates have to cover for you.'

And of course he was right about that. But in my book, that didn't justify him overloading me with more tasks, just to break my spirit and 'prove' that I'd have no time or energy left to run.

So I was feeling fierce and hungry. I felt great relief whenever I was able to break free and run—and even more so when I was able to race.

I'd done well in the Senior National before, notably in 1979, when I'd finished fifth and made the England team for the second time. At the World Cross Country Championship in Limerick that year, I'd finished ninth and was the first English guy across the line, leading England to the team title, though I am unhappy to report that Welshman Steve Jones—another RAF man who was both my good friend and deadly rival—finished two places ahead of me that day.

In 1981, I hoped to do well again and make the team that would go to the World Championship in Madrid. I had reason for optimism: Shortly before being posted to Harrogate, I'd run in the International Athletes Club cross country race at Crystal Palace in south London, where I narrowly beat Steve, edging him out for third place behind two Africans. But two months later, after the upheaval of my move to Yorkshire, Steve beat me in the RAF Championships by 25 seconds or so. Nevertheless, I was encouraged by the way I felt, if not the result, and I knew I was getting back to form.

Then, eight days before the National, I got injured.

In those days, we often raced in shoes that resembled sprint spikes and didn't have much of a heel on them at all. I was racing in the Inter-Services Cross Country Championships in Portsmouth. The course was flat and fast, and I was really flying. On the first lap, we had to run through a large puddle that straddled the course. That's common enough in cross country; you run through the water and pray there's nothing lurking under the surface. This time, though, I was unlucky: I stepped on a brick and bruised my heel. I came up limping a little, but it wasn't too bad.

Next time round, on the final lap, Steve and I were battling each other for first place. And, once again, it was a pretty good battle. 'If I am still standing at the end of the race, hit me with a board and knock me down, because that means I didn't run hard enough,' Steve once said, according to a May 2007 article in *Runner's World*. Steve was a strong, tough, genuine guy—exactly the kind of rival I liked to have. Over the years, I'm sure our friendly rivalry drew out the best from each of us, both for the RAF and for the Great Britain team.

When we reached the big puddle on the second lap, I tried to avoid planting my foot where I had stepped before. But it happened again! A different brick, maybe, but the same heel. This time the pain was so bad I had to stop for a few seconds.

There was only a mile left in the race, and I got going again. Steve beat me by 10 seconds.

I didn't really mind losing the Inter-Services Championships to my RAF team-mate, but I was concerned about overcoming the injury before the National. It was quite painful. Painful to run, painful to walk—painful even to stand on it—and I only had seven days to recover.

The injury happened Friday. The National would take place on Saturday of the following week.

You're always looking for the perfect build-up before a big race. That's invariably affected by several factors: the other races on your schedule, how you feel, and even the weather. But normally, preparing for an important event like the National, I would have put in a longish run the Sunday before the race. And I would still have trained twice a day as the race approached.

But on Saturday I couldn't run a step. So that kind of build-up was out of the question. I iced the heel and hoped for the best.

By Sunday, although it was still painful to walk, I found I could run on my toes round the carpeted lounge at my in-laws' house without pain. Encouraged, but still a bit desperate, I decided to risk a short jog and managed an easy two miles.

But I was still in pain. And the National was now just six days away.

I had a circuit round the Army base at Harrogate where I trained in the evenings. On Monday, although my lunchtime jog on grass had been a bit painful, I thought it might be worth trying to run on a smooth, well-lit road. When I gave it a go it that evening, I discovered I *could* run—and that it was actually more comfortable to run fast than to run slowly, because when I ran fast I was more up on my toes.

So I didn't want to go at a steady pace, and I didn't want to run far. The only option was a short, sharp session. I tried three times one lap, each about 1,400 metres, with two minutes rest between. My heel, well cushioned in trainers, felt OK. I was encouraged. Though I did some short lunchtime jogs on soft grass that week, my real training had to be fast—weight forward, up on my toes, really going for it.

Heartened that I'd had no adverse reaction, I tried just two of the same 1,400-metre efforts on Wednesday, pretty much flat out this time, with a good four minutes of recovery in between.

It was Thursday, just two days before the race, before I tried running in my spikes. This would be the acid test because I knew I would have to run the National in spikes, if I could run it at all. That lunchtime, I did a fast, sharp workout—six times 600 metres hard, with the last 200 flat out each time—on mercifully soft, muddy grass on the Stray, the beautiful open space that runs alongside Harrogate. If I'd suffered an adverse reaction after that session, that would have been it. No National.

So for better or worse, that was it. No long Sunday run and not my normal volume of training, either. Just three short, sharp sessions—quite tough—on the Monday, Wednesday and Thursday before the race.

The championship that year was at Parliament Hill Fields, just north of London, only a few miles from where I lived at the time. Formerly known as Traitors' Hill, it's the entry to Hampstead Heath, 790 acres of hilly heath criss-crossed by paths. I'd been running on Hampstead Heath since I was 13, in school races and for my club, Shaftesbury Harriers, and had won many races there over the years. And for the past three years, up until my move to Yorkshire, I had been training on the Heath two or three times a week. I knew it like the back of my hand.

On Friday I took a day's leave from the RAF to go down to London and check out part of the course, walking and jogging around in trainers, just trying out the heel and seeing how I felt.

'Bit lethargic', I wrote in my training diary. 'Don't feel great. Heel a bit iffy'.

The heel, though it had improved, still hurt. The ground was frozen, and I was worried. If the ground was still hard the following day, I would probably not be able to run. I was praying for a thaw—a thaw and lots of rain.

The next morning the heavens opened and during the Youth and Junior races the Heath became a quagmire. It was, I thought, a wonderful, glorious, beautiful day. Maybe I'd be able to race after all.

All the best runners in the country turn up at the National Championships, of course, and the field that year was particularly strong. Following our recent results, most people predicted Steve Jones would win. He was a terrific runner who went on to set the world record for the marathon in Chicago, and he won the London and New York City marathons, as well.

Being Welsh, he had no need to run the English National, because he would automatically be selected to run for Wales in the World Cross. Indeed, as a Welshman he would normally not even have been eligible to run in the English National; his national race was the Welsh Championships, which he won a record number of times, However, in 1981 the rules allowed him to join an English club, Bristol, and thus become eligible to run in the English National, a much more prestigious race, and a title he clearly wanted to win.

Then there was Mike McLeod, the Elswick Express, who went on to win an Olympic silver in the 10,000 metres in Los Angeles in 1984. Not to mention Dave Moorcroft, who'd won gold in the 1,500 in the 1978 Commonwealth Games and would smash the world record for the 5,000 in 1982. And Dave Clarke, who would finish ninth in the World Cross Country Championships in Rome the following year.

A number of other great names in British distance running were there, too— Mike Tagg, Bernie Ford, Tony Simmons, and up-and-comers Steve Binns and Roger Hackney. Plus nearly 1,800 other runners, as well. I think the only big name missing was Nick Rose, who had won the National the previous year but was running the U.S. Championships this year instead.

After a gentle warm-up with Pat Collins, one of my Shaftesbury teammates, I put on my spikes and tried a few harder efforts. The ground was so soft that I put in my 18-millimetre spikes—the longest you could get—for better grip. All around, runners were doing their pre-race strides. I suddenly recognized one of them, an old school friend named Ben Brown, who had beaten me in the English Schools Championships 10 years earlier. I had hardly seen him since. He recognized me, too, veered in my direction—and promptly fell flat on his face in the mud. It was that slippery and, unbelievably, he was wearing only plimsolls. He got up, we wished each other luck and, to my regret, I never saw him again. But I don't think there's any way he could have got round the course in those shoes.

I felt strong and loose doing my final prerace strides. But the warm-up doesn't tell you much. At Parliament Hill, the point when you know what kind of day you're going to have is after the first three minutes or so of the race. The start is about half a mile uphill. And that can be one hell of a long half mile if you don't feel good, knowing you've still got eight and a half miles to go. Sometimes you get to the top of that first hill and feel like you're ready for the race to be over.

But there's no holding back at the start. In a field that huge, it's important to get near the front right away. If you get trapped in traffic, you're in trouble.

'The start of a world cross country event is like riding a horse in the middle of a buffalo stampede', the American marathoner Ed Eyestone once said after competing in one. 'It's a thrill if you keep up, but one slip and you're nothing but hoof prints'.

And that was certainly true of the National.

The gun sounded and we were off, 1,800 of us, thundering away in a muddy herd. Well, 1,799 of us, actually—Moorcroft was still getting his tracksuit off and he missed the start by half a minute or so. Unaware of this, I reached the top of that first hill in second or third place, feeling comfortable! Then a little dip, a run up another small hill, and I was in first place, only three quarters of a mile into the race. *Without any effort!* What in the world was happening?

I remember telling myself, 'Don't take the lead now.' The plan had been to wait until the start of the third lap, when everybody would be tired and I could use my strength to try to break away. But the way I felt that day, I just couldn't go any slower. It would have been uncomfortable. So I thought to myself, 'It's OK, I'm moving well. Don't worry. Just keep your rhythm and keep going.'

Normally in a race you have to really put the boot in and make a positive move if you want to shake off your rivals. But now I just kept running—and nobody came with me. 'I'm not even trying', I thought. 'Where *are* they?' I can remember the feeling even now, over 30 years later. Absolute magic!

I never look round during a race, so I didn't know how closely people were following me. But a good sign was that I couldn't hear anyone, so I knew I was pretty well clear. But just how far, I could not tell.

I had friends and family around the course—my wife, Sue, and her parents; my coach, Harry; my best running friend, Phil Stamp; and many Shaftesbury Harriers members and supporters, including Dave Bedford and Bob Parker, my old coach. They would yell to me as I passed so I could get some idea of what was going on behind me.

When I came by at the end of the first lap, I found out later, I was a full 40 seconds in front of the next man. 'Take it easy, Julian!' I heard Phil shout nervously. 'Don't get carried away! You've still got six miles to go.'

I knew what was on his mind. He had watched me blow it on the track in a 10,000-metre race at Crystal Palace in 1978—the selection race for the Commonwealth Games that year. In that race, I had intentionally taken the lead early to avoid the puddles and splashing after an absolute deluge just before the race. I had run quite fast for a while. But by the halfway point Brendan Foster had stormed past on his way to setting a new European record of 27:30.5. Mike McLeod and Bernie Ford also came by, and I finished fourth—with just three to be selected. The first of several near misses on my part.

Now Phil was worried I was doing the same thing again. He was trying to encourage me, but I knew what 'take it easy' really meant: The translation was, 'Don't be an idiot! Don't make that same mistake again!'

But I kept to my strong, relaxed rhythm. On the second lap, I heard Phil again, sounding somewhat less worried and rather more exited.

'You're still pulling away!' he shouted. 'It's fantastic! You're a minute ahead.'

He sounded like he couldn't quite believe it—and I certainly couldn't. It was like being in a dream. Absolutely no effort and no distress—I was hardly breathing!

By the end of the second lap, actually, my lead was 68 seconds, which was unheard of. I had three miles left to run and I felt strong as ever. I kept flowing along, easily able to pick my line and avoid the worst of the quagmire, which during the race had spread like a brown scar across the green landscape.

It was surreal. Normally, a race is physical and noisy, with elbowing, heavy breathing and the clamour of rival supporters. The miles fly by in the intensity of the battle. This time everything was eerily quiet round most of the course. Instead of having the battle on which to concentrate, all I could do was maintain my rhythm. It was like riding a wave.

On that last lap, I began to hear shouts of jubilation from everybody—friends, relatives, and even strangers.

'There's no one in sight!' someone yelled.

'You're so far ahead you can stop and have a cup of tea!'

'Well done, Goat! Are you sure you haven't taken a shortcut?'

There were even a few slightly grudging shouts of, 'Well done, Julian', from the Steve Jones supporters.

People meant well but these comments weren't especially helpful. I was in the zone, and I didn't want to switch off and start smiling and waving my arms. I still had a job to do. I remember talking to myself, trying to keep my focus.

'Keep riding that wave', I said.

With nobody pressuring me, I never got out of breath. Up the hills, down the hills, it was all the same—feeling good, my rhythm quick, loose and rangy. If only you could run like that every day!

In the end, spattered with mud, I crossed the line in first place. I was English Cross Country Champion! I had won by miles and followed in the footsteps of my clubmate and one-time training partner, former 10,000-metre world record holder Dave Bedford, one of my heroes.

My first comment to the press was, 'The easiest race of my life. It was just like a club championship.'

Mark Shearman, Athletics Images

The easiest race of my life—but also the best.

It seemed to take ages for other runners to come into view. One newspaper reported that I was in my tracksuit and signing autographs before Dave Clarke, the second-place runner, finished the race.

At any rate, my time was 44:39. Dave Clarke finished in 46:34. I had won by almost two minutes—a record that still stands. Mike McLeod was third. Dave Moorcroft finished fourth—a brilliant run, considering he had missed the start by 30 seconds. My old rival, Steve Jones, took fifth.

And my heel? It never troubled me at all. It was healed.

It's impossible to say exactly what led to such a special day. But *something* had happened: I had run 13 seconds per mile faster than some of the finest runners in the world. And if I wanted to run as well as possible in the future, it was important to figure out why things that day had clicked so well.

Some of it always comes down to factors beyond your control. I was pushed along by anger at not having been selected for the Olympic team the year before and by outrage at my boss at Harrogate. The rain, of course, was a gift. And I found that the overwhelming relief at being able to run, following the fear of being unable to run, produced a powerful mental state.

Beyond that, though, there's no doubt that the different prerace build-up forced on me by my injured heel—my emphasis on faster sessions rather than longer ones—had left me sharp and ready to go. I had to acknowledge that if I hadn't hurt my heel—and had instead followed my normal prerace build-up—I might not have won that race.

I learned a lot from that experience: In future years I tried to replicate that kind of prerace schedule. Although I didn't win any more races by two minutes, I often succeeded in racing better than my fitness would have indicated.

And that is what I want for you. Running, you see, is not just a matter of pure bull-headedness, of just churning out the miles and hoping for the best on race day. You can train smarter and learn what works for you. You can adjust your training so you peak at certain times. This is the holy grail—to find out how to get in the zone, how to harness the power of the mind together with your fitness at just the right time.

A significant part of running smarter is good technique—which means running in such a way that you don't waste precious energy working against yourself.

It's funny. Everybody recognizes the importance of technique in swimming and cycling. Yet many people think it makes little difference in running. But how do the best runners make it look so easy? They flow, their feet lightly touching the ground, seeming almost to fall into the next step. They don't squander their energy; they use it to run faster. These are matters of form, technique, timing, and balance.

And if your aim is to run fast, why practice running slowly? Why perfect the art of plodding? If you want to kick past rivals at the end of a hard 10K, why rehearse slowing down as you get tired? Shouldn't you practice speeding up?

And a lot of runners think stretching is only about preventing injuries. They touch their toes a couple of times, then head off on their 10-mile run. But stretching is also about enabling you to run in a looser, rangier way. When your back and hamstrings are tight, each of the several thousand strides you take in a 10K requires a little more effort. Each stride is a little shorter, too. If two runners have the same level of fitness, the more flexible one will run more easily—and go faster, further, with less effort.

It is also important to think about what, in particular, holds *you* back, what prevents *you* from running faster? Is it your breathing? Your legs? Your core strength, arms, or maybe even your stomach, both in terms of your stomach muscles and your intestinal fortitude? Is it your basic speed that lets you down? You can design sessions to break through those limitations. Which routines have led to have good races and which haven't helped at all? Perhaps you produced your best performance in a training session. Why did it happen then rather than in a race you worked so hard to target?

We live in a so-called technological age, when we expect to be able to explain everything in terms of science—pure cause and effect. We're bombarded with the science of peak performance and the jargon that goes with it: anaerobic thresholds, blood lactate levels, heart rate zones, and so on. But this knowledge by itself does not make you any fitter, nor does the measurement of any set of parameters guarantee a particular performance. You still have to go out and produce the goods on race day, even if the session you did last week was the best you'd ever done. Of course your performance on race day depends on your level of fitness. But many other factors come into play that allow you to get the most out of yourself on the day.

Nobody has yet succeeded in determining the link between any one training session and an improvement in performance. And I don't believe anyone ever will, because the ideal amount and intensity of training, and the speed with which it takes effect, varies from person to person. In fact, these factors even vary at different times for the same person. Sometimes a less intense session can be more beneficial than one that's more intense.

Relying on science alone also ignores the mysterious mental and emotional aspects critical to performance. Visualisation, concentration, psyching yourself up and other people out—that's all well and good. But what stimulates the real power of the mind? How can you harness this power to unlock your true potential?

Even worse, relying only on the science of what makes us run faster creates an inexorable drift toward chemically aided performance—an increasingly depressing trend that is threatening the credibility of top-level competition and harming the image of almost every professional sport.

A welter of scientific studies is available. They often give ultra-technical, complicated, and contradictory advice on how to train and how often and how hard. But there is no magic formula; there are no magic sessions. We are all individuals with different strengths, weaknesses, and lifestyles; and we have different environments in which we train.

I believe a good 50 percent of training is art, not science. It's about intuition and feelings, confidence and belief, tactics and motivation, relaxation and concentration. You need to find what works best for you in order to get in the zone and reach your potential.

When I competed internationally, I had the good fortune to run with a number of superb athletes. Dave Bedford and I ran for the same club and shared the same coach, Bob Parker. Steve Jones and I were friends and rivals in the RAF. Steve Ovett and I also shared a coach, Harry Wilson, and trained together. And we were similar as runners: All of us were strong, we all ran cross country well, and we took similar approaches to training. We worked hard—but we were good at making the hard work fun. Unfortunately, only Ovett could sprint!

I learned a lot from them, and you can, too: Throughout this book I'll illustrate important points with anecdotes from their careers or from my own or from other world-class runners I was privileged to know. More recently, I've also learned a lot from my years of coaching runners of all abilities, and I'll share some of those stories, too.

My hope is to get you to think more about your own running. My aim isn't so much to prescribe as it is to get both your brain and your feet moving a little faster. This makes running less arduous and more varied, less draining and more invigorating. Running should be about challenge, not drudgery. Above all, it should be enjoyable.

I want to help you reach that state of grace where every component of fitness—physical, mental and emotional—comes together to produce a magical performance of which you never would have thought yourself capable. I'd like you to have days when you exceed your expectations, when running feels effortless—when, whatever your level, you feel the way I did on the day of the 1981 National Championships. I'm going to try as best I can to offer insight into not just the science of performance but also the art of running, for top athletes and ordinary mortals alike.

BUILDING THE BASE

Welcome to part I, which is about building a base that will serve you well as you seek to become a faster runner. You might be surprised by some of the chapters I've included here.

One of them is on running technique. That's something that's rarely considered important for distance runners, but it's critical to practice proper technique from the outset. Otherwise, it's like spending your first year or two holding the violin bow the wrong way or using the wrong grip on the tennis racquet: You develop terrible habits that are difficult to break.

And I start to discuss speedwork in chapter 2, where I talk about fartleks—speed play—as a way to begin to get used to running faster. People who believe building the base involves little more than extended plodding will find it difficult to break out of that slow rhythm later on. The idea that one day your feet will move faster, your knees will come up higher and your stride will lengthen when you've never before practiced running fast is a fallacy. Speedwork isn't something to be delayed until after the base has been established. Speedwork is *part* of the base.

So start out on the right foot: Practice running well, and practice running fast.

Pushing the Limits

Before we go out for our first training session, I ask the runners who come to me for coaching advice a simple question: What is it that stops *you* from going faster? What stops you from going with a runner who overtakes you? What does it *feel* like?

Often, they haven't thought about it or they find it difficult to put into words. Is it your legs, I ask? Your breathing? Maybe your arms? Or your stomach?

And after they give it some thought, perhaps for the first time in their running careers, more often than not they decide it's their breathing. Their legs may be willing, but the out-of-breath feeling tells them: No faster! They feel they are leaving their comfort zone.

'If I go any faster', they say, 'I'm not sure I'll be able to make it to the finish.'

'Well, how often do you get out of breath in training?' I ask.

'Oh, I'm not *meant* to get out of breath', is the surprisingly common reply. 'I read a book that says I'm supposed to keep within certain limits. Am I *supposed* to get out of breath in training?'

And I say, 'Yeah, you *are* supposed to get out of breath. Absolutely. You should get out of breath—at least some of the time—in most of your training sessions. Even on a steady run, you can work a little harder up a hill or do a little speed play. Work, then recover, preferably without stopping—but don't hesitate to stop if you need to. Just use the break to have a quick stretch.'

Of course, when I take these runners out for their initial session on the roads or through the woods of southern England, where I live, it is not difficult for me to determine what holds them back the most. But I ask them the question first because I want them to start thinking about it and feeling the feedback they get from their bodies. We're all different, which is why sticking slavishly to a schedule you found in a magazine or maybe on the Web is not such a good idea. It wasn't designed for *you*.

This is one of the places the runner's art comes in: To create a training program that helps your running progress, you have to pay close attention to what it is that particularly limits you. If you want to go faster, you've got to extend those limits. Otherwise, they're going to stay right where they are, keeping you from going faster than you go now.

Take for example the runners who decide they're held back most by their breathing. If they take the cautious approach—'Oh, I should *never* get out of breath'—they won't get much of a training effect on their lungs, which is precisely what they need most. They won't learn to cope with being out of breath, nor will they learn how to recover after having been out of breath, which are abilities they'll need if they're going to race well.

Not only that. They will also need these very abilities if they are to get fit enough to train more effectively and more specifically—and gain a wider variety of training effects. In other words, it will not only be their ability to race, but also their ability to train effectively that will be limited if they simply stick to a regimen that advocates never going above a certain heart rate, never getting out of breath, or always staying in the 'fat-burning zone'—which itself is a bit of a misconception.

A runner who trains without getting out of breath won't give his heart much of a workout either. And if his breathing is the first thing that tells him he's working too hard, his legs won't be getting stronger, because they won't be put under any pressure.

The result will be that nothing much changes. Next year and the year after, those limiting factors will be just as limiting. And that runner will still be posting the same times he does today.

Maybe you're one of the runners who's stuck on home base. Staying at the same level is not what you want, or you wouldn't be working so hard—or looking for advice. This book is designed to help you get going, and start making real progress.

Here's a key principle to remember as you develop your training plan:

‘ To run at your best, you need to improve on a variety of fronts. Although distance running is largely about endurance, there are six primary components of fitness, *each* of which can help you run faster. They are the five Ss: *speed, suppleness, strength, stamina,* and *skill*—plus *psychology.* If you progress in any one of these areas, your performance will improve. If you work on all of them, you'll have a breakthrough. ’

But many runners' training is one-dimensional. 'When I started off, I could only do five miles', you'll hear them say. 'I'm certainly progressing—I'm now up to 15 miles.'

Well, clearly that is progress, but only in the sense that they can go longer, not that they can necessarily run faster. Their times for the 5K or one mile may hardly have improved at all. The aim of these runners never seems to be to run faster but simply to manage a longer race. Their progression is 10K, half-marathon, and full marathon. And then what? Just more of the same. There's nowhere really for them to go.

I'm saying, go back to a 5K or even a mile. Aim to get faster at these distances, even if your real target is the longer races. But many of these runners think going faster is the hard option and going further at a nice comfortable pace is the easy option.

Wrong. Whatever the race distance, the easy option is to get it over ASAP. Arguably, a five-hour marathon is harder than a three-hour marathon. And 25 laps of the track—10,000 metres—in 50 minutes rather than 28 minutes sounds pretty painful to me.

'Even in long races, you know you can manage the distance', I tell them. 'What you need is to be able to go a little quicker. Are you getting any better at going quicker?'

'Hmm, maybe not', they'll say. 'I haven't tried that.'

Well, it is definitely worth trying. A few years ago a 65-year-old lady named Cecilia Morrison came to me for coaching advice. She was aiming for the European and World Masters championships. She considered herself a 10K runner—5K was a little short for her, and she definitely felt she was not fast at 1,500 metres.

Now, five years later, having markedly improved her technique and changed the balance and variety of her training to include more speed-work and strength training, she has won several gold and silver medals at 5,000 metres and 10,000 metres in the World Masters Championships. Even more unbelievable (to her), she has set a world best for age 70 for the 1,500 metres—running it in 6:04, nearly eight seconds faster than the previous record. And—no surprise to me—she also smashed the record for 5K. She ran it in 22:19, a massive 32 seconds faster than the previous world record.

She never thought that she could run that fast. But by concentrating on the shorter distances, she improved still further at the longer ones. By getting stronger, she actually improved her speed—and her stamina.

Like Cecilia, most everyday runners who train longer but not necessarily faster are trying hard to get

Courtesy of Lesley Richardson/www.rikko2photo.co.uk

Work on strength as you get older—and you may even improve with age, like Cecilia Morrison.

better. They may in fact be trying a bit too hard: They're slaves to distance and effort rather than thought, art, and skill. They think the only way to run faster is to try harder rather than to train smarter. Some are following to the letter advice they've read in books telling them that the best way to train is never to run too fast, but instead just to run longer and longer.

Others are so concerned with effort that their runs are ruled entirely by their effort meters—their heart rate monitors. They're so concerned with keeping their heart rate at, say, 155 beats per minute for the whole run that they lose sight of all the other critical components of fitness. They let their heart rate monitors govern their training.

Still others may fear that if they run too fast, they'll have to stop before they've finished that day's route. And stopping in the middle of a training session would mean failure, right? We all know that.

Well, I think all of that is nonsense. Let's take these misconceptions one by one.

A heart-rate monitor has some value, to be sure, but it's only a tool, not the be-all and end-all of training. The best use of a heart rate monitor in training is allowing you to measure how quickly you recover to a heart rate you've set as a target—say 120 beats per minute.

In a racing situation, perhaps in the first 20 miles of a marathon, you can also use it as a governor: You can set your effort to a particular heart rate to help with your pace judgment and prevent you from going too fast early on. But a heart rate monitor should absolutely not govern your training, although it can provide valuable feedback.

Really, it's better to judge your effort level based on your breathing, rather than on your heart rate, because (a) you actually feel your breathing, and (b) because calculating your max heart rate and any percentage of it is fraught with errors and misunderstandings. The correct formula for determining what percentage of your maximum heart rate is appropriate for different levels of intensity is so complicated that I think it's better skipped.

The bottom line is that there is nothing wrong with getting your heart rate up towards its maximum, working as hard as your breathing will allow. Get a feel for what you can manage. Experiment! If you feel you overdo it, just ease down or stop altogether.

And what in the world is so terrible about stopping? In my book, when you're training you can stop as often as you like. Just make sure you *need* to stop. Maybe you started your run too quickly. In that case, you've learned something about pacing. You've discovered where the edge of your ability lies at that moment, which is something you'll never find out if all your training is conservative. Or, of course, you might be doing a session where you actually plan to stop and have recovery periods because they enable you to work harder than you otherwise could—pushing the limits, which is the point of training. Either way, stopping for a rest is no big deal. Use it as an opportunity to get your breath back, stretch, and maybe enjoy the view.

The bit about never running hard in training will pretty much eliminate all hope of progress. Like a hamster in a wheel, you can run and run without getting anywhere.

This takes us back to the five Ss: You're not just looking for stamina. You're not just looking to go as far as you possibly can. You want to race better. And even if you are aiming for a stamina event like the marathon or Ironman triathlon, the key to making progress is remembering that a number of factors limit your ability to go faster. Your training should address all of these factors: Improvements in your speed, skill, and suppleness will also help improve your stamina.

And it is this that lies at the root of my thoughts on learning to run more quickly:

‘ More than anything else, you need variety in your training. Add as many strings to your bow as possible—not just stamina, but speed, strength, suppleness and mental toughness. It's that combination of weapons that will help you race better and finish ahead of one-trick ponies. Train differently almost every time out. Vary the speed, the distance, the terrain and the pattern of your sessions. By mixing in hills and fartleks, all manner of speed sessions, longer runs and short recovery runs you can progress on many fronts at once. This is the key to making dramatic improvement and discovering what you are really capable of. ’

That's how the best athletes reach their full potential. They're strong *and* supple, they have speed *and* stamina—and they run with skill, which means running efficiently to make the most of the fitness they have. And their training has made them fit psychologically, which is just as vital as the other strengths they need, if not more so.

All these factors are no less important for club runners. Why develop all that stamina if your body is so stiff that it takes twice as much energy as it should to push it down the road? Why develop your psychological strength if your lack of skill means you're putting on the brakes with every stride you take? That's just fitness gone to waste. It's not about being a world-class runner; it's about being the best you can be. And I think you'll find that variety keeps you fresher, and makes running more fun, too.

Throughout this book, I'll offer advice on how to improve all five Ss as well as the mental side, psychology. Your basic conditioning needs to cover all of them.

And always remember this: All of your training should be done with a specific aim in mind—to improve one or more of these factors. Aimless training won't help you, and it may even be detrimental.

Let's look at each of these ingredients to success in a bit more detail.

SPEED

It should be obvious that speed is essential to running faster, but many runners do nothing to improve it. 'I'm aiming for the marathon', they say. 'I don't need to work on my speed. I'm a long-distance runner.'

I think that's a cop-out. People who think that way should bear this in mind: There are only two ways to run faster. You need to either increase your cadence—your leg speed—or increase the length of your stride. There's no other way to get down the road quicker. Whether you want to move your legs quicker or run with a looser, rangier stride, you need strength and suppleness.

And learning to run with a fast cadence will help you run a better time at any distance. Always start with a quick cadence, even as a beginner. If you start out running with long, slow strides, it is difficult to increase your cadence later on. Sometimes you will want to increase the length of your stride, as well, but *not* at the expense of slowing your cadence unless your cadence is so fast it's inefficient. A quick cadence will help you put on a burst of speed when you need to. Try accelerating in top gear in a car. It doesn't work—you need a lower gear for quick acceleration.

Want to run faster? Think quick feet.

'Some runners, particularly beginners, have the misconception that to get faster, they need to cover more ground with every stride', Jeff Galloway, who once held the American record for 10 miles, wrote in *Runner's World* in March 2007. 'But for distance runners, that's seldom the right formula for faster times. In fact, it can lead to overstriding and a greater risk of injuries. The real secret to improvement at distances from the 5K on up is faster turnover, or cadence.'

Look at any top distance runner, whether on YouTube or by watching the New York City or London marathons on TV. Count the number of times the right foot touches the ground during the course of a minute. Multiply that number by two—the guy's got a left foot, too—and you are likely to find out he's taking 180 steps a minute, maybe even a bit more. That's quick feet for you: three steps a second.

This is true of cyclists, too. Cyclists are often classified as mashers or spinners—those who pedal slowly and those who pedal quickly, whatever gear they're in. Lance Armstrong revolutionised cycling training in part by emphasizing training at a high cadence. He knows what he's talking about: He won the Tour de France seven times and—perhaps even more impressively—finished third at the age of 37, after a three-and-a-half-year layoff. He didn't do that by being a masher.

And a quick cadence—180 steps a minute or more—is common to all top-class distance runners, from those who specialise in shorter distances on up through marathoners. Elite 5K racers are moving quicker than marathoners by using a longer stride, which is difficult to maintain for very long, but the top marathoners are moving their feet just as quickly. A video of the New York City Marathon showed that the top 150 runners all ran with just about the same cadence—184 to 188 steps a minute.

That might be a little more than novice or intermediate runners can manage. But try to come close. In running, we don't talk about mashers and spinners. The concept is the same, though. Just change down a gear or two! Instead of being a plodder, be a floater: quick feet, no matter the distance. Patter along, and ingrain this quick rhythm in all your running. How do you do this? Not by thinking about your legs, but your arms. If you move your arms quicker, your legs will have no option but to move quicker, too, whether it be in speed sessions, long runs, training, or racing.

Of course, our potential for pure speed is limited in part by our ratio of fast-twitch to slow-twitch muscle fibres—and to be honest, I would have liked a few more of the fast-twitch variety myself. That ratio is something we're born with, although it can be altered to some extent by training.

But beyond that accident of birth, speed is limited by other factors we have a much greater ability to affect.

Strength is an exceptional example. Remember that you can go faster only by increasing your cadence or your stride length. What if you could do both at once? That would be a double whammy and *really* increase your speed. Taking bigger strides while increasing your cadence requires more strength: If you get stronger, you'll run faster. And the converse is also true: If you practice running faster, you'll get stronger.

How fast you go is also limited by how supple you are. The looser you are, the less effort it takes to make each movement. The same effort will produce a bigger stride and faster feet.

Speed is also limited by skill. To run skilfully is to run efficiently, using the least amount of energy to propel yourself forward rather than squandering your forces by putting on the brakes or twisting from side to side. Running skilfully also allows you to relax, breathe comfortably, and use your energy to good effect.

Speed is limited by stamina, too. Nearly everyone who can maintain a steady pace of seven or eight minutes per mile can go fast enough to run a mile in five minutes. They have the basic speed necessary to do it. But they can only keep up that pace for maybe 200 or 300 metres, so the challenge is to learn to maintain that speed over longer distances. For those runners, long runs at seven to eight minutes per mile will improve their endurance, but not their *speed endurance*. And to race well over longer distances, they need specific sessions to develop speed endurance.

Speed, in other words, is limited by all the other Ss—strength, suppleness, skill, and stamina. Work on them *all* and your speed will improve.

If you have slow legs, sprint drills can help you. Try quick-feet drills. While running on the spot, move your feet as quickly as you possibly can, like raindrops bouncing off the pavement, and hardly lifting them. Keep this going as you move slowly forward. See how many steps you can take in the space of 10 or 15 metres. The split second your feet come off the ground, put them down again. It's like trying to see how fast you can clap but with your feet. At the same time, pump your arms, not moving them far, but quick-quick-quick-quick-quick.

Don't time yourself. If you're in a group, the winner is the *last* person to get to the 15-metre line. It's very tiring. Then walk back and do it again, two or three times.

Admittedly, it's difficult to do these drills on your own, but in a group they can be quite a laugh, and they are very effective. They help develop proprioception in the muscle fibres—what you might call muscle memory, the ability to move by autopilot rather than relying on the much slower messages coming from the brain. When you first try this drill, you will find it difficult to control your movements. One foot may come up higher than the other, and it will be difficult to keep your feet and your arms in sync. But keep at it: This drill develops timing and coordination as well as speed.

And don't just stick to the quick-feet drill. The next step in the progression is to try to get a feel for using that quickness in your normal running. Get your cadence to its absolute maximum, hardly moving forward for the first 10 or 15 metres. Then hang onto that ultra-quick cadence, take the brakes off gradually and lengthen your stride, then lengthen it more and more while still putting your feet down very quickly. All at once—*wow!*—it's like an aircraft at the end of the runway: The engines are full on, the brakes are on, you're not going anywhere, and then suddenly you take the brakes off. With those high revs—those quick feet—you'll feel maybe 30 or 40 metres of acceleration. It's not so easy to do, but try it. Practice it regularly and you will find it does improve your speed and skill.

If your stride's too short, one remedy is high-knee drills. This is almost like running on the spot while lifting your knees as high as you possibly can, keeping the cadence reasonably quick and making a little forward progress. It's also crucial to not lean back during this drill. Try doing this for 20 metres, then walk back—again, two or three times.

Like the quick-feet drill, the high-knee drill is most likely something you will include as part of your warm-up before you start a session, or as a warm-down after the session. And, as with the quick-feet drill, you can end by converting the high-knee drill into actual running, which is the reason to do the drills; you're not just doing them for their own sake. Do the drill for 10 or 15 metres, then—still keeping your knees as high as you can—take the brakes off, open up, and pick up speed, reaching up and forward with your knees. What you're trying to do is incorporate the drills into your regular running and learn to run differently by concentrating on those two simple elements of speed—cadence and stride length.

STRENGTH

For some reason, many people don't associate strength with distance running, so they don't work on getting stronger. They don't run any cross country events. No press-ups, either. No pull-ups, no sit-ups, no trips to the gym, and no running sessions designed to make themselves stronger. Endurance, not strength, is the key, right?

Maybe skinny runners don't look strong. But they are, especially in terms of their power-to-weight ratio. It's true that the kind of strength you need varies according to your event. If you look like Hulk Hogan or Arnold Schwarzenegger, chances are you won't run the marathon very well. Pure strength won't help you much unless it can be harnessed effectively for your specific event.

But strength is a vital part of running well. If you want to power your way up a hill, it will take strength to do it. *Something* is lifting your body all the way from the bottom of the hill to the top. And that something is you. Weakness is not going to get the job done. The key is to improve your power-to-weight ratio.

The same is true on the flat. Taking longer strides requires greater strength: Each stride has to do more work to cover more ground. Eating up the ground with big quick strides the way top runners do—or the way you want to do at the end of a race—means you have to be strong.

By contrast, weakness in the legs or stomach muscles will shorten your stride, meaning you'll cover less ground with the same number of steps. Contrary to what you might think, your abdominal muscles play an important role in picking up your knees and creating a strong stride. Many ordinary runners do not realise that abdominal exercises are crucial to developing good form, stride length, and strength.

But it's not just leg and core strength you should be interested in. As we'll see in chapter 3, you really want to run with your whole body. Your arms and your upper body are also vital to running well. Your arms act as your accelerator pedal, and your legs will never be able to go faster than your arms.

' **If you want to run your best, strengthen your arms with presses and curls. To strengthen your legs, core, and back, run some hills, run through sand, or do some abdominal exercises—and, most definitely, take up cross country.** '

Your core strength provides the crucial link between what you do with your arms and what you do with your legs. Strength training isn't an extra; it's an integral part of running to your capability. The British runner Kelly Holmes, who won gold in the 800 and 1,500 metres at the Athens Olympics in 2004, used to do hundreds of sit-ups in a single session.

Martin Cushen/Actionplus/Icon SMI

Strength allows runners like Kelly Holmes to maintain good form at the finish.

Holmes was inspired in her running by another Brit, Sebastian Coe, one of the most successful middle distance runners of all time. Coe won four Olympic medals—including golds in the 1,500 in Moscow in 1980 and Los Angeles in 1984—and set 11 world records.

Coe thought distance runners make a mistake in neglecting strength training, which he felt was critical to his success. It was only when he discovered how much his core muscles helped him, he often said, that he really made progress with his running.

STAMINA

Stamina is the area where many runners focus their efforts to the exclusion of all the other Ss. Stamina is the ability to continue running at a certain effort for long periods. If your idea of progress is to go for longer and longer runs, you are working on stamina to some extent. But if those long runs are all quite gentle, you might not be working on stamina all that much. And the better you become at the long gentle runs, the more the law of diminishing returns sets in.

To improve stamina, try some steady runs—short and often. Add in just one or two long continuous runs each week. And, although they have often been branded speedwork, your stamina will be greatly improved by running fartleks, interval sessions on the road or on the track, and hill repetitions.

SUPPLENESS

Doctors say they can recognise runners by their tight hamstrings. This is not as it should be: Tight hamstrings shorten each stride and make each lift of the knee a little more difficult. It would be better if doctors recognised runners by how supple they were.

Suppleness is about being a better overall athlete. It's crucial to developing speed, strength, and stamina. I'll discuss it in detail in chapter 5. It's also crucial to preventing injuries. Don't make the mistake so many other runners do by failing to recognise its importance. Increase your suppleness and you'll increase your range of movement, increase your efficiency—the ability to go the same speed with less effort—and reduce your risk of injury, which means your training will be more consistent.

Don't stretch when you're cold. Jog the first 5 or 10 minutes of your session, then stop and have a good stretch with your muscles warmed up. Be sure to loosen your upper body, including your chest, neck, and shoulders, as well as your legs, because you need to be relaxed and loose from head to toe in order to run your best.

And remember to stretch *after* your run as part of your warm-down. That will prevent muscles stiffening up, reduce injuries, and aid recovery rate.

SKILL

If suppleness is neglected by too many runners, skill—technique—is neglected by even more. But it is critical to running as well as you can.

I have developed my own ideas on technique, and I have seen them help runner after runner improve dramatically—often far more than they ever thought possible. I'll discuss these keys to success in full in the next chapter. You don't want to practice running inefficiently any more than you'd want to practice tennis for the first couple of years while holding the racket incorrectly.

' For now, remember running is like cycling, not walking. Keep these basics of good technique in mind:

- Bend your knees.
- Don't land on your heels.
- Feel as if you are falling into your next step. '

PSYCHOLOGY

Here we come to the big unknown, the hardest to understand, the X factor. But it might be the most important factor of all. If you put 10 equally fit athletes on the starting line, the one with the best mental state is sure to win. In fact, the winner might even be someone who's less physically fit than the others, but psychologically stronger. I'm convinced psychology played a role in my victory in the 1981 National Cross Country Championships. Various things had made me angry. Several factors had made me feel I was on a mission to 'show the bastards'. And I was exhilarated to be over my injury and able to run pain-free. So I was relaxed and happy, too. I just took off and never slowed down. My mental state allowed my physical fitness to come through. It was not a case of trying harder. Quite the reverse.

The elements of psychological fitness are diverse. We're talking about inspiration and determination, self-confidence and motivation, and concentration and the ability to cope with both setbacks and success. All of these can have an enormous effect on your performance—for better or worse. Training can improve your strength in these areas.

Psychological training takes place in every session you do. Each session you complete, each challenge you rise to, adds to your confidence. But every session you miss or fail to complete undermines your belief in yourself. And that can be very harmful, so make your targets demanding and progressive, but also realistic and achievable. Once you've set them, don't disappoint yourself. Just do what you set out to do.

DOUBLE YOUR OPTIONS, TRAIN TWICE A DAY

Well, now, all of that may sound like quite a lot to work on, all those limiting factors. And if the key to a breakthrough is to work on all of them, how can anyone possibly do it all at once?

This brings me to the benefits of running twice a day. Don't be daunted. This is something I think a lot of runners misunderstand. It's not so much about increasing your volume of training as it is increasing your number of sessions.

Let's say you're a fairly serious runner and you're trying to run 70 miles a week. Putting in a 10-mile run every day is pretty tough. But in comparison, doing two five-mile runs in a day is a piece of cake. And the training effect is more beneficial.

First of all, you get the benefit of having a higher metabolism throughout the day by running little and often. Secondly, you will feel nicely loose and warmed up for your second run, even if you're a little tired. And thirdly, and even more important, you will build a routine with many more pegs to hang different sessions on. Which means you can work on a greater variety of sessions, allowing yourself to address more limiting factors in any one phase of your training.

And not only that: If you're running twice a day, you can work in more easy runs, which pick you up, help you recover, and put something back in the tank—a really nice feeling, both physically and mentally. If you're only training once a day, or maybe just three times a week, it's difficult to find time to fit in those recovery runs. They end up being long runs instead, or all your sessions end up being recovery runs without having done the hard sessions to recover from.

Training twice a day opens a lot of doors. You might do an easy run in the morning and some hills in the evening—and it won't feel that tough. Often you'll discover you feel better in your second session than you did in your first.

Perhaps you raced the day before, or trained very hard, and you're feeling depleted. You might limit yourself to just three miles in the morning, then do seven in the evening. That's still 10 miles. And you'll say to yourself, 'Oh, that was *easy*.' The three miles were just a recovery run. After that you get a rest, and by evening you feel like you are starting to pick things up again. That really is much easier and more beneficial than just doing a 10-mile run straight off.

I started by discussing someone who's running 70 miles a week. But people who run far less than that can reap great benefits from training twice a day as well. Let's say your runs are normally about five miles. Instead of one five-miler, try two three-milers. All of a sudden you, too, will have more pegs to hang your training on—a greater ability to mix in different kinds of training and to include those invigorating recovery runs, too.

So it's not just about running more miles, it's about doing more sessions. That will put more variety in your program, bring you greater benefits and leave you mentally fresher.

I know some people will be sceptical. I've seen it many times. When I was at Oxford University, I shared a flat with several other runners. They just refused to believe me or even try it.

'We're going to do a 10 tonight', they'd tell me. 'That's much better than one of your short runs.'

I was quite a bit quicker than they were, but younger—the new kid on the block—and they weren't inclined to listen to me.

'Twice a day—that's risky', they'd say. 'You'll get too tired; you'll get injured.'

But it's quite the reverse. After your first run, your metabolism is raised for several hours afterwards, so you continue to get the benefit and training effect as you recover. That means you're *less* likely to get hurt: You'll actually feel looser before you start the second run of the day. And you'll probably run two different sorts of sessions, which means you won't repeat exactly the same motion or take exactly the same stride as many times as you would if you combined your training into one long run. And you'll stretch twice in the day, as well.

Perhaps their real reason for only training once a day was the thought of wasting time—changing clothes twice, showering twice, and so on. Not to mention the extra washing! Suffice it to say that the old guard had lost to Cambridge in the annual cross country varsity match. But the newer group of runners, who had a much more open-minded approach to twice-a-day training, beat Cambridge convincingly the next two years.

I admit to having tried training *three* times a day at various times but honestly I can't really recommend it! It started when I was a schoolboy. I used to run to and from school, and my dad, who was a schoolmaster there, would bring my books and clothes to school in the car. Sometimes I would run in the middle of the day, too, perhaps in a PE class, so I was occasionally doing three three-mile runs a day and, although that's not a lot, I admit I found it quite hard. And basically, it was too much hassle. You spend too much time getting changed. And I'm not sure there's any extra benefit to it.

But twice a day—believe me, it's extremely beneficial. Get into the routine and you'll feel fantastic!

Sure, running twice a day might take a little getting used to. You might have to drag yourself out of bed earlier in the morning—though two 5K runs can be easier to fit into your schedule than one longer one. And you have to work out a lifestyle that permits it, perhaps by running to work or at lunchtime.

But in terms of the benefit to your running, the difference between running once a day and running twice is enormous. Everyone I have spoken to who's changed to twice a day has said it was the key to making a big leap forward.

So how do you get into it?

Some people recommend dipping your toe in cautiously. If you're used to running six or seven days a week, try running twice a day once per week they say. See how you feel. Then maybe you can build up to doing it twice a week.

I have never thought you get anywhere by taking that approach. I think you just make it harder for yourself by trying to get used to it gradually. That way, running twice a day is the exception rather than the rule, and you're more likely to have arguments with yourself over whether to do it: Oh, no, I have to run *twice* today. That makes it a bit daunting, unless it's your normal routine.

‘ Take the bull by the horns and start running twice a day at least three times a week, and ideally five—every weekday, for example. ’

This works because a lot of your training is about routine. If it's normal to go out twice a day, then that becomes easier to do most days than just once or twice per week. It's a regular part of your day. And to start with, you need hardly increase your mileage; instead, make the sessions shorter, more manageable, and easier to fit in.

Within the broad categories I've discussed are more specific limiting factors, and there are specific ways to address them. You'll want to work into your training remedies for the problems that limit you in particular. I'll talk about them throughout the book.

And as you train, always remember that you want to improve your fitness on as many fronts as possible. You want speed, stamina, strength, suppleness, skill, and a strong mental approach—and the ability to use these attributes together under race conditions. Don't go out and do the same sessions over and over, time after time. You don't add strings to your bow that way. Variety is the spice of life, and it's also the essence of good training.

KEY POINTS TO REMEMBER

- The six components of fitness are the five Ss—speed, suppleness, strength, stamina and skill, plus psychology. If you work on all of them throughout the year, adding as many strings to your bow as possible, you'll have a breakthrough.

- Always have an aim as you train: to improve one or more of the six components of fitness—or, very importantly, to have a recovery run. Aimless training—lots of junk miles, all steady paced—won't help your performance and may even be detrimental. If the aim is a short, easy run, stick to the plan. Don't get diverted by allowing it to become longer or harder than you planned, just because you feel good. If you feel good—hold it. Conserve it! Bottle it! That's the feeling you are after. Save it for your next hard session, or next race.

- To fit in the variety of training sessions you need, run twice a day most days. Not necessarily more miles—just more sessions, many of them short. It's the key to a major advance in your fitness.

Aiming True

The heat was on, but Crammie was cool.

The year before, in 1982, the young British runner Steve Cram had won gold in both the 1,500 in the Commonwealth Games in Brisbane, Australia, and the European Championships in Athens. He was a comer—someone to watch.

Now, in August 1983, going into the first World Championships in Helsinki, a film crew was there to do the watching. They followed Crammie from March through the World Championships in August—producing a documentary that was called *Steve Cram: Good for the First Mile*. As the championships arrived, the crew trailed Crammie through the athletes' village, keeping an eye on his preparations for the big event, the 1,500-metre final.

It's common for athletes in that position to still be doing quite a bit of training even though the race is close at hand. In the athletes village you know your rivals are watching you, even if there doesn't happen to be a film crew. Maybe you want them to see you out on the track, running fast and looking good.

Most athletes, myself included, would probably want to stick to their normal training routines as much as possible. With so much time on your hands, you feel much better going out for a run, rather than just whiling away the hours worrying. You can read, sleep, play cards and listen to your music, but sticking to your normal pattern of training is the best way of maintaining the structure and focus of your day, and—crucially—that stops you from just drifting from one meal to the next, over-eating, and feeling increasingly lethargic.

It's terrible if you start to feel heavy, tired and lethargic, and you have to find a way of avoiding this. With the benefit of hindsight, although I was quite good at easing down for the important races, I probably did too much mileage during the summer track-racing season. It may have made me much stronger in the long run, but I definitely went into some races more tired than I should have been.

My early training partner, Dave Bedford, who held the world record in the 10,000 for four years, was always running, and this approach probably rubbed off on me. Even before a big race, Dave would be out in the heat, still wearing his tracksuit, running like hell and trying to impress people—usually quite successfully.

Looking back, Dave was probably lacking in confidence, in stark contrast to Steve Cram's cool demeanour. Crammie was in Helsinki, just 22 years old, facing the World Championships with the added pressure of being tailed by a film crew. But he stayed cool and relaxed, watching TV and strolling about the village—and not doing very much running at all!

But come race day, he produced the goods.

Despite lacking Seb Coe, the world record holder, people were calling the line-up in the final a dream field. It included Cram's British teammate, Steve Ovett, the reigning Olympic 800-metre champion; the American Steve Scott, at the time the second-fastest miler in history; and the Moroccan runner Said Aouita, who would win Olympic gold in the 5,000 the following year in Los Angeles.

At first the pace was slow—it would clearly be a tactical race, which would suit Ovett and his devastating change of pace. Then, with 500 metres to go, Aouita took off. Cram went with him. As the bell sounded for the final lap, Aouita continued to accelerate, really winding it up on the back straight. Still Cram stayed with him. And with 180 metres to go, Cram unleashed a blistering kick, taking the lead and showing what he had left in the tank. He held the lead through the finish, just edging Scott for the gold. Aouita finished third. Ovett, who had let himself get boxed in on the inside, finished fourth.

Crammie—calm, cool, relaxed, and rested—was world champion, which goes to show that the aim of your training should not be to grind yourself into the

Cool as you like! Steve Cram winning the World Championships 1,500 metres, Helsinki, 1983.

Mark Shearman, Athletics Images

ground. Sometimes the aim is to recover and just feel good. Even when you're training hard, the aim should always be to leave yourself ready and able to run the following day. But as a big race approaches, things change. You should now be training not so much for fitness—it's too late for that—as for feelings. You're trying to reach race day not just fresh and rested, but mentally desperate to race. Far from dreading the start, you feel the gun gives you a release and sets you free. At last you can uncork that bottle and let the fitness, the emotion and the exhilaration pour out. This is what you have been training for—the performance after all the rehearsals. And your training leading up to the big race should be about building up, saving and bottling these feelings.

Whenever you go out, whether a race is approaching or not—you should keep in mind what you're trying to accomplish in that session.

‘ Always have an aim as you train. Each session should have a specific purpose.   ’

Just getting in one more medium run is fine at certain times of the year, when perhaps your aim is to get your mileage up. But mileage isn't everything, and you need to do more specific sessions if you are to gain the full range of desired training effects.

This is where many novice or intermediate runners make their biggest mistake. Their recovery runs are a bit too hard. Then, because they haven't allowed themselves to recover properly, their hard sessions are a bit too easy. Their long runs are a bit too short and maybe a bit too fast, their short runs are a bit too long, and their training can easily wind up all levelled off, all medium, and all ho-hum. Sure, it all counts as mileage, but some of it ends up as junk mileage: They're doing what they can already do. It's enough to make them tired, but not specific enough to really extend their limiting factors.

That's not an effective way to train, it's not an efficient use of time, and it's not going to lead to much progress.

Keep your aims specific: You might want to work one day on increasing your speed, perhaps; another on enhancing your endurance or boosting your strength; and yet another on teaching your body to recover quickly. Also, your aim might be to recover with a very short, easy-paced, comfortable run that leaves you feeling refreshed at the end.

‘ You should try to include four key sessions in your weekly training. To maintain a balanced program, each week should include a long run, a fartlek, repetitions either on hills or on the flat, and at least one recovery run.   ’

Of course, at certain times of the year, you may wish to emphasise endurance—more mileage—or strength or speed. But you can still include these types of session each week and adapt them to the phase of training you're in.

Let's take them one by one.

RECOVERY RUNS

Maybe you expect me to start by describing a big blowout on the track or hill repeats that set your knees to trembling. Well, I could, of course. At the right time of year and with sufficient rests, those sorts of sessions can do you a world of good. But I'm going to start by talking about recovery runs.

It's true that the recovery sessions are most beneficial only after you've done the harder sessions. But it is equally true that you can only do the harder sessions properly if you are disciplined about sticking to the aim of your recovery sessions—to *recover*, to leave yourself raring to go, feeling almost deprived because you know you could have run more. It's the same as being strict on yourself and resisting that extra pint or second helping of pudding.

But all too often, people who think they'll do an easy run on a particular day don't wind up doing it. They say to themselves, 'Oh, it's a lovely day. My mates are going for eight miles. I'm only supposed to be doing four, but I can't resist it. I'll go slowly, and that way it'll still be a recovery run.'

Well, eight slow miles is *not* a recovery run! Especially when the plan said four. Then the next day they're more tired than they should be, not quite up for something that's harder, like hill repeats or a session on the track.

OK, I'll miss that and do a fartlek or a hard five-mile run instead, they tell themselves.

Well, that's OK, but still not part of the plan. And their training all becomes watered down and levelled out.

' The aim of a recovery run is to feel better at the end of it than you did at the start. Run at an easy pace, but keep your feet quick. You'll end up invigorated. And keep it short—you'll doubtless vary it from time to time, but 20 to 30 minutes is ample. '

If you have a spare 20 or 30 minutes on a recovery day, you'll do yourself far more good if you spend it on a stretching session or a swim rather than on extending your run.

Going for a recovery run does not mean plodding. Many people find themselves thinking, 'This is supposed to be an easy run today. And these are nice, soft shoes. I'll just run on my heels and feel nice and comfy and slow.' They shift their weight back, almost sitting down over their heels, and their legs slow down. Their footfalls become heavy and ponderous.

On a recovery run, even though the pace is slow, still move your feet quickly. Take smaller strides—*much* smaller strides—and keep your centre of gravity forward, try to stay up on your toes and patter along with your feet nice and zippy. And bend your knees: You want to put some spring back in your legs.

To start, you may feel this quicker cadence is a bit harder work than sitting back and plodding along as you're used to. It's hard to avoid going faster in this low gear, and your breathing may well be a little heavier and your heart rate a little higher, so slow down even more: Take shorter steps. But don't slow down by taking *slower* steps. Running with a slow rhythm is a hard habit to break, so don't allow yourself to revert to it. Keep a good, quick rhythm, even on recovery runs. Running with quick feet will be much more beneficial because you'll get used to what running really ought to feel like. That quick rhythm will become ingrained and stick with you in all your runs.

Of course, you can also recover with an easy swim or an easy walk, either of which would be great. But, if you're going to run, keep it quick and relaxed. Stop and stretch a bit. You might mix in a few 100- to 150-metre strides. Think of the whole session as a chance to practice your form and keep that sense of being springy on your feet. At the end, you should feel that you can't *wait* to run again.

Unfortunately, many runners think that feeling means they haven't done themselves any good because they haven't worked hard enough. Usually at the end of their runs they like to congratulate themselves on how tired they are, thinking it means they've done great work. The more wiped out you feel at the end of your run, the more you've done for your fitness, right?

Well, no. Which brings me to another of the four key sessions to include each week—the long run.

LONG RUNS

This is the only one of the four key weekly sessions that intermediate runners tend to include in their training. It's the one S they work on—stamina. But even this they do in a way that may hold them back rather than help them progress.

' Remember, the main aim of any session, whatever training effect you're going for, is to be fit to train again tomorrow. '

If you wear yourself down so much on your long run that you can barely go up and down stairs for the next two days, think of all the faster-paced sessions you're going to miss. And the aim is to learn to run fast, right? You don't want to deaden your legs; you want to become quick-footed and energised, with a spring in your step. Don't go at it so hard that you injure yourself and feel overtired or flat mentally. That's no help at all.

Let's say your plan is to run an hour and a half, perhaps on Sunday. Too many runners set off at the same speed at which they would normally do their 40-minute runs. And then—oof—they can probably keep it up for an hour and a half, with a lot of effort. But they suffer the next day: They're too tired to do the Monday hill session. They wind up spending almost the whole week recovering, all their runs become steady, and pretty soon they've swept all their training into one big pile of medium again. And that's not to their benefit.

In a long run it's very easy to overdo it. Try to avoid that; it sets you back. Go out for anywhere between one and one and a half hours. But take it easy. Run your long endurance sessions at a pace that allows you to converse fairly easily. The aim of the long run is not speed, but time on your feet. Chat with your friends. Catch up on the gossip. Keep your feet quick but your pace reasonable. Work up a thirst. And don't try to incorporate all your training aims into that one session. You can't do everything all in one go.

Bear in mind that the best evidence you're making progress is not how fast you do your training runs, it's how fast you recover. If you get up the next morning and your legs don't ache and you go up and down the stairs just fine, surely that's a big improvement from when you first started. If you find that you're itching to get out and train again, that's a big improvement, too. And *that's* the road to progress.

Many recreational racers may already be doing some of their long runs at a conversational pace. They make significant progress when they first start. At first they gain the initial effects of endurance training: They probably will have lost some weight, improved their cardiovascular efficiency, and increased their endurance. But this improvement quickly tails off.

Runners often come to me for coaching advice, telling me that they've worked up to doing a 12- to 15-mile run every week, maybe even longer, and they're up to racing half-marathons. But somehow they just can't get any faster.

There's a reason for this. It's the law of diminishing returns. Or, in training terms, train the same and you'll race the same.

Yes, they've increased the distance they're able to run. But are they any stronger? To a limited extent, maybe so. Are they more supple? Almost certainly not. Are they better at coping with being in oxygen debt? No. Can they recover quickly after having gone beyond this anaerobic threshold? Maybe, but only marginally.

Often they've got into the marathon scene, so it's trundle, trundle, trundle all the time. It's plodding in training and in races. They keep thinking that they've really got to go far, so they'd better run slowly, and that usually means moving their legs slowly. They never experience the sessions that produce the training effects they really need. They don't even give themselves a chance, because they think it's more important to do more miles than to learn to run fast.

FARTLEK RUNS

But there is a very effective way to make the transition to running faster and doing the kinds of training that will lead to significant improvement—fartlek. And this type of running is something to incorporate in your training early on, not some kind of sharpening to be saved for later, after you have practiced the art of plodding for a year or two.

Fartlek running is absolutely fantastic: It's fun, effective, and sets you free! It's the vital first stage in getting used to running at different speeds. It's running how you feel and learning about your body's capabilities by experimenting. How fast dare you go, and for how long? And then let's see how long it takes you to recover before you feel ready for another effort. It's not about running certain distances a predetermined number of times at a particular speed or heart rate on a nice flat surface. You don't need to use your watch. It's unstructured speed work—stress-free and exhilarating. And very beneficial.

Fartlek, as many runners know, is Swedish for 'speed play'. That's just what it is, playing around with different speeds on different terrain, getting accustomed to running much faster than race pace over various distances, and varying your recovery times as you feel.

This type of training was developed about 75 years ago by a Swedish athlete named Gösta Holmér. Holmér had won Olympic bronze in the decathlon in 1912 before his home crowd in Stockholm. Later on, he was named coach of the Swedish cross country teams, which were in dire need of help. In the 1920s, they'd been beaten consistently by the great Paavo Nurmi—the Flying Finn, he was called—and his countrymen. For the Swedes to be dominated by their neighbours was, of course, unacceptable. Something had to be done.

Enter Holmér.

He soon realised that the runners he was working with had problems with their basic speed and with speed endurance. So in the 1930s, as he took his teams running through the pine forests of Sweden, he came up with the idea of speed play—incorporating bits of much faster running into some of the steady runs.

The results were astonishing and must have left the Finns wondering what in the world had happened. Within a few years, the Swedes were demolishing the Finns on the track. And Swedish runners who had incorporated fartlek training in their programs claimed world records for the 2-miles, 5,000 metres, and 10,000 metres. Still later, in 1942 a Swedish athlete named Gunder Hagg—a devotee of fartlek training—broke 10 world records in a single summer.

Sometimes fartleks can be coached, with the harder sessions preplanned and maybe a whistle blown to start and finish each effort. But what we're talking about here is essentially *un*structured. It's just running how you feel—having fun with speed, experimenting and learning how fast you can go and for how long.

Initially, many runners are wary of doing any kind of speedwork. Never having done it, they find it hard. They're not used to it physically or mentally. Maybe, too, they think of it as something to be done only for a month or so before a race, a form of sharpening to be attempted only after having built a huge base of long, slow miles. And speedwork—you can get injured doing that, right? Really, they tell themselves, it's so much simpler and safer to go for an easy run.

Well, of course it's easier to go for an easy run. And I'm not decrying it. People enjoy just getting out for a run, which is not a bad thing to do. It's very therapeutic.

But runners who want to experience the feeling of making progress, who want the excitement of discovering there can be more to running than just the social side, need to do these other kinds of sessions. If you want to run faster, then learning how to do that is *part* of the base, not some finishing touch to be applied later. And learning how to make this harder training fun—that, too, is a vital part of the art of running.

Not only that. I think varying the speeds at which you train actually *reduces* your chance of injury. Many of the ailments that runners suffer are repetitive-stress injuries: They result from making the same exact motion over and over. The motion doesn't have to be strenuous at all—just ask journalists and others who keyboard all day long and end up with splints on their wrists.

If all of your miles are run at the same speed in the same shoes using the same stride on the same surface, that's going to be a heck of a lot of repetitions of the exact same movements with the exact same stresses on your body. Let's say your stride is one yard long. That's 1,760 strides in a mile, 14,000 strides in an eight-mile run—and more than 70,000 strides in a 40-mile week. But by running at different speeds, you vary your stride length and change the movements you're making. There's less repetition of precisely the same motions.

So How Do You Run Fartleks?

Start as you would for a steady run: Run easily for 10 minutes or so, then stop and stretch. Continue on your way, and throw in bursts of speed. Not sprinting—just strong running but, crucially, faster than race pace. Pick out a tree or some other feature in the distance and tell yourself you'll run fast and hard until you reach that point. When you get there, drop back to a jog to recover. Then, when you're ready, pick another target and do it again.

Don't make all your efforts the same. Vary the speed, the distance and the terrain on which you run. And vary the amount of time you give yourself to recover, too. Keep the hard efforts between 20 seconds and 3 minutes, and try to keep jogging in between.

Running short faster efforts (up to one minute) with long recovery times is a way to work on pure speed, which may well not be your primary aim. Doing them nearly as fast but with shorter recovery times (less than one minute, and possibly as little as 30 seconds) teaches your body to recover quickly, in part by getting rid of lactic acid, the stuff that slows you down and makes your legs burn. When you keep the recoveries short, your body adapts and you end up raising your anaerobic threshold level. That's the level of exertion beyond which your muscles start using more oxygen than the body can inhale, absorb, and transport. You end up in oxygen debt as the muscles produce more lactic acid than the body can cope with. If you can increase your anaerobic threshold level—in other words, if you can train yourself to run faster without accumulating lactic acid and to disperse it more rapidly—that's a huge benefit to you. And it's not one you get from your steady runs alone.

Running longer efforts—90 seconds to 3 minutes each—really starts to develop your speed endurance. But of course take longer rests after these, perhaps as long as 3 minutes.

Some people might think of speed sessions as being a bit too serious for them, all work and no play. Nothing could be further from the truth. Do them with your friends and they're good fun, jocular and convivial. That makes them easier to do, and much more fun than doing them on your own. The fact that you're all in it together helps everyone through the session. Jogging the recoveries together gives you a chance to chat and joke between the hard efforts. Take it in turns to lead, and learn—about each other, but especially about yourself. Fartlek is the best way to experiment and discover what you can do. Which in turn enables you to plan, identify strengths and weaknesses, and alter and fine-tune your training to make it specific for you—and of course, it will allow you to plan your race strategies against other runners who will have different strengths and weaknesses to you.

Fartlek sessions can be easily adapted to suit runners of different abilities going out together, too. Just make sure you all start and stop the efforts at the same time so you each get the same amount of rest. The faster runners can jog back to regroup with the slower runners after each effort. And sessions like this usually leave you fresher and more stimulated than a long, steady run.

One way to do a fartlek with friends is to take turns leading the group. Go out with six or eight friends and run along in single file, 10 to 15 metres apart. The runner at the back has to increase his pace to overtake the pack and take the lead and then drop back to a steady pace. Then the next runner charges up to the front, and so on. It gives you a good feeling to stride out strongly past the other runners, one after the other. And when you get to the head of the pack, you get to ease down and recover. This type of training makes you feel you're part of a team, helping each other instead of racing against each other.

A fiercer way of doing a fartlek session with a small group of runners of similar ability is to again take turns to lead, but without knowing how far the leader will go at that pace. Your job is simply to stay with him. He may be going for 50 metres or 500 metres, you don't know; it may be at a steady pace or an ever-accelerating pace. And when the leader calls time for a rest, it is not him but the next runner who decides how long the recovery jog will be, and then it's that runner's turn to lead, again as fast and for as long or short as he or she decides. It becomes a game of bluff and counter bluff—running poker—which, of course, is what racing is all about. This kind of session isn't just about fitness, it's also great for race preparation and developing tactics.

There are endless ways to do fartleks. Be creative. Run how you feel. Yes, you're working on speed. But don't forget the play. And remember the skills, as well: Maybe sometimes you can practice going faster by increasing only your cadence, while keeping your stride length the same as when you were running slowly.

HILLS AND SPEEDWORK SESSIONS

The other important session to include each week is a repetition session—either hill reps or fast reps. The benefits of these are so significant that I've devoted a separate chapter to each later in the book. For now, I want to emphasise that these sessions, too, can be good fun—especially if you do them with friends.

And you can structure them in many different ways, as well. There's a place for traditional repeats, of course: doing X number of 800s at a certain pace, for example, with a specified amount of recovery time. And you can do much the same thing on the roads, without measuring the length, around a circle of streets near your home.

But relay races are also a fun way to train. They're not as serious as true races, but having other teams running at the same time can motivate you to push harder, especially if you're a faster runner chasing down a slower runner, or a slower runner starting ahead of a faster runner. Each team will have runners of different abilities—say, one slow and one quite fast. Or there might be at least one vet on each team. Or each team might be made up of both men and women. Anything you think will be fun and create a close match.

If each team has two people, in what's called a paarlauf relay, you can take turns running hard and recovering. One person will run 400 metres, for example, then the other will run the next 400 while the first runner rests. It can go on for as many laps as you decide so that each runner completes four 400s, or six or eight or whatever you want. Having a fast partner is both a blessing and a curse. He or she will help your team overtake the others, which is what you want. But having a fast partner also gives you less time to recover between your laps. When you see Mr. Speedy striding down the home straight not all that many seconds after you handed over to him, you might not know whether your heart should jump or sink.

But if necessary the session can be altered to give the faster runner more distance and less rest. He can jog back and take the baton earlier so the slower teammate has less distance to run.

I often lead warm-weather training camps at Club La Santa in Lanzarote, one of the Canary Islands. One year, I was running a two-week camp for triathletes.

One of my wife's running friends, Jo Staples, and her husband came down for the second week for some sociable training in the sun. Jo is the nicest person you'd ever want to meet. But she's not one in whom the competitive fires burn bright. She's perfectly happy with her back-of-the-pack Sunday running with friends—and why not?

Club La Santa organises various low-key races each week. It's the ideal place to get a free introduction to triathlons, duathlons, and so on. This particular time, there was a duathlon on—run, bike, run—and I wasn't able to run at the time.

'Well, look, Jo', I said. 'We'll do a duathlon together as a team. You run the first run, I'll bike, and you run the second run.'

'Oh, no, no', she said. 'I don't know, Julian. I'm no good at these competitions. I get too nervous.'

But I persisted. After all, that's what a coach is for. The way she remembers it, I said these competitions were informal, and there would doubtless be children participating and grandmas, too.

When she arrived, though, there were no children. No grandmas, either. Just people who looked to her a whole lot like athletes.

But by this time she was committed. For once, she was actually doing an event, so there was a little bit of pressure on her first run. It was short—just 2.5K—and that gave her the idea she could do it at a fast pace. And off she went.

'About 100 yards from the start, my chest was pounding, and I was—"Oh, my *word!*"' she recalled recently.

She kept at it, though, and finished. In last place—but without stopping. Absolutely fine! No one was expecting anything else. But she *did* it!

And that was perfect for me. I like a challenge, so I hopped on the bike, rode hard, and when I finished, we were back in front.

'I was still catching my breath when you zoomed into the stadium', Jo recalled. '"I'll kill that Julian," I said to myself. You looked like you'd hardly broken a sweat.'

So—much too soon for her liking—it was Jo's turn to run again. But this time it was different. She had a head start! This was good!

'It was quite an exciting feeling', she said. 'Hey, I'm in the *front!*'

It was an experience she'd never had before. She had a lead to hold onto! Other runners were trying to catch her! And she really gave it a go. We got her to do some work *beyond* her comfort zone, and it was great.

She admits there were times during the race when she was taking my name in vain. But in the end, she was happy to have done it and felt a great sense of achievement.

Who won or lost in the end isn't important. These aren't serious races. But they're an excellent way to mimic situations you'll encounter in real races—situations for which, it would seem obvious, you need to train. You can't expect to handle them well in a race if you've never done them before. Sessions like these give you a chance to improve your speed, try out different paces, and discover your capabilities.

> **'** Pacing in training is different to pacing in races. The goal in races might be to stay a bit on the conservative side and run at an even pace, or to plan your big push for a certain point in the race. In training, often the aim is to experiment, throw caution to the wind, and find out what you're capable of doing. What you discover might surprise you. **'**

Throwing caution to the wind isn't the goal 100 percent of the time: When you're running repetitions, the goal can be to hit exactly the same time 8 or 10 reps in a row. But in a fartlek, you can feel free to run as hard as possible. You might find when you get to the telephone pole you've picked that you've run faster than you thought you could or that you recover more quickly than you would have done a few weeks earlier. You'll feel ready to take off again sooner than you expected. You can't find out what you can really do without pushing against your limits. Besides, you need to run at various paces to produce the wide range of training effects that will help you improve.

And in relay races, there's no room to be conservative. If your team is behind when you take over, you need to run as hard as you can to chase down the runner in front of you. Just take off at top speed and hope you can keep it up. Again, you might well find you're capable of a whole lot more than you thought.

These discoveries carry over into normal races, when you all line up together. If you've learned that you can now run, say, six minutes quite hard even when you're tired, that gives you the confidence to start much faster or to push for home in a race well before the finish line comes into view. The runners around you may hold back—not necessarily because they're incapable of pushing that hard for that long, but because they don't realise they can do it. They're too cautious to try.

BALANCED WEEKLY TRAINING SCHEDULES

A balanced weekly training schedule should include the sort of variety that these four sessions provide—a fartlek, repetitions of some kind, a long run, and one or more recovery runs. Examples of these kinds of weekly training schedules can be found in the appendix on page 189. But there's another question: How do you balance your training with the rest of your life?

The answer varies from person to person. For most people, running is a hobby. It's not the most important thing in their lives, nor should it be. But if they want to improve, running can't be the last thing in their lives, either, something to be squeezed in only as an afterthought, after everything else is done.

A lot of training is about routine. To balance your training with other parts of your life, the training needs to be not first, not last, but an integral part of your daily routine—something you don't debate with yourself every day: Should I or shouldn't I? Training needs to be a habit.

There are various ways to fit training in. If presidents and prime ministers can find time to stay fit, others of us can find ways to do it, too. Some people run to work or get in a short run before work. Others get in a run at lunchtime. Getting out of the office and away from the computer for a while makes you more alert and productive. It's just a matter of routine.

It's normal to get tired from the shopping, the gardening, the housework, your job, and looking after the kids. But don't allow daily fatigue to level out all your training. Maybe you get home at 7:30 or 8:00 at night, and you can't face anything more than a half hour or so. Fine! Make *that* your recovery run. And feel good about it. You will certainly feel better for having got out for a run, rather than slumping in front of the TV.

That's where, once again, training twice a day helps. You can do short sessions. You don't need to tell your family you're going for a run and that's the last they'll see of you for an hour or two. You can be back in half an hour. You can do more sessions, add more strings to your bow, and do yourself more good without going out for so many long runs. The shorter runs will fit more easily into the gaps in your schedule. And when you find the slots where training does fit in, be sure to make it an unquestioned habit. Routine is an absolute key.

And remember to leave yourself feeling pleasantly tired. You want to be fit to train the next day, yes. But more than that, you've got to *look forward* to training the next day. I said earlier that you should always have an aim as you train. Well, the overriding aim, whatever standard of runner you are, is to enjoy it. Don't go so far or so fast that you wipe yourself out.

And don't get caught up in trying to distract yourself by hiding between your earphones: Why blot out the real world? Be aware of your body and your feelings. Wherever you are, there will be something to be savoured. Enjoy the sounds and smells around you—the twitter of birdsong, the whisper of the wind, the salty tang of the sea, and the sweet aroma of the rhododendrons. Whenever you're running, your senses will be heightened. Allow your running to be a pleasurable, sensation-filled experience. And don't get overly tangled up in the technicalities of training regarding heart rate monitors and training zones.

No, you're not on a treadmill. The aim is to enjoy it, to have a good time, and to *feel good*. There has to be fun and repartee, some good times. And then the training, I think, will look after itself.

KEY POINTS TO REMEMBER

- Balance your weekly training with four key sessions: a long run, a fartlek, a repetition session, and at least one recovery run. Include other steady runs as you wish.
- The aim of a recovery run is to feel better at the end than you did at the start. Keep the pace easy but your feet quick, and keep these runs short.

- Run your long endurance sessions at a pace that allows for conversation. It's not how fast you run that matters, it's the time you spend on your feet.
- Fartlek running is the vital first stage in getting used to speedwork. It's unstructured but very beneficial.
- Pacing in training is different to pacing in races. In races, you will probably want to maintain a steady pace. But in training, run at different speeds. Use some training sessions to push the boundaries and find out what you're capable of. If you don't try, you'll never know.
- Make training an integral part of your daily routine, an unquestioned habit.

3

Running With Skill

With 200 metres to go and glory up for grabs, Steve Ovett pulled alongside the man leading the race, the Soviet runner Nikolay Kirov. It was the final of the Olympic 800 metres being run in Moscow's Central Lenin Stadium, Kirov's home turf. From back in the pack charged Sebastian Coe, the world record holder. The crowd roared. Everything was shaping up for a razor-close finish.

But as the leaders rounded the final bend, Ovett shifted into another gear and pulled away. Feet flashing, arms pumping, he flew down the straight at a speed the others could not match, winning Olympic gold and writing his name into the history of international running.

If you want to understand how you can reach your potential, it helps to have a picture in your mind. A picture of Ovett would be a good one to have. Go to YouTube and watch some of his races. He was one of the greatest Britons ever to grace a track, and there was more to admire than just his results, spectacular as they were. He was magnificent to watch: His coordination was perfect. All parts of his body moved in sync. His balance was spot on, and his centre of gravity was forward of his hips. His feet flowed; his strides, fast and long, ate up the ground in front of him. He had an aura, a sense of menace, that created fear in his rivals and space in the pack.

For a more recent example, watch the relaxed and rangy way the great Ethiopian athlete Haile Gebrselassie, or his countryman, Kenenisa Bekele (winner of three Olympic golds), runs. Get a

Mark Shearman, Athletics Images

With 'eyes like chips of ice', Steve Ovett beats favourite Sebastian Coe in the 1980 Olympic 800-metre final in Moscow.

feel for their overall timing, balance, and coordination before worrying about whether you're moving your arms properly or landing correctly on your feet.

When Ovett came on the scene, he was definitely the one I wanted to emulate. I wanted to run taller and rangier, with that kind of cadence and strength. Later on, when we shared the same coach, Harry Wilson, Steve and I sometimes trained together. Watching Ovett on the telly was one thing. But running alongside him was an altogether more vivid experience. He was so stylish, relaxed, and powerful that again I thought, 'Jeepers, *that's* how to run! Thank God he's not doing the 5 and 10K!'

If you want to run your best and make the most use of all the miles you put in, you'd do well to carry a picture of a top runner in your head, as well.

Of course, runners come in all shapes and sizes and have different strengths and weaknesses, so to some extent each person will have a unique style. But that's not the same as saying everyone will naturally find the best way to run. Is that how people learn to swim—by getting chucked in the water so they can develop their own style? Every swimmer has idiosyncrasies, but all swimmers appreciate the importance of timing, balance, relaxation, and coordination, and almost without exception, swimmers are taught how to swim. How many runners are taught how to run?

❛ Just as it is in swimming, technique is vitally important in running. It only takes an understanding of the little things you're doing that slow you down—and how to correct them—to make a breakthrough. The way you run, far from being unimportant, can make a world of difference. ❜

The thing is, nobody is ever taught to run. There's a widely held perception that distance running doesn't require much skill. Sprinting takes some skill. Pole vaulting, hurdling, jumping, and throwing—even more so. But distance running? You just put one foot in front of the other, and what's so difficult about that? Besides, tinkering with someone's style, the thinking goes, would be wrong. Look at Emil Zatopek, the Czech runner. He looked so ungainly, but he won Olympic gold in the 5,000 metres, 10,000 metres, and the marathon in Helsinki in 1952. Obviously, the way to run is just how you naturally do it.

It would be easy to lay all these misconceptions at the feet of coaches. And they do bear some responsibility, concentrating on mileage and times as they so often do. But runners bear some responsibility, too. When I was an international athlete, I couldn't help taking it a bit personally if someone—often even my dad—told me I was a plodder who'd lost out at birth on any fast-twitch muscle fibres and just couldn't sprint. (Being a biology teacher, he did at least admit that was partly *his* fault—and apologized for failing to pass on his own ability to sprint!) Or if someone suggested I could only run well in the mud, as the BBC athletics commentator David Coleman implied in a brief conversation in a hotel lift at Gateshead in 1981, shortly after I'd won the National Cross Country Championship in extremely muddy conditions.

'What are you doing here, Goater?' he asked, referring to the Golden 5,000 metres invitation race being held at Gateshead the following day. 'The only chance you've got is if they plough up the track!'

Well, they didn't, and I finished a respectable fifth in 13:25, beating many more-fancied runners, including Dave Moorcroft, who would smash the world record for the 5,000 less than a year later. But Coleman was right in that the race highlighted my lack of a sprint finish—and the difficulty of winning without one.

Looking back, I should have taken more notice of some of the criticisms, at least those that were well-intentioned efforts to help me run better. But the trouble was that none of those people actually had any idea how to help me run faster. They could see that I was a plodder, but all they could suggest was harder training not better technique.

That's still true for most runners, even today. Go to any local club, watch the members go out for their group run, and you'll see plenty of evidence that no one has ever taught these dedicated competitors how to run skilfully. Even among the club's top performers, you may see people with heavy legs and a slow cadence. Many have hardly any knee lift and land on their heels with the lead foot well in front of their bodies, in effect braking with every stride. Many have tense postures and poor balance, perhaps holding their heads to one side or running with one shoulder higher than the other. In a vain attempt to ease this tension, some dangle their arms or flap their hands—or even do different things with each arm. Some bring their arms across their bodies, twisting themselves until they really start rocking and rolling. The harder they work the more ungainly and off-balance they get.

In other words, runners who are training hard to run as fast as possible often end up doing all manner of things that actually slow them down. They're under the misapprehension that effort is everything and that all they need do is to train harder and run more miles.

❛ Practice makes perfect, right? Well, wrong, actually. Practice bad habits, and they'll become ingrained. Only perfect practice makes perfect.   ❜

Running correctly is not so much about looking good as feeling good, though it's hard to run correctly without looking pretty good too. And there are compelling reasons to learn how to do it. First off, if you run correctly, you'll be less likely to get injured. That means your training will be more consistent—and that might be the single most important factor in making progress.

Secondly, the ability to maintain good form will allow you to go faster or keep up the same speed for longer distances. Efficiency is critical to distance running. You need to avoid working against yourself. In distance running, people often talk about the need for an economical stride, meaning for example low knee lift. I disagree. An economical stride means a quick cadence, spinning, pattering along in a fairly low gear, like pedalling briskly while using a low gear on a bike. Running economically does not mean shuffling along at a fast walk.

Running is a simple activity, even though running fast entails a lot of skill. Let's try and keep it simple.

I have ideas on how to run correctly. As a coach, I've seen them help runners of all ages and abilities improve dramatically. Many of these ideas I have not heard discussed by any other coach or read in any other book. Unfortunately, they didn't help me in my own running career. I wish they had, but I developed them largely after my career ended.

It became clear to me as my 30s wore on that my career as an international-class runner was coming to an end. I've always been competitive, and I began to wonder what else I could do—something at which I could improve rather than just watching myself decline as a runner.

In the late 1980s, we started going to Club La Santa in Lanzarote, one of the Canary Islands, for warm-weather training. It's not such a great place for running—Ovett took one look at the harsh and rocky terrain and promptly left. But it has great biking and swimming facilities, as well as a 400-metre tartan track, and it's an absolute mecca for triathletes. Despite my inability to swim, I tried my hand at triathlon and gradually got hooked.

And that, oddly enough, is what got me into thinking about running technique—listening to swim coaches. They talked about timing, balance, and coordination. These may be obvious things, but they were never stressed for distance runners.

Swimming, for example, is not just about your arms. You use your whole body, not only for power but also for balance, timing, and to minimise drag by maintaining a streamlined body position. If you're swimming properly, you're harnessing the power of your back.

Funnily enough, it's really very similar to running.

‘ Running is not just about your legs. Doing it well involves using your whole body—for relaxation, timing, and power. What you're doing with your head, shoulders, arms, and hands makes a huge difference. ’

As in swimming, your back plays a crucial role. A tight back will limit the range of movement in your hamstrings, shortening your stride and causing injuries if you try to run fast. It will also affect the way your feet land, which in turn can tighten up your leg muscles. And that can lead to problems in your ankles, knees, and hips—not to mention exacerbating the original back problem.

Before we break down the different parts of your body, let's think of it as a whole. First off, think about how you feel, not how you look.

' You'll help yourself if you feel you're running *tall*, *relaxed*, and *balanced*. You should sit, stand, and walk that way, too, for that matter. '

Running tall gives you room to breathe. Your chest has more room to expand. You can take in more air than if you're hunched with your chest collapsed. Running tall also allows you to take longer strides. You can't take long strides if you're tight and sort of sitting down as you run. Other things being equal, if each stride is longer, you'll get to the finish line sooner. Whatever your stature, picture yourself running as tall and rangy and relaxed as possible. Plenty of small men run fast with long, rangy strides. Haile Gebrselassie, a very small but very fast man, is a good example. He's only five-foot-five, but he runs with the long and loose strides of a much taller man.

Staying relaxed saves energy. Each of us has only so much fuel to burn. You don't want to waste it tensing parts of your body that should be relaxed, almost fighting against yourself. Fighting against yourself is like trying to ride a bike with the brakes on.

AP Photo/Thomas Kienzle

Poetry in motion: Kenenisa Bekele, Sileshi Sihine, and Haile Gebrselassie showcase fabulous technique in synchronization during the 2004 Olympic 10,000 metres in Athens.

> ‘ Here, above all, are the key things to remember as you run: You should feel like you're falling forward and that it is only by bringing your legs through quickly that you stop yourself from falling. Your head should be still and looking straight ahead. Your arms should have the feeling of pulling back, one at a time—not by any exaggerated arm movement, but by using your shoulders, which at all times should be loose and relaxed. You should reach forward with your knees bent and your heels coming through fairly high, so your legs move almost like those of a cyclist. And your feet should land quietly and move quickly and lightly.   ’

Reading this, many people might think I'm echoing the so-called 'Pose method' of running, which has gained considerable popularity in recent years, particularly in the United States and in triathlon circles.

But that's not the case. I developed these ideas on running long before the Pose method came along. I think the Pose method gets a lot of things right. For example, it's the only other method that echoes what I've been saying all along about falling into the next step and not landing on your heels. But in my view, the Pose Method makes running technique sound unnecessarily complicated. It recommends that runners do convoluted exercises, some of them involving a coach controlling your leg action with elastic cords. The suggestion is that it can take years to learn proper technique. I think that's a money-spinning hook. Technique doesn't have to be so complicated; learning it doesn't have to be so regimented. In some ways, you still need to run how you feel, in an uninhibited way. And somehow many African runners have managed to learn to run well without using rubber bands. I like to keep things simple, too.

Now that we've looked at the whole picture in a nutshell, let's examine the different components of running with skill.

KEEPING YOUR HEAD

Your head is heavy—about 12 pounds on average. That's a significant portion of your body weight. If you're tiny, like Gebrselassie at 117 pounds, it's 10 percent of your total weight. If you're larger—I'm over six feet—it's a bit less. In any event, what you do with an object that heavy, where you carry it and how you hold it, has a significant effect on your running.

If you run looking at the sky, letting your head hang behind you, that's like putting the brakes on. It really holds you back. It also constricts your throat, making it harder for you to breathe. So don't do it.

And if you let your head rock from side to side, that unbalances you and creates torsion throughout your body, wasting your energy. Don't do that, either.

But don't look too far down or let your head lean too far forward. If you do, your backside will stick out, you won't be running tall, and it will be hard to pick your knees up because you're leaning too far forward.

❛ You should hold your head tall, with your neck relaxed and your eyes looking straight ahead and slightly downward, focused on the ground 10 or 15 metres in front of you. That will help keep your centre of gravity forward, enabling you to fall into the next step and keep the rapid, rolling cadence that will help you run at your fastest and most efficient. ❜

GIVING YOURSELF A HAND

Quite early in my career, I was with a squad of British distance-runners, warm-weather training in Spain. Charlie Elliot, one of the coaches, suggested I needed to make some changes in the way I ran.

'Has anyone ever taught you to run?' he asked. 'Come down to the track and we'll do a session. I can help you'.

To be honest, I was a little resentful that he was criticizing my natural way of running. Especially as he wasn't even my coach. I knew I had talent, and I'd been posting excellent results since I was 16 or 17. But I thought, OK, I'll give it a try.

He was the first person—perhaps the only person—who tried to get me to run differently and more strongly by using my arms more effectively. He and I were chatting before our session started, and he said, 'You need to think much more about how you use your arms. Don't just swing them or, even worse, flap them. You want to feel you're *pulling,* first with one arm, then with the other. Remember, your arms drive your legs. It's your arms that help you maintain your stride length and your endurance'.

Up until then, I'd thought all I needed to do with my arms was to keep them relaxed and balanced.

'I've really never felt like I'm pulling with my arms,' I said, a bit doubtfully. 'But I suppose I see what you mean'.

I tried my best, but this new style of running didn't feel comfortable. 'Oh, God', I thought, 'it's harder this way.' What Charlie didn't say to me—although I wish he had—was, 'Of *course* it's harder, partly because it's different to what you've been used to and partly because your upper-body strength is so puny! Stick with it, because it's going to work'.

We only had one session together, and Charlie was only looking at using my arms to maintain stride length. Even he didn't emphasise the most important use of your arms—to maintain a quick leg cadence.

Still, I'm grateful to him, because he was the first person to tell me how to use my arms, and what it should feel like. The germ of an idea came to me, one that would take shape more fully when I turned to triathlon.

As you would expect, my swimming coach, Robin Brew—a former Olympic record holder in the 200-metre individual medley—talked a lot about technique in the front crawl. As I listened, it struck me: He could be talking about running.

He told me where most of the power of the stroke comes from. It's not in front of you or even underneath; it's behind you. A swimmer should push his hands right back along his thighs before letting them exit the water. This *push* phase of the front crawl is just like the long *pull* phase with your arms when you're running that enables you to get a powerful drive off the rear foot. Cut it short, or do it too slowly or too fast, and you won't maximize the power of the drive. Timing and co-ordination are vital.

Before we get into exactly what pulling feels like when you're running, let's talk about the things you want to avoid.

You can let your arms dangle, which is great for relaxing your shoulders but bad for power and balance. You might do this to loosen up and facilitate recovery between repetitions. But avoid it if you're trying to run strongly and with speed.

Some people move their forearms vigorously, bending them at the elbows to produce a flapping or even a hammering action. That uses a lot of energy without helping move you forward at all.

Other people avoid that pitfall, keeping their arms nicely bent at the elbows, but fall into another: They stick their elbows out and bring their arms almost sideways across their chests. This limits the expansion of their chests and constricts their breathing. Even worse, the more effort they put into this sideways arm action, the more they knock themselves off balance. This creates torsion through the trunk, knees, and ankles. Not only is the whole thing wasted effort, but people who do this also increase their risk of injury.

Many runners simply don't think much at all about what they do with their arms or how fast they do it. Your arms will move as fast as they need to in order to keep up with your feet, right? Actually, it works the other way.

❛ **If you move your arms quicker, you'll automatically change weight quicker from one foot to the other. Faster arms mean faster feet—your arms, not your legs, are your accelerator pedal.**   ❜

And since they're so critical, you'll almost certainly benefit from working on your upper-body strength.

But moving your arms quickly is not the whole story. As in nearly every sport, the key to success is your timing. In swimming, it's vital to catch hold of the water and pull those arms right back—quickly, but not *too* quickly. If you move your arms too fast, they slip the water.

It's similar in running: You want your arms to move quite vigorously, with that feeling of pulling, but the timing is all-important if you want the pull to be effective. You want to move your arms fast enough to keep a high cadence but not so fast that you get ahead of your stride. If you do that, you'll pull your arm all the way back before you've developed the drive off your rear foot. Your arm will be behind you and you'll be ready to change weight to the next leg before you've got the drive from a full leg extension. And you'll lose the vital connection between the pull of your arm and the push off your back foot. It's your stomach and core strength that are the crucial link between what you do with your arms and the power and drive coming from your legs.

How can your arms help instead of hinder? When you run, hold your hands loosely clenched. Keep your shoulders loose and your arms relaxed but not floppy, elbows bent at an angle of less than ninety degrees. Use your shoulders to move your arms in a forwards and backwards plane, not across your body. There should be virtually no movement at the elbows or wrists. You want to have the feeling you're pulling, one arm at a time—not just backwards, but *downwards* and backwards, and it's important to remember that you're pulling from the shoulder, not the elbow. Think of it as if you were trying to elbow someone behind you, not someone beside you.

6 Unless you're sprinting, almost all the effort of your arm action should be behind your body, not in front. The action is all pulling back. Your front arm just needs to stay bent, and it will continue forward and upward with no active push, just as long as the other arm is pulling. 9

This may be difficult to feel at first. I remember once when I was at Oxford, and I was trying to get back from an injury. When I was well on the way to recovery, one thing I tried was skipping on the grass, almost like the skip phase of a triple jump—skip and skip and skip. And I remember feeling the connection between the arms and the powerful drive you can develop off the rear foot. 'Much more useful, and less risky, than bounding', I thought.

Try it. Skip. Long and loose and rangy. If you're not pulling, you'll wobble: You can't skip with both arms in front of you. And the pulling of your arm behind you contributes to your lift. Try to feel and develop the connection between the arm pull all the way back and the drive off the back foot.

That connection is exactly what you're looking for when you're running but with much quicker legs of course. You'll feel it, and be able to practice it, not just by doing skipping drills, but by running fast up steps and up hills.

KNEES, FEET, AND ANKLES

It's obvious that what we do with our legs affects the way we run. But no one teaches us how to move them. So let's talk about it now.

When you run, reach forward with your knees, not your heels. If your centre of gravity is behind your foot as it hits the ground—if you're reaching forward with your heel—each footfall creates a braking effect. That's definitely not what you want. Instead, bend your knees and lift and reach with them. And make sure your hips are above your foot as it hits the ground, not behind it. Running is like cycling, and your legs should move in a cyclical motion. It is *not* just a quick walk, where your legs are straight and you land on your heels.

What you do with your feet is also important, though no one talks about that, either. Your feet should work exactly the way they do when you're running on the spot. There's no need to land on your heels. Try running on the spot and landing on your heels—it's very difficult! It's much more comfortable to land correctly, on your forefeet. Your feet should have a quick double action, serving as shock absorbers as you land and as springs as you take off, in a quick rebound action.

That means landing on your forefoot and, as the shock-absorbing effect sets in, allowing the rest of your foot to lightly touch the ground, then springing off your toes again. All that takes place in a fraction of a second.

❛ The best indicator of whether you're using your feet correctly is the sound they make—preferably very little. If they slap the ground or bang it, or if you seem to be stubbing your feet as you land, you're putting on the brakes, wasting energy and risking injury. You want your feet to be quiet, and quick, too—at least two steps per second and three if you can. ❜

I can hear some readers saying, 'Wait a minute. Some of us are just natural heel-strikers. And, secondly, running on your toes is for short distances. Anyone who runs longer races will land on his heels. That's why running shoes are designed the way they are. They're meant to absorb the shock of landing on your heels. The guys in the shop even *told* me to land on my heels!'

There's no doubt: Much of the perceived wisdom today, often promoted by running shoe manufacturers and endorsed by podiatrists, is that you should hit the ground with your heel, then roll onto the ball of your foot. But are running shoes designed like that because of how everyone runs? Or does everyone run that way because of how the shoes are designed? I think it's largely the latter. Some running shoes have such built-up heels that you can't avoid landing heel-first. I can understand why some of the best African runners—like Zola Budd, the South African athlete who set two world records at 5,000 metres—prefer to run barefoot instead of wearing those clumpy old shoes. And there have been several studies recently that support this view and even claim that running shoes are a major *cause* of injuries.

I dispute the claim that anybody is a natural heel striker. It's true that the faster you run, the more likely you are to be up on your toes. But it's possible to run long distances without landing heavily on your heels. If you run on the spot without landing on your heels, why can you not go forwards the same way?

And what happens when you run uphill? Do you still think you're a natural heel striker?

Consider the great Ethiopian runner Abebe Bikila. He won Olympic gold in the marathon in 1960, running barefoot over the streets of Rome with some of the course winding over the cobblestones of the Appian Way. There's no way he ran 26.2 miles landing on his bare heels. That would have hurt too much.

I understand the impulse to say, 'Hey, that's just my style.' When I was a competitive runner at university for a number of years, I noticed that my shoes were wearing out on the outside of the heels. I must have been sitting down a little as I ran, swinging my legs through long and low, reaching forward with my heels and landing on them. But I could still run quite strongly—and when you can win races you tend to think that's just the way you run.

The thing was that I kept getting injured. I was getting Achilles trouble, my calves were very stiff, and my back was taking such a pounding that I wound up with a misaligned pelvis. I thought long and hard about how I was running compared to Ovett, and I decided to change my style. I also decided to race—not only on the track but also at cross country—in shoes that almost prevented me running on my heels, because there weren't any heels to run on. And over time I found I used my feet better, and ran much faster.

There are a couple of ways to practice landing on your feet properly and getting the feel of the spring effect. One is to run uphill. That same session at Oxford, when I was skipping on the grass, I ran up and down the steps in the grandstand. I found I was getting more bounce and becoming more confident in my landing. In the same way, if you run uphill, you're going to land on your toes and get that feeling.

Or you can try running on the spot. You won't be landing on your heels that way, either. And remember as you run the roads—don't slap your feet down and don't stub your feet as you land. But don't worry too much. Don't keep thinking, 'Am I landing right?' Just listen to your feet. If your feet are quiet, you'll be doing well.

BALANCING ACT

Now that we've looked at technique from head to toe, let's put the different components back together into a coherent whole. In the end, all the actions we've been talking about need to work together to achieve a style that's powerful, relaxed—and balanced.

Running with balance is vital to being the most efficient runner you can be. You don't want to move side to side and waste energy righting yourself with every stride. Your energy should be devoted to propelling yourself forward. Would you wobble your head or flap your arms if you were racing on a bike? Balance is no less vital when you're on the run.

Go back to what I said about having a picture in your mind of how you want to run. Who are the best distance runners today? Africans, without a doubt. Consider Gebrselassie, perhaps the greatest distance runner of all time. In 2008 in Berlin, he ran 2:03:59, becoming the first person to break 2:04 and setting the 26th world record of his fabulous career.

And who broke that record? Patrick Makau, a Kenyan, who ran 2:03:38 in Berlin in 2011.

At the 2008 Olympics in Beijing, Tirunesh Dibaba, another Ethiopian, became the first woman ever to win gold in both the 5,000 and the 10,000. Kenenisa Bekele, yet another Ethiopian, won gold in the same two races on the men's side, following his domination of the World Cross Country Championships, which he'd won six of the last seven years.

Also in Beijing, Samuel Wanjiru, a 21-year-old Kenyan, sadly no longer with us, defied all predictions that Beijing's heat and smog would prevent fast times in the marathon and ran 2:06:32 to win.

And that doesn't even scratch the surface of African running accomplishments. Look at the lead pack in any world-class distance race today, and you're bound to see several Africans jostling for position—quite often more runners from Africa than from any other continent.

What do all these runners have in common? Many things, not least of which is enormous talent. But another is that they can run at tremendous speed while staying perfectly poised and balanced. There's no wobble to be seen.

Many come from countries where balance is part of everyday life, where people carry earthenware pots on their heads for long distances as if there were no trick to it at all. If you think your balance is good, try putting a cushion on your head and walking across the room. You might find you're quite jerky, either from side to side or forwards and backwards—or both.

When Africans do it, it looks easy. But it involves skilful, finely tuned interaction between almost all the muscle groups of the body. These athletes are aware of, and have control of, what their entire bodies are doing, from their feet right up to their heads.

Walking with something on your head involves balance and posture at a slow pace. If you could run as smoothly as that, you'd be much more relaxed and efficient.

As a coach, I've never tried to get my runners walking around with things on their heads. You don't have to do it too much to get the idea: It's just useful to show people they don't move as smoothly as they might think.

But there are some exercises you can do to improve your balance. One is to stand first on one leg for 30 seconds and then the other. Not so hard? Try it with your eyes closed, for 10 seconds on each leg. You might find that quite difficult at first. But with practice, your balance and awareness of your entire body will improve markedly, even with your eyes shut.

Another recommendation is to get a wobble board. Your job is to stand on it and control the wobble without allowing the edges to touch the floor. Quite easy with two feet, a lot harder on just one foot. When you master that, stand on the board and throw a ball against the wall, catching it on the rebound while still keeping your balance. Make it as difficult for yourself as you like.

Balance is mostly a matter of being aware of your entire body. Observe yourself as you run. Is your head hanging forward or wobbling from side to side? Are you holding one of your shoulders higher than the other? Are your arms coming across your chest or working unevenly? All of which are undesirable. Or are you running tall, with arms pulling and your centre of gravity over your front foot as you land? Are your feet moving quickly and quietly? If so, good. Because that will allow you to run faster and further, whatever your level of fitness.

READY TO ROLL

Bearing in mind that if you want to feel tall, relaxed, and balanced as you run, it is vital also to allow yourself to roll forward with every step.

As all cyclists know, the aim is to maintain contact with the pedals through each revolution. They want to have equal contact with the chain ring, applying force all the way round the cycle at a tangent rather than just pressing down with one leg and then with the other. Cyclists sometimes think they're pretty good at it—but then as an exercise they try to cycle smoothly with only one foot clipped into the pedal. It's very difficult. When they do it with two legs, they don't notice how bad they are. But doing it with one leg, they realise there *is* a dead spot. And they practice minimizing that.

‘ You want something similar to a cycling feeling as you run. Each step should produce almost zero braking and as little up and down movement of your body as possible—as if you were carrying something on your head. To achieve this smooth, rolling effect when you're running, you should constantly strive to avoid landing on your heels. ’

When you're running, don't give your leg time to swing all the way forward until your heel hits the ground. That's what causes a braking effect. Instead, bend your knee, almost fall forward, and put your next foot down quickly, not too far in front of you. Apart from the split second as you land, you want to keep your centre of gravity forward of the foot you're landing on, not behind it.

You can't achieve this by bending at the waist. If you lean forward too much with your upper body and leave your backside sticking out behind you, your centre of gravity will still be behind your front foot. You'll land on your heel with your leg in front of you, applying the brakes.

On the other hand, if you run with your body upright and sit down a bit as you run, that won't help either. Your footfall will be flat, not springy, and your centre of gravity will still be behind your front foot. The brakes will still be on, and most of your energy will go into upward lift rather than forward drive.

' **You want to run tall and barrel-chested, with your hips forward and your feet springy. If you get the feeling that you'd fall forward if you didn't hurry up and take the next step, that will keep your cadence brisk and allow you to use gravity rather than fighting it.** **'**

Often, as I coach runners, I ride beside them on my bike. Sometimes when I see someone having trouble taking the brakes off, as it were, I give him a gentle push at the base of his spine. It's not really a push, just a touch sufficient to make him overbalance. All of a sudden, he gets the feel of what he should be striving for, the hips forward and the sensation of almost falling that makes the feet speed up simply to ensure he doesn't actually fall over. That, combined with the circular leg motion, like that of a cyclist, creates the all-important rolling effect. Once you've got that momentum, don't fight it, just maintain it. It's like running downhill—even on the flat!

KEEPING IT SIMPLE

There you have it: the basics of skilful running. Some runners might think technique is an extra—something they'll work on if they have some spare time next month or the month after that. More likely, they think it's something only top-class runners need to worry about. Not so. You can—and should—practice good technique every time you run, not just when you're doing drills or special technique sessions.

' **Just be aware of what you're doing and what you're trying to do. You can practice and improve your technique on every run, and if your technique improves—even without any increase in fitness—you will run faster and with less risk of injury.** **'**

Altering your style will feel awkward at first, but stick with it. It will feel natural and fluid after awhile. If you're not sure what you're doing wrong—and most of us aren't—run on a treadmill in front of a mirror. Or, better still, get a friend to video you while you're running. You could be in for a nasty shock, but unless you identify a fault, how can you correct it?

And always remember these key elements: Run tall, relaxed, and balanced, falling into the next step. Head straight and still, pulling with your arms and reaching forward with your knees so your legs move like those of a cyclist. And keeping your feet quick and quiet. As I said, it's simple—and a simple checklist to go through while you're running. It's not all about complicated drills and special sessions.

Skilful technique can help runners post faster times than they ever thought possible and surge past rivals who have beaten them in the past. To some extent, that's what we're all looking for when we enter races. It's part of the fun of running. And the faster you go, the more fun you'll have.

KEY POINTS TO REMEMBER

- Technique is vitally important: It's not about looking good, it's about running faster. The point is to move efficiently, making the best use of your energy. Good technique allows you to make the most of your fitness, whatever your level. Work on it every time you run.

- Run economically—not with long, slow legs, but with short, quick strides. Reach forward with your knees so your legs move almost like those of a cyclist.

- You should feel like you're falling forward and you need to bring your legs through quickly to stop yourself from falling.

- Faster arms mean faster feet. Your arms, not your legs, are your accelerator pedal and control your cadence.

- When you run, you want to feel tall, relaxed, and balanced. Keep your shoulders loose.

- Hold your head straight and still. Your eyes should look straight ahead and slightly downward, focused on the ground 10 or 15 metres in front of you.

- Your arms should feel like they're pulling back behind you, one at a time.

- Your feet should move quickly and land quietly, as when running on the spot.

4

Gearing Up
for Success

In 1993, Graeme Obree, the Flying Scotsman, decided he would try to break the one-hour cycling record—one of the sport's most prestigious achievements. The world record of 51.151 kilometres had been set nine years earlier by the Italian rider Francesco Moser.

Obree reserved the Vikingskipet velodrome in Hamar, Norway, and gathered the officials necessary to certify a new world record. On July 16, he was ready for his attempt. He normally rode Old Faithful, a bike he'd built himself. But at the last minute, he was persuaded to change to a copy of Old Faithful, but one that had a different gear ratio.

After an hour of all-out, intensely painful riding, Obree failed. He'd covered 50.690 kilometres, missing the world record by 461 metres.

But he was still convinced he could break the record. And he felt sure his mistake had been to switch bikes. But he only had use of the velodrome for 24 hours. The officials were getting ready to leave. And he felt he would never have the chance again.

So he announced he would make another attempt the very next day.

When morning dawned, the stadium was nearly empty. Many of the journalists had packed up their pens and gone home, certain he would fail.

A mere 18 hours after his first attempt, his legs still aching, Obree mounted Old Faithful, with the gear ratio he had originally thought best. He ran ahead of Moser's pace all the way. The collapse many had predicted over the last 15 minutes never came. He stayed strong. And by the end of the hour, he had covered 51.596 kilometres—a new world record!

He had ridden nearly a kilometre further than the day before. The only change had been the gearing he used. What a difference!

It might sound odd, but this applies to running, as well. Counterintuitive as it seems, runners can also improve their performance by finding their optimum cadence and stride length—in other words, by using the right gear ratio.

‘ Gearing is critical to running well, no matter your ability. Whether you are going uphill, downhill or running on the flat, you are looking for the ideal balance between stride length and cadence that you can sustain for the period of your race. ’

As I mentioned in chapter 3, the Pose method of running gets some things right: falling into the next step and not landing on your heels. But it has a couple of huge omissions. It doesn't talk about gearing, which is essential if you're going to run your best and beat your rivals. And it discounts the contribution your arms make: Your arms are the key to setting your cadence and timing.

Let's think about it for a minute. Do you think Lewis Hamilton could win Formula 1 races if his car had only one gear? Could Lance Armstrong have powered his way through the Alps to seven Tour de France victories riding a sleek, state-of-the-art, fixed-gear bike?

Nobody talks about it and nobody teaches it, but gearing is critical in running, too. You can't use the same gear for attacking up a hill as you would cruising on the flat. And gearing is far less complicated than you might think.

'If you were going uphill on a bike', I sometimes ask the runners I coach, 'what would you do if it were getting tough?'

'Stand up' is one common answer. Fine, but it's not really a sustainable option to pedal standing up all the way to the top. Clearly, at some stage it will be necessary to drop down a gear or two.

'So what can you do when you're running up a hill?' I ask.

'Well, you can't change gear!' they say. 'You haven't got any gears!'

'Of course you can', I tell them. 'Just take shorter steps. But at all costs *keep the same cadence.*'

Obviously, you don't want to run up a hill with the maximum possible stride length. That becomes very hard, unsustainable work and, as with cycling or driving a car, you feel the need to change down a gear.

But if you take steps that are too small, you'll find you're putting in a lot of effort and still not really getting anywhere. A comfortable gear lies somewhere between those two extremes.

However, what is most comfortable may still not be the most efficient or fastest. The proper gear makes a big difference, as we saw with Graeme Obree. Lance Armstrong also pedalled at a much higher cadence than had been the accepted norm among the cycling elite—and found he could go faster *and* save his legs in the process.

And I found the same in running. Training with Dave Bedford in the 1970s, I was always aware of his enormous stride—the big gear—that he managed to maintain in relentless fashion over tough cross country courses and round the track. But he couldn't change pace: He found it difficult to quicken his stride after pushing this big gear for so long. In driving terms it would feel like trying to overtake a car at 40 miles per hour in top gear—sluggish.

Two other British 5,000 and 10,000 runners at the time, Dave Black and Tony Simmons, ran very differently, with a much quicker cadence. It looked like they were just pattering along, and yet their times proved they were covering the ground much faster than it looked. A quicker cadence can mean you'll breathe a little harder—just as a car running at a higher rpm might use more fuel—but a lower gear will still save your legs from becoming overtired and give you a zippy change of pace.

So not only do you need different gears—a different balance between stride length and cadence—for uphills and downhills, but also the proper balance will vary from one runner to the next.

So how do you change gears? Many runners, when they try to go faster or climb a hill more strongly, have no picture in their minds as to how to achieve that. They think they just need to push and keep doing exactly the same thing they were already doing, only with more effort. Doing the same thing is not going to get the job done.

Instead, think of what you're going to do differently. Not more effort, but more skill and better timing. Making your arms work that little bit quicker will have the effect of changing down a gear.

The best thing to imagine is the gears on a bike. When you shift into a lower gear to ride uphill, each revolution of the pedals takes you less far down the road, but you keep pushing the pedals at the same number of revolutions per minute.

To shift into a lower gear when you're running, think arms not legs. Pulling more urgently with your arms will force your legs to also move more quickly— but of course with a slightly shorter stride length. You'll be able to power up hills more economically.

Somewhat longer strides—again, keeping the same quick cadence—can give you good cruising speed and help you eat up the road ahead. This is great if you're not climbing a hill or trying to put on a sudden burst of speed.

Selecting the proper gear is critical. If you try to run the entire race in too low a gear, you're not going to have a fast enough cruising speed to run your best. But don't try to push too big a gear up a hill—or even on the flat unless it's the sprint finish—because you'll come undone! You might get up the first couple of hills but you won't make it all the way through the race in very good shape.

Of course, there are times when you do change gear *and* change your cadence too, just as you would if you were cycling.

' To put on a burst of speed, maybe even uphill, and leave a rival hurting in your wake, shorten your stride and put yourself in a lower gear—but pull more quickly with your arms to increase your cadence, using the extra power of the lower gear for quick acceleration. Then change up to a bigger gear—and you're away! '

That's the same thing you'd do to overtake another car on a two-lane road: downshift and floor it. Try it when you're running. It works wonderfully well. If you're climbing a hill with other runners in a race, odds are they'll find their legs stuck in a slow cadence, as they try to push too big a gear. Downshift, keep a quick cadence, and you'll power past them.

If you have slow feet, practice moving them quickly. Try fartlek runs where you sometimes increase your speed by deliberately not taking longer strides, but only taking quicker ones—just like biking on a turbo trainer where you try to get up to 130 rpm.

A low gear is great for hills, but selecting the proper stride length for the long, flat sections of a race is critical, too. Too low a gear—too short a stride—and you won't cover the ground as fast as you could, no matter how hard you work. Too long a stride and you'll crump out before the race is done. Try, just by feel, to run with a stride length big enough to allow you to cover the ground quickly, but not so big that you can't sustain it over the course of the distance you're running.

All the other elements of technique come into play when you change gears, too—balance, timing, keeping your centre of gravity forward, and moving your legs as if you were cycling. And when you think about speeding up your cadence—whether to accelerate quickly in a lower gear or to power down the home straight in a higher gear—think about what you're doing with your arms. Remember: Your arms are your accelerator pedal. They control how quickly you move your legs.

Once you try it, you'll discover that gearing—especially downshifting—is quite easy to apply to your own running. It comes down to stride length and, above all, keeping your quick cadence.

Here's a guide to using the proper gear as you go through a race:

On the flat, choose the highest gear—the longest stride length—at which you can maintain two or preferably three steps per second for the entire race. Please note, however, that's if you're running a time trial or an even-paced race. If it's a tactical race, and you're running slower than your top cruising speed, you will want to be in a lower gear, feeling you have lots of power in hand, rather than labouring in too high a gear—just as when driving a car in traffic at 30 miles per hour, you will want to be in third gear rather than fifth.

This will take a bit of experimentation, but it's critical. Too long a stride—too high a gear—and you'll tire out and your legs will slow down. Too short a stride, and you won't be able to run the race to your potential. It will be like trying to win a Formula 1 race in first or second gear: No matter how high the rpm—no matter how quick your footfalls—you're not going to go very fast.

On the hills or running into the wind, shorten your stride.

You'll cover less ground with each stride but, like a cyclist powering up a hill in low gear, you'll have more strength and the ability to keep your cadence quick. You'll find yourself pushing past other runners who keep their stride length the same but find their legs moving more and more slowly.

If someone overtakes you, check his or her cadence. If you're not moving your feet as quickly as your opponent is, try matching his or her cadence.

Of course, if you are moving your feet at the same rate, that means he or she is taking longer strides and is simply strong enough to push a bigger gear faster than you are. Well, there's not much you can do about that in the middle of a race short of moving your legs even more quickly.

When it comes to the finish, change down a gear—like downshifting a car into third—and try to quicken your cadence. When you get your speed up, try to open up into the longest stride you have the strength to push *while still maintaining your quick cadence.*

Cyclists can't win sprint finishes in too low a gear, no matter how hard they try, and it doesn't work in running, either. Downshifting to climb hills is very easy; using a bigger gear to sprint at the end of a race is intensely difficult. I couldn't do it very well. Neither could Dave Bedford. Maybe a lot of it comes down to genetics.

Icon Sports Media

Seb Coe maintaining good form all the way to the finish to win the 1984 Olympic 1,500 metres in Los Angeles. In contrast, Steve Cram has started to labour and over-stride.

But if you watch, you'll notice that when Olympic champions finish with a blistering last lap their legs are moving fast. But that's not all—they have opened their stride way up as well. A quick cadence plus long strides will get you around the track in a hurry.

Whether or not you can sprint well at the end of a race, always try to choose the right gear for the conditions and the terrain. If you know how to use the proper gear, you'll have a big advantage over one-geared runners. You can zip up a hill while another runner labours up in too high a gear, like a car trying to climb a mountain in fourth, his legs getting slower and slower and his eyes starting to bulge out of his head. And you'll know how to open up your stride a bit and get the best out of yourself on the flat or going downhill.

Get the gearing right, and you'll finish ahead of other runners with the same level of fitness as yours. And they'll be wondering how in the world you did it.

Gearing is also crucial going downhill. Taking lots of short choppy strides—running in a low gear—will create a severe braking effect, just as it would in a car. But if you are strong enough to open up and run rangily down a hill, there will be no braking effect and you will rapidly overtake those runners who are stuck in a low gear.

KEY POINTS TO REMEMBER

- Gearing is critical to taking full advantage of your level of fitness, whatever standard of runner you are. It's a matter of feeling the correct cadence, and therefore the correct gear, for that particular surface, gradient, and part of the race. Choose the right gear for the right occasion and you will see a big improvement in your results.

- Gearing properly means varying your stride length—shortening it for the tough bits, using a somewhat longer stride for the flats, and lengthening it to go faster—all the while keeping your feet moving at the same quick cadence.

- Shorten your stride (in other words, change down a gear or two) while keeping your feet fast to power up the hills.

- The speed and intensity at which you move your arms is critical to mastering gearing. If you only concentrate on your legs while switching gears, you're only controlling half your gear box.

- When training, sometimes deliberately choose either too big or too small a gear. Practice building leg *strength* by slightly over-striding, and improving leg *speed* by under-striding. Experiment. But generally, avoid plodding by selecting the proper gear that allows you to maintain a quick cadence every time you train, so it's second nature when you come to the race.

Chapter 5

Flexible You

When I started out as a runner, I was often told I was a bit stiff and ungainly. I didn't worry about it too much, as it didn't seem to stop me from running fast at cross country or playing football well on the school playground. But I didn't really like rugby or other sports that involved a lot of sliding tackles and falling over. I tended to land heavily because I wasn't lithe and supple, so I quickly showed a preference for noncontact sports. Looking back, I must have seemed like a bit of a wimp—but to me the aim of sport was to get stronger, fitter, and faster, not to end up getting hurt all the time.

Beyond that, I'm not sure that being a bit inflexible really troubled me. Distance runners were expected to be stiff. That was just one of the side effects of the training you had to do in order to be good.

But I learned along the way how wrong that was. Flexibility is critical to performing as well as you can: If you want to run fast, you've got to be loose and supple. You've got to flow. Even more importantly, suppleness helps prevent injuries, meaning your training becomes more consistent—which means, in turn, that you can make better progress and run faster. Which, after all, is the goal.

All my club and school coaches encouraged us runners to stretch, of course, but the stretches my mates and I could do on a five-mile road run in the dark of a winter's night were very different to those the track and field athletes would be doing indoors on mats in a warm gym. It was not until we distance runners joined in with those athletes at various training camps that we saw how unsupple we really were.

One guy who really got me into stretching was our coach at Oxford, a colourful former Polish soldier known as Captain Mack. He used to gather us for occasional sessions of advice and philosophy—and not always on the subject of athletics, for he had views on other matters as well.

As elite athletes, he expected us to feel super-fit and full of energy all the time. Train hard and play hard was his approach—although probably even he would not have approved of the excessive levels to which my club mate and training partner Dave Bedford would take it, on both counts. Bedford was something else.

'Of course you can have a social life', Captain Mack would tell us in his wonderfully expressive Slavic accent, 'as long as it doesn't interfere with your training. Girlfriends—no problem! When I was an athlete, I had seven girl-friends—*all aktiv!*'

It didn't have much to do with running technique, but it had everything to do with building up his athletes' feeling of being almost superhuman and indestructible. And he himself exuded fitness and well-being from head to toe—from his voice and his posture to his enthusiasm. That's how he was—absolutely inspirational.

The inimitable Captain Mack used to coach the entire university athletics team on weekends. Everyone knew that jumpers, hurdlers, sprinters, and vaulters needed to do some serious stretching, but Captain Mack encouraged distance runners to do it regularly, too. But perhaps, not surprisingly, many of them weren't keen on it at all. They just wanted to lace up their shoes and go out and get another 15 miles in the bank. Never mind the other stuff.

But sometimes we were persuaded to go to Captain Mack's sessions, and he showed us how to stretch. I found, to my dismay, that many athletes were much more athletic and supple than I was. I also found that when I went for a run after stretching for five or 10 minutes, I felt a lot better—and ran a lot better, as well. That pretty much convinced me that, yes, improving my suppleness and regular stretching, especially before and after a run, was a necessity.

Before I go any further, a disclaimer: I'm not an expert on stretching. No one's ever called me Mr. Flexibility or thought of me as a human pretzel. I'm not a stretching maniac or a yoga fanatic. I'm just one runner writing for other runners, based on what worked for me over a 12-year international career.

But that may be a good thing. Sometimes I think the experts can confuse more than they help. Half the time, when you pick up a book on stretching, you open it and find 60 stretches in there. Who has time for that? The temptation is to shut the book, put it on the shelf, and never open it again.

You don't *need* that many stretches. Nor do you need to do all the weird and wonderful stretches you might see top athletes doing before a big competition. But you *do* need to stretch—regularly. As with many things, a little and often is best!

For starters, the worst thing for any runner is to be injured. Conversely, most runners would agree that breakthroughs normally come not because of any magic training sessions but simply as a result of consistent, injury-free training.

In my experience, regular stretching is the key to avoiding injury. Being loose, quite apart from allowing you to run faster and rangier, allows you to train hard without getting hurt.

In the end, though, it was not a coach—not even Captain Mack—but a group of fellow runners who gave me the most practical advice about stretching. In 1975 I spent a few weekends up in Birmingham, Britain's second biggest city, training with some of the university athletes. Birmingham University has long been a hotbed of athletics, and back in the '70s and '80s it had a policy of recruiting athletes to enable them to compete with the specialist sports colleges of Loughborough and Borough Road College, as it was known then.

Several of the guys up there—Ray Smedley, Mike Kearns, Andy Holden, and Ian Gilmour to name but a few—trained regularly with the Birmingham-based Scottish runner Ian Stewart.

Ian was running well after a couple of lean years during which first Dave Bedford and then Brendan Foster had been getting the better of him. Although he represented Scotland in the Commonwealth Games and World Cross Country, Stewart was as Brummie as they come—Birmingham through and through: He was dour, blunt, and fiercely competitive.

He had won the 1970 Commonwealth Games 5,000 metres in Edinburgh—refusing to give way to his fellow Scot Ian McCafferty in the finishing straight by forcing him across the track, eventually crossing the line in lane 6!

From 1969 through the mid-'70s, Stewart was one of the top distance runners in the world. 'First is first, and second is nowhere' was his mantra (cleansed of its usual string of expletives). 'This country is full of bloody good losers; what this country needs is a few bloody good winners!'

You can be quite sure that Stewart was not a good loser. He finished third in the 5,000 metres in the 1972 Munich Olympics, behind the great Finnish runner (and eventual winner of four gold medals) Lasse Viren—a thrilling race in which the first four finishers all broke four minutes for the final mile. Stewart finished strongly, surging in the final few metres to snatch the bronze out of the hands of the American cult hero Steve Prefontaine.

Most runners would have been elated. Not Ian. He told a TV interviewer that he'd run 'crap' and would probably throw his medal in the river.

We knew Ian was back running well in the winter of 1975. He and the other Birmingham-based athletes had a considerable advantage in those days: They were able to include track sessions in their schedule, running on the only indoor track in the country, at the nearby Air Force base, RAF Cosford.

That winter, back to his best, Ian won the European indoor 3,000-metre title one weekend, and then went on to win the World Cross Country Championships over 12K in Morocco the following weekend. Quite a double!

Ian Stewart's 'crap' run. Stewart (309) edges Steve Prefontaine to win bronze in the 5,000 at the 1972 Munich Olympics.

Mark Shearman, Athletics Images

I'm sure I learned a lot going up there and getting to run with him now and then. But it was Ray Smedley who gave me the best advice on stretching. He had made the Great Britain team at 1,500 metres for the Munich Olympics in 1972, and was England's first finisher—twice—in the World Cross Country Championships in the '70s.

'Look', he told me once, 'I just read this book, *The Six Simple Stretches That Really Help Prevent Injuries*.' At least I think that was the title. Judging from the Web, it seems to be long out of print—not surprising, considering how many years it's been since then.

Anyway, the stretches in the book were very simple to do. They could be done virtually anywhere—at home, out on a run or even at work, and they would take only a few minutes. And I've been doing them, or variations of them, pretty much ever since.

You should, too. Because if you're supple, you can run with more spring in your step. You can stay more relaxed, which helps you breathe easier. You'll take longer, looser strides and be more resilient when you land. Experts say that every footfall puts the force of three and a half times your body weight on that leg. If they're constantly landing heavily, it's no wonder runners get injured.

But the whole feeling of running is different when you're relaxed and loose as opposed to when you're stiff, heavy, and crashing down on your heels. You may still be landing with the force of three and a half times your body weight, but if your calves are springy and your back is loose enough to absorb some of the shock, landing feels much lighter and more sustainable.

The vast majority of fun runners don't realize they can avoid these stresses by running loose and limber, with a flowing, rangy stride. They do the exact opposite: They know each landing will be jarring, and to minimise the impact, they run tightly, with virtually no spring in their step. They barely get beyond a fast shuffle. Instead of relying on their joints to cushion the impact, they simply rely on the heavily cushioned heels of their trainers. And that can lead to other problems, as detailed in chapter 11.

Of course you can cover the ground like this, but it's not really running, in my view. It's a lot slower than running—and probably even slower than the top race walkers walk! By shutting down and running tightly, these runners deny themselves the chance of learning how to really run. And the more they practice running like this, the harder they make it to ever learn to run properly.

Stretching is the first step towards escaping from this cycle. If you improve your suppleness you will gradually take longer, rangier strides and build up the strength and resilience necessary to cope with the landings. Running on soft ground is the key to building up this strength and minimising the shock of the landings. You should aim for loose but stable and strong joints, and muscles that are stretchy but not overstretched.

Beyond that, a looser runner is a faster runner.

I went through a spell of working very hard on my suppleness, often stretching for 10 or 15 minutes before I even left the house—doing stretches there that I could only do on the carpet, for example. It made a huge difference. I can remember how supple I was. I could feel it in my running. I got injured less often, too, and so enjoyed two years of consistent training. During that period, I won the English National Cross Country Championships, finished fourth in the World Cross Country Championships, won a bronze in the Commonwealth Games 10,000, and ran personal bests of 13.15 for the 5,000 metre and 27:34 for the 10,000 metre. The combination of stretching and strengthening exercises was at the heart of these performances, so I can't recommend it highly enough.

  You want to be loose from head to toe. You want your hamstrings, calves, and thighs loose, of course, and also your hips. But above all, make sure you don't neglect your back: If your back is supple, you'll be able to run faster and more freely.

If your back is tight—and, most probably, tighter one side than the other—you'll inevitably run unbalanced. That means you run the risk of one injury leading to another and another until you finally grind to a halt.

A supple back makes a big difference in the way you feel. If it's loose and flexible, you can run in a way that's lively. Your footfalls are springy; you land without jarring yourself.

I'm talking about your entire back being loose, including your lower back. Too often, people, even those who stretch regularly, neglect the lower back almost by accident: When they stretch their heads toward their knees and reach for their toes, most of the bend is in the upper back. The head is coming toward the knees and curving only the top half of the back. But it should be your chest that is coming down toward your knees. *All* the vertebrae, including those lower down, should have a little movement to them, a little bit of spring, rather than feeling as if they're fused together. The lower back is vitally important: If it's loose, your stride will be freer, more relaxed, and rangier. If it's tight, you'll feel a jarring with every impact, and will not be able to run fast.

Be sure to stretch evenly, too. Often, runners develop injuries because they're naturally tighter on one side of their backs than the other. It's almost an unavoidable consequence of being right- or left-handed. But it's exacerbated by your posture, by normal activities such as driving, and by specific activities like running round the left-hand bends on the track.

This imbalance can make runners' feet land differently from each other. And that can be like running on a camber. Pretty soon they've got a hip problem or a knee problem. They pronate more, and because of that they may develop trouble with their calves or their Achilles tendons. It's just one thing leading to another, all the way through, a constant series of knock-on effects. Your back is *so* important: Take care of it. Stretch it—and strengthen it—evenly on both sides.

When should you stretch? As often as you can. More than once a day, if you want to make progress. It's very easy for people to go to yoga, or to Pilates, or whatever. And they're proud and think they're as loose as a swami, so they don't need to do anything else. There's nothing wrong with yoga. But most people go just once or twice a week, and really that's not nearly enough. Stretching, whether you're running that day or not, should be part of your daily routine.

If you do one stretching session a week, you might manage to get fairly loose during that session. But the next day, you'll wake up all stiff again. And if you do nothing about it, the following week, when the time for your yoga class rolls around again, you'll be back to square one.

Try to stretch two or three times a day. You might only do it for five minutes each time. That's OK. Just do a couple of stretches in the places you feel tight. Stretch when you watch TV or when you go up the stairs. Stretch when you walk into the kitchen for some tea or a glass of water. Make staying supple a part of your lifestyle. That works much better than having to think: 'Oh, I'm training now; therefore, I've got to stretch.'

Rather than having to stretch because you're running, I would almost think of it the other way round: Whether I'm training or not, I'd stretch anyway, just to keep loose. You don't even need to get changed. The worst thing is to be sitting for hours on end in a car or at your desk. You stiffen up! But your body is designed to move, so get up and stretch as a matter of course and then fit in a run or some other exercise in between. And if you're running twice a day, it's easy to stretch four times a day—before and after each run.

Of course, people's time is limited. A lot of people say to me, 'Oh, I don't stretch before I run, but I do afterwards.' Maybe they've read in a magazine that that's the best way to do it. Well, that's another aspect to it: Stretching after you run does help you recover. But stretching before your run is equally important, if not more so. I don't like to feel tight when I run, and I think it's risky.

❝ Your aim should be to run while you're loose and relaxed so you don't get injured. Stretch early into the run, when you're warmed up a bit, rather than just running first and then stretching only at the end. ❞

And don't limit your stretching routine to your legs and lower back. You want your neck and shoulders loose and relaxed, too.

Remember, the thing that stops you from going faster is nearly always that you're out of breath. You see a lot of everyday runners who look very stiff and tight in their shoulders. One shoulder is up around their ear, or their arms are in so tight to their chest they can't breathe properly. It all looks so uncomfortable. If you're tight in the chest and shoulders, you can't take in all the air you should. The ability to breathe freely is kind of important in distance running, to put it mildly.

As you run, you want to feel tall, rangy, and relaxed. The relaxation should flow in two directions—from your neck and shoulders on down, and from your feet coming on up. You want to be springy and un-tense from top to toe. You want to land nice and light on your feet.

Look at elite runners like Kenenisa Bekele who, with three Olympic golds and six World Cross Country Championship victories, is the best distance runner in the world today. He and others at the top are running really fast, just flying around the track or almost skimming over the cross country course. And they really don't look stressed out at all.

But go to your local road race, and you'll see people going half as fast while looking twice as stressed. Some of these people would run a lot faster if they could figure out how to relax. They'd burn less energy, that's for sure. And they would free up their stride. It's a matter of running tall, relaxed, and balanced. You need to allow yourself to be loose even when you're moving fast.

HOW TO STRETCH

Before we get into the best stretches to do, let's talk about the best way to do stretches in general.

Your muscles have a reflex that inhibits your ability to get loose and become more supple. Simply put, when you get close to overstretching a joint, your body's instinct is to protect the joint rather than the muscle. It does this by reflexively contracting the muscle, a response known as the stretch reflex. This reflex is triggered by Golgi tendon organs, which are located where muscles meet tendons. They reflexively prevent a stretch from going any further and damaging the joint.

To get more supple, it really helps to inhibit this stretch reflex, and there's a simple technique that allows you to circumvent it—in essence to fool your body into allowing the stretch to take place. It's called PNF stretching, for proprioceptive neuromuscular facilitation, and if you forget what it stands for, don't worry. I had to look it up again myself. If you support a muscle by giving it a resistance to work against, the Golgi tendon organ senses it no longer needs to do its work, and eases its reflexive grip. Then you can gently stretch the muscle a little further than before. (You can also relax the Golgi tendon organs by tensing the opposite muscle, depending on the stretch you're doing.)

Though it may seem counterintuitive, PNF stretching involves pushing gently *against* the stretch. Here's how it works: Let's say you're trying to stretch your hamstrings by lying on your back and using your hands to pull your straight leg up toward your shoulder. You should be holding your leg below the knee, otherwise the knee will bend.

Try gently pushing your leg against your hands—*away* from your shoulder—breathing out and relaxing as you push against the resistance. Use your hands to keep your leg in place; don't let it actually move away from you, despite the push.

After pushing against your hands for several seconds, relax and use your hands to pull your leg even higher. Because your hamstrings have been supported as you pushed against your hands, the Golgi tendon organs have relaxed. They've sensed that there's no danger to the hip and knee joints and accordingly have released their grip on the hamstrings, allowing you to stretch them further safely. Repeat this procedure three to four times and you'll find you're able to progressively increase the stretch each time.

You can do this alone or, even better, with a training partner, who can provide the resistance and help you with the stretch. This is a very effective technique for increasing your suppleness and range of movement.

Now let's talk about the most important stretches to do regularly. They are probably best carried out in the following order: back and hamstrings; quadriceps and hip flexors; adductors; calves; and piriformis and ITBs, or illiotibial bands down the outside of your thighs.

I. BACK AND HAMSTRINGS

As I mentioned earlier, your back is vitally important, and you should think of your hamstrings as being an extension of your back. Here's an exercise that stretches both. I used to do it using a steeplechase barrier but a three-foot-high wall, fence, dining room table, or even stair banisters may do just as well—just depending on how tall you are.

How To

Rest your entire leg in front of you along the table's edge (or steeplechase barrier, if there's one handy) which, one hopes, is nearly waist high. The other foot is planted flat on the floor. Bend your upper body toward the leg that's resting on the table, breathe out gently and reach towards your toes with your hands (figure 5.1). Remember, don't just curl to get your head toward your knee: That loosens only the upper back. Get your chest down toward your knee so that you feel a gentle and comfortable stretch in your lower back and hamstring.

Coaching Point

Having the entire leg on the table is better than just resting your heel on a fence rail or the stairs. When your whole leg is

Figure 5.1   Back and hamstring stretch.

supported, there's no danger of hyperextending your knee—so your body can relax instead of reflexively tensing to protect itself. You'll feel the stretch in your back and in the hamstring of the leg that's up. The hip flexors in the front of the standing leg will get a good stretch as well, if you keep that leg straight—in other words if the table or wall is the right height.

2. QUADRICEPS AND HIP FLEXORS

Runners cannot avoid working their quadriceps and hip flexors (the muscles in front of the hips and thighs which you use every time you lift your knees), and so it is important to keep these muscles stretched and loose.

How To

First, stretch the hip flexors by holding a lunge position (figure 5.2), allowing the heel of your rear foot to come off the ground and keeping your body upright. After that, it's good to stretch both the quadriceps and hip flexors at once. Start with your right quad by standing on your left foot (figure 5.3). Hold your right foot with your right hand and pull it straight back and up behind your backside. Here's the key: Pull on that foot so your thigh moves back behind you, too, and gets a good stretch. The hip flexor in the front of your hip will feel a stretch, as well—unless you allow yourself to lean forward. Don't. Keep tall, with your torso upright, reaching towards the sky with your left hand.

Figure 5.2   Hip flexor lunge stretch.

Figure 5.3   Quadricep stretch.

Take Care!

You are *not* trying to crush your knee joint. Stretch the front of your hips and quadriceps.

Coaching Point

Often you see people pulling on their foot while leaving the knee pointing straight down, right next to the other one. That's not a complete or sufficient stretch; that's just holding onto your foot. Be sure to pull your leg back so your knee is pointing somewhat behind you and you feel the stretch along the front and top of your thigh. You can gain the PNF effect by pushing your foot against your hand and slightly straightening you knee. Then, of course, switch legs.

Quad strength and elasticity is vitally important in running downhill. When people who haven't run it think about the Boston Marathon, they tend to think of Heartbreak Hill. It does have an ominous-sounding name and, granted, it does come after the twenty-mile mark. But it's only 600 metres long. The challenge of the Boston Marathon isn't that half-mile—it's that the course is primarily *downhill*. The first 13 miles are downhill, there's a sharp downhill in mile 16, and it's all downhill between miles 21 and 24. And those who finish often complain about the punishment all that downhill running inflicted on their quads.

In a typical example, Lucas Meyer, Connecticut's top finisher in 2010, thought he could run a 2:16. But he ended up jogging across the line and posting a 2:21.

'My quads are a mess,' he told the local paper. 'At Mile 20, my quads just shut down.' And he had done a lot of downhill training, trying to get ready.

3. ADDUCTORS

Runners often avoid stretching their adductors because they don't seem to work very hard when running. But ignore them at your peril! They perform an absolutely vital role when you're running, and if you strain them you will not be able to run. The simplest, and best, ways to stretch are to use the sideways lunge and a hurdler's stretch.

How To

To perform the sideways lunge (figure 5.4), keep the rear foot sideways and flat on the ground, and bend the front leg gently until you feel a gentle stretch along the inside of your leg. Keep your body upright—there is no need to lean forward.

Figure 5.4   Sideways lunge adductor stretch.

The second stretch (shown in figure 5.5a and 5.5b) not only stretches the adductors but the whole hamstring, hip, pelvis, and lower back areas as well. It's an extremely beneficial stretch often used by hurdlers. To perform this stretch, stand on one foot, sideways to a table. Rest the other knee and foot on the table, bent at ninety degrees at the knee and ankle. You're going to look a lot like a hurdler just as he clears the barrier. Now bend forward at the waist, gently reach down towards the floor, breath out, and relax. Don't bounce!

Figure 5.5a   Hurdler adductor stretch side view.

Figure 5.5b   Hurdler adductor stretch front view.

Coaching Point

Very few distance runners do this, but I used to find it tremendously helpful. Many runners get sciatic nerve problems as a result of a tight, bruised or mis-aligned sacroiliac joint. This is the joint in the pelvis that supports the base of the spine and gives your pelvis a vital bit of cushioning as you take your weight on each leg. This hurdler's stretch is a great one to free up the muscles and joints around your hips, pelvis, and lower back.

4. CALVES (GASTROCNEMIUS)

There are two important stretches for the calf muscles. First, we'll talk about the larger of the two, the gastocnemius.

How To

To stretch the large calf muscle, the gastrocnemius—the one that forms the thickest part of your calf—lean against a wall, post, tree or whatever (figure 5.6 on page 66). Put the foot of the leg to be stretched on the ground behind you, toes pointed forward. The other leg will be closer to the wall (or tree), with the knee bent because you're leaning forward over it. Keeping the heel of your back foot firmly on the ground and the knee straight, lean gently forward and feel the stretch in your calf. Don't allow your backside to stick out. Keep your body in a straight line, from the rear heel up through your neck and head.

Coaching Point

Hold the stretch for 10 or 15 seconds, as long as it feels comfortable. Remember to stretch evenly on both sides: When you switch, put the other foot back as far as the first one was, and hold the stretch for the same count. Ideally, do two or three stretches on each leg, progressively increasing the stretch and slightly varying the angle of your foot. Control the stretch by adjusting how much weight you put on the front foot.

Figure 5.6 Gastrocnemius stretch.

5. CALVES (SOLEUS)

The other muscle in the calf is the soleus, which is deeper than the gastrocnemius. To target the soleus, as opposed to the gastrocnemius, you need a slightly different stretch.

How To

To stretch the soleus, in the lower part of your calf, bend the knee of the leg you're stretching while keeping your heel on the ground (figure 5.7). Keep your back upright. The other leg is behind you for balance, also bent, bearing hardly any weight. Bend the knee of your front leg more deeply, bringing the knee forward and down toward your toes, while keeping the heel flat on the ground.

Take Care!

It may be difficult to sense the stretch at first, but gently bend your knee even more deeply, and you'll feel it. Again, don't stick your backside out.

Figure 5.7 Soleus stretch.

Coaching Point

Hold the stretch for 10 seconds or so, relax, and stretch again, progressively, several times. Do it equally on both sides.

As well as being an important pre-run stretch, this is a very good stretch to do after a session or a race. This is because during a tough run your calf muscles will have worked hard and may well stiffen up afterwards if you don't stretch them afterwards. Not only this, if your calves remain stiff you'll be much more prone to developing tightness in the Achilles tendon, which can easily develop into full-blown tendinitis. This is serious and it can take a long time to recover, possibly even requiring injections or surgery. So don't let it happen in the first place! As always, prevention is better than cure. Don't react to the problem—foresee it, and prevent it happening!

One function of your calf muscle is to lift your heel up and drive off the ball of your foot. The other function is to cushion your footfall, to absorb the shock of landing on the ball of your foot before the heel very briefly touches down and lifts off again. But if you allow your calves to lose their elasticity, you will find landing more painful, making you run more on your heels and possibly leading to other injuries in the hips, knees and back.

6. PIRIFORMIS AND ITB

Lots of runners experience problems with their piriformis muscles and their ITBs.

The piriformis is a small muscle in your bum that runs from the base of the spine to the femur, the thigh bone, about where the crease in your buttock is. If the piriformis is tight, your knees tend to point out slightly, resulting in the outside of your foot and leg taking too much strain as you land. This can cause major injuries. Firstly, as you bring your leg through, you can strain the adductor muscles on the inside of your thigh. And secondly, as you land, you can strain the outside of your thigh—the ITB, or iliotibial band.

The ITB is a ligament-like band of tissue that runs down the outside of your thigh from the hip to just above the knee. It adds stability to the knee, preventing excessive side-to-side motion, and in runners it really gets a workout. Sometimes it becomes quite tight, and inflammation of the ITB can lead to severe knee pain, as well.

A tight piriformis muscle can also put pressure on the sciatic nerve, causing your buttock to feel like it's on fire and sending pain radiating down your leg. This is called piriformis syndrome. It's sciatica that's not been caused by anything serious like spinal injury or deterioration.

All these problems can largely be prevented by loosening and stretching the piriformis muscle and the ITB—and, of course, by paying attention to *how* you run. Technique is very important in running; I've described it in detail in chapter 3.

How To

To keep both your piriformis muscles and your ITBs healthy and supple, sit on the floor with your left leg straight in front of you. Put your right foot flat on the floor outside of your left knee, gently pull your right knee to your left shoulder, and hold it. You'll feel the stretch on the outside of your bum and along the outside of your thigh. Try it two or three times using the PNF stretching technique described earlier (i.e., pushing your knee against your hands), gradually increasing the stretch each time. Then switch legs.

Coaching Point

Most runners only think of their piriformis muscles and their ITBs after they're injured. Often, that's the first they ever hear of these parts of their body. But regular runners are at risk of problems with both, and you know what they say about an ounce of prevention. Keep the piriformis and ITB relaxed and loose and they'll be good to you.

Figure 5.8   Piriformis and ITB stretch.

Finally, let me give you some extra stretches that weren't in that book Ray Smedley told me about so long ago. I talked earlier about your back and the importance of keeping it loose. Here's a good stretch that's also best done on the floor.

To keep your lower back free, lie on your back and—keeping your left leg flat on the floor, toes up—pull your right knee up to your right shoulder. Hold it there for a good stretch. Now pull your right knee over to your left shoulder and again hold it and give it time to stretch. Then swing your right knee and foot across so they touch the carpet on the outside of your left knee.

Sometimes you may notice a few little pops in your back as the sacroiliac and lumbar region of the spine loosens up. It's not painful, and the relief can be immediate. Suddenly you feel loose and relaxed and you can breathe easily again.

You can also loosen your back by kneeling, reaching far forward onto the floor with your hands and, almost catlike, flattening the spine—especially the upper back between your shoulder blades.

You'll also want to keep your neck and shoulders loose. Even they can get tight, not just from running but from normal, everyday life. And running can exacerbate those problems.

To free up your neck once you've warmed up, nod slowly forward and back a few times, and move your head side to side, from one shoulder to the other. Don't roll it round and round as so many runners have done in the past. That's a bit risky!

Similarly, keeping your neck relaxed, rotate your shoulders three times or so with your arms out straight. Make sure not to hunch your shoulders up near your ears. Then rotate them three times in the opposite direction.

Another good way to stretch and loosen arms and shoulders—one I often suggest to the athletes I'm coaching—is by swimming. Do both front and back crawl, but not breaststroke. These two strokes loosen your shoulders. Your body is supported by the water; everything's nice and relaxed; your muscles are warmed up. And you're stretching and reaching forwards underwater. If you're doing the front crawl, breathe alternately to each side to keep things evenly balanced. Running is such a balanced activity compared to other sports: Golf, cricket, tennis, and baseball are all one-sided activities. Apart from running around left-hand bends on the track, everything in running should be equal and symmetrical, first one side and then the other. So do your stretching, your training, and your swimming (and your briefcase-carrying) equally on both sides.

In the end, you want your whole body to be as supple as possible. That's a big part of being an athlete. It's about injury prevention and better performance. Moving a stiff, tight body down the road takes far more effort than it should.

Being loose and free will help your balance. It will free up your stride and your breathing. You'll just feel better and more natural as you run. If you're rangy and relaxed, you'll flow on by your running friends who put in the same amount of training as you but don't think stretching's all that important.

Make working on suppleness a regular part of your routine—do just a quick stretch or two between activities. Turn it into a habit. When you finish this chapter and put the book down, stretch your back or your quads before you go on to the next thing. Maintaining suppleness and keeping a good posture will enhance your sense of well-being as you go through the day. You'll feel sharper at work. You'll move more easily. And you'll be able to pick stuff up off the floor without grimacing.

Suppleness is essential to running well. But its benefits extend much further than that. Feeling good is all about keeping your body loose and free.

KEY POINTS TO REMEMBER

- Make stretching a part of your everyday routine, not just something you do before or after a run.
- Be sure to stretch evenly on both sides to avoid imbalance, which often leads to injury.
- Ideally, stretch before and after your training session. You want to feel loose and free and easy as you train.
- You can stretch in between sessions as regularly as you like. You don't have to get your running kit on. Just stretch!

Chapter **6**

Take a Deep Breath

Here's something I think might surprise many everyday runners: When I was at my best, reeling off 12 consecutive 63-second laps in the 5,000 metres, I wasn't gasping for air. I was working as hard as I could, believe me—going the whole way at 4:15 per mile. But I was still able to keep my breathing relaxed and controlled: generally a nice, evenly balanced rhythm of three steps for each breath in and three more for each breath out.

When I set my personal best (13:15) that night in 1981, I wasn't gasping for breath even on that all-important last lap. To be honest, I can't remember exactly how I regulated my breathing on that final trip round—I was probably too busy with other things, like trying to figure out how in the world I could sprint faster this time. But I can promise you that, even then, I wasn't breathing any more often than two steps in and two steps out. Neither was Henry Rono, who beat me that night in a U.K. all-comers record time.

Over my career, I was privileged to run against many world-class runners—world record breakers, Olympic medallists, and world champions. I don't recall any of them gasping. I trained regularly with Dave Bedford and Steve Ovett—world record holders both. They didn't gasp, either—and it wasn't just because they found it so easy to keep up with me!

The same cannot be said for most everyday runners, though. Many of them have only two ways of breathing—two steps in and two steps out if they're going at a comfortable pace, and one step in and one step out if they're pushing hard or going up a hill. A few of them try to find a halfway point between those two, breathing in for two steps and out for one, for example. That's unbalanced and even more undesirable.

There's a reason the top runners don't puff in and out with every step, even when they're exerting maximum effort: It doesn't help. It would use too much energy. It would keep them from running as fast as they're capable of doing.

And the same goes for you.

Panicked puffing makes you tense when you want to be relaxed, which means you can't use your lungs to their fullest capacity. You're too tense; your chest is too tight; your breaths are too shallow. All you're doing when you breathe that fast is blowing out unused air. You're absorbing less oxygen than you would if your breathing were slower, deeper, and more controlled.

❝ **Run tall and relaxed. If your posture is poor, if you're tense, or if your chest and shoulders are taut, your breathing will be constricted. Keep your shoulders relaxed, loose, and flexible to allow your chest to expand.** ❞

Just as no one teaches you how to run—although I think they should—no one teaches you how to breathe. Like running, the thinking goes, breathing is not a skill; it's just something everyone does naturally, right? Well, fast running *is* a skill. And so is controlled breathing. My experience as a coach has shown that neither of these skills just comes naturally to people. And the most difficult and unnatural aspect, if you want to put it that way, is breathing control. But it's necessary. Quite simply, if you can't breathe in a controlled and relaxed manner while you're running at speed, you're going to grind to a halt.

It's exactly the same as in swimming. The first priority is to be able to control your breathing. Only when you can do that can you start to make progress.

Fortunately it's much easier with running, when your head's not underwater and you're not feeling like you're about to drown. But the principle is the same: Develop that skill, and you'll increase your top cruising speed. If you can control your breathing and feel comfortable going fast, suddenly running becomes much easier and more enjoyable.

The way to start is to convince yourself that you *can* control your breathing much more than you thought. Try it and you'll see. You can breathe slowly and deeply in circumstances where you would have thought it impossible.

I know a lot of people say they can't. If they've just charged up a hill, for example, or done some fast repeats, they have no choice but to heave and pant. There's a panic to the way they feel when they're out of breath. They think that if they don't gasp they might pass out from lack of air. The panting is a reflex; it's involuntary; it's just what the body does when it needs oxygen. They're convinced they can't control it.

But I think they can.

There's a little trick I use to prove it to people, often with groups of kids, but it works with anybody. I give them all some brisk workouts to get them well out of breath, after which they gather in a group, puffing like Vesuvius. Then I tell them they need to know their heart rates, so they all have to count their pulse for 10 seconds.

Lo and behold, silence falls. The gasping stops as if by magic. They can't hold their breath for 10 seconds at that point; instead what you're left with is strong, quiet, controlled breathing while they concentrate on their counting—proof that people *can* regulate their breathing to a much greater extent than they think. Which is actually much more important than knowing what their heart rate was!

Now that you know it's possible to transform ineffective panting into a strong controlled breathing pattern, let's talk about how you can get better at it, even while you're running at speed.

The problem many people encounter when they get out of breath is that they don't breathe out sufficiently, and therefore there's very little room for more air to get into their lungs. This is the feeling that leads to gasping, panic attacks, and sometimes exercise-induced asthma.

When you're running the key to breathing control starts with the *exhaling* phase. Breathe out slowly and fully, and you'll create more space for new, oxygen-rich air. The inhaling phase is the reflex action that will happen automatically; it is the breathing *out* that requires most control. When you're running, unlike swimming where you only have time for a quick gasp, the inhaling phase should last as long as the exhaling phase, and again this takes an element of self control. I think the best advice is to measure your breathing against your footsteps, always keeping to an even pattern of four steps in, four steps out, or three and three, or two and two, depending on how hard you are working.

‘ You need to master the skill of effective breathing. And the main way to improve your ability to control your breathing while you're working hard and under pressure is to practice it. From time to time on your steady runs, try sticking to a four steps in, four steps out breathing pattern. And on your harder efforts, try to hold a rhythm of three in, three out. ’

This breathing pattern may be quite hard at first if you're not used to it. Changing a pattern you've used for years is bound to be difficult. You might panic a bit and think you can't keep it going. Maintaining your control whilst breathing out at a slow and steady rate will be most difficult. You may reach a stage where you're desperate to breathe and suddenly you manage a deep sigh, almost like someone who's been crying and then sighs deeply. This will give you a huge sense of relief and you will then be able to relax again and feel that things aren't so bad after all.

I don't quite understand what happens with your body when you do that, but I found it a very helpful thing to practice. Because after a big sigh, I'd feel everything was OK. I was still going fast, I was still able to keep my stride length, and I was still breathing four steps in and four steps out, which is how I did much of my training.

I have said that none of the top-flight athletes I ran with gasped as they ran. Perhaps I should have said almost none. Zola Budd, the talented (and often barefoot) South African runner and world record holder, was an exception.

For all her ability, Budd is best known for having collided with the American runner Mary Decker, another world record holder, in the 3,000-metre final at the 1984 Olympics in Los Angeles. Decker fell heavily, the field rushed on, and the hopes of gold she had cherished for so long were forever gone. Initially, Decker blamed Budd for the collision. Even though many years later Decker changed her tune, Budd will never live down that moment and will always have to suffer the hurt of being disqualified in an Olympic final.

Earlier that year Budd had come to the U.K. to train. South Africa was banned from the Olympics because of apartheid, and she wanted to qualify for selection to the British team so she could compete—which she did. She was only 17 years old at that point, and I trained with her several times.

Before the fall, Zola Budd, Wendy Sly, and Mary Decker in the 1984 Olympic 3,000-metre final.

Running alongside her, it always seemed to me as if she were running too hard, puffing and puffing and puffing. It was very noticeable, and you'd think 'Surely she can't keep this up, she must slow down soon.' But she never did! She just carried on. But every quarter mile or so, she would take one huge deep breath, and then let it out like an enormous sigh. And then immediately she'd be back to her puffing. It was really strange. I'm not sure she even knew she was doing it. But it did seem to help her keep her breathing under control and enable her to keep up such a fearsome pace.

I've been talking so far about matching your breathing to your steps. And controlled breathing is vitally important. But actually, it can be very helpful to think of it the other way round: Try matching your steps to your breathing. Instead of using your steps to slow down your breathing, use your breathing to speed up your steps. If you've read this far into the book, you'll know that quick feet are essential to running fast. If you don't allow yourself to breathe in until you've taken four steps, that's a powerful incentive to move your feet fast. And you can also practice opening up your stride a lot while keeping your feet just as quick—which is the essence of running very fast. Use your breathing to help keep that quick, urgent cadence.

I remember my normal lunchtime run round the Stray at Harrogate—a massive L-shaped green that stretched along two sides of the town, probably more than four miles around. I always had little checkpoints on my regular runs that let me know how I was doing. On this one, I'd warm up and stretch in the first half mile, and then there was a road to cross to get to the Stray. Normally, it would take four or five steps to cross it. But sometimes, without any effort, I found myself doing it in just three. What a feeling—no effort, and just eating the ground up! So that was the first little check on the run, a real indicator that I was in the groove and moving well.

I would usually do my lap round the Stray at a fairly steady pace, running mostly on the grass. And at the end, there was a quite a long, slightly uphill finish on the pavement, which consisted of large, evenly spaced paving stones. Even though it was uphill, I would try to land only on every third slab—forcing myself to marginally overstride while still maintaining a four steps in, four steps out breathing pattern. It wasn't a sprint, but it was quite fast and, being uphill, extremely difficult. What an incentive to keep that cadence quick! And maintaining that degree of breathing control was a killer, I'm telling you. Definitely not sustainable for very long.

In a sense, I was trying to mimic altitude training, where your body is deprived of oxygen. Nowadays it's called hypoxic training. It's thought to increase the ability of the muscles to work better when oxygen levels are low, like at the end of a race. Coaches have swimmers do it—they tell the athletes they're only allowed to breathe once every six strokes—or not at all for a whole length. That's a killer, too, and it's the same sort of thing I was trying to do on that little bit of the run all those years ago.

If you want to keep your breathing controlled, it's important to increase your lung capacity. Like your heart, your lungs adapt to the demands placed on them in training. And just as a big heart needs to beat less frequently than a small one to pump the same amount of blood around the body, so a large pair of lungs needs to inhale less frequently than a small pair.

Long steady runs will enhance your body's ability to absorb oxygen. But your Mini-sized lungs will only develop Rolls Royce proportions if your training is intense enough to stretch not only their efficiency but also their capacity and power.

If you're tight when you run or your posture in general is bad (whether you're running or not), that can make your back, shoulders, and chest stiff. That, in turn, restricts your breathing so that inhaling takes more effort. You take shallower breaths, using only a small portion of your lung capacity and expelling the air before much of the oxygen's absorbed. Accordingly, you will feel out of breath before you should.

In the old days of *Chariots of Fire*, athletes used to fling open the bedroom window first thing in the morning and do some deep-breathing exercises.

Sometimes that would be it for the day. They were on the right lines—they just needed a bit more exercise!

You can loosen and strengthen your upper body by swimming—the front crawl or back stroke—and by doing press-ups, bench presses, and other exercises with light weights. Exhale strongly as you lift the weight and breathe in slowly as you let it back down.

In addition to bench presses—lying on your back on the bench and pushing the barbell straight above your chest—two other weight exercises are particularly helpful, not so much for building strength as for stretching out your chest and shoulder muscles and opening up your chest to enable you to breathe more easily. You only need very light weights:

• Lying on your back, as you would for the bench press, extend your arms upward with a dumbbell in each hand. Keeping your back flat on the bench, gradually inhale and lower your arms until they're extended beside each side of your head, horizontal to the floor, with elbows slightly bent to avoid injuring your shoulders. Exhale strongly as you lift your arms back to the starting position.

• Lying in the same position with your arms straight up from your chest and a weight in each hand, lower your arms until they're out to your sides and horizontal (again with elbows slightly bent), then slowly return them to the starting position. Remember: Steady, controlled breathing—breathing in as you stretch and out as you lift—is crucial.

Remember, upper body strength improves your running in many other ways, as well, so you're doing more than just helping your breathing. Flexibility and power are helpful in allowing you to breathe correctly, but on their own they're not enough.

Just as you can develop your muscles, you can develop your lung capacity by breathing deeply and stretching the chest muscles to allow your lungs to fully expand. Your lungs have millions of alveoli, tiny air sacs where the oxygen you breathe in is exchanged for the carbon dioxide you breathe out. It is here that oxygen is absorbed into the blood stream. These alveoli have a large total surface area—the size of a tennis court if they were spread out. But if you don't breathe deeply—or if your chest muscles are not flexible enough to allow your lungs to expand fully—many of the alveoli aren't used at all. Your ability to absorb oxygen is diminished and certainly not developed to its full potential.

Most sedentary people use only 20 or 30 percent of their potential lung capacity. Many runners use only about 60 percent. You want to get as close to 100 percent as possible.

And not only in a race, but also in training. The alveoli are surrounded by a network of pulmonary capillaries. As with your muscles, exercise dramatically increases the capillarization of your lungs. But that only works for the portion of your lungs that are getting used regularly. It's no good developing more capillaries to only half your alveoli. You want to work on them all.

❝ To increase your lung capacity, it is important to breathe deeply, whether running fast or slow. In addition, it is important to do some sessions in which you breathe deeply—and rapidly. The most effective sessions are short repetitions with very short recovery times. ❞

In these sessions it is not the speed you run that matters, so much as the short recovery, so you don't need to hammer your legs or fear injury. As a starting point, an ideal session would be five sets of four times 100 metres, run at about 90 percent effort, with only 15 seconds rest between each 100m, and two-minute recoveries between sets. This makes you get out of breath—and recover—20 times. Yet you've only run two kilometres, and soon afterwards your legs will feel comparatively rested.

From this starting point, you can progress in two different directions: You can work toward eliminating the 15-second rests until you end up running five (or more) times 400 metres at nearly the same speed and with the same two-minute recoveries. Or you can progress toward five sets of four times 200 metres, with the same 15-second rest. An intermediate stage would be to alternate sets of 100 metres and 200 metres.

Fifteen seconds is not a lot of rest. After just 15 seconds you'll still be out of breath, and thinking you're not yet ready to go again. But force yourself: Once you do get going, you'll feel OK, and your breathing will settle down again. It's strange but true—you will feel more out of breath during these short 15-second rests than when you're running fast. And remember, in a race you don't get any rest at all. So you should be confident that you can run at a good speed and sustain it. You'll know that you've run 20 repeats much faster than your race pace and that, if you push hard during a certain part of the race, you can recover very quickly. Keep your breathing controlled and relaxed, perhaps by taking one of those big sighs at the top of the hill, and you'll be on your way again while the other runners are taking a half mile or so to get themselves back together.

There's another benefit to quiet, controlled breathing: It psyches out the other runners. If the runner next to you is puffing away like mad, you sense that he or she is suffering a lot more than you are. And you feel like you can make a move anytime you want. And that runner's impression of you will be of a super-fit athlete who's just cruising along!

To be honest, although that's true 99 percent of the time—I do remember an exception. One year in a Middlesex Cross Country Championships, a seven-mile race, I wasn't running particularly well at the time, but I was in the leading group of three. After about two miles, one of the other guys was heaving away, sounding for all the world like a steam engine. I heard him next to me, rasping noisily, 'Uhhh-huhhh, uhhh-huhhh, uhhh-huhhh.' I thought, 'My God, that guy is running *way* too fast. He's never going to last at that pace.'

And, what do you know, the darn guy ran the whole way like that and eventually pulled away from me and won the race! I could *not* believe it. But I have to say that's extremely unusual, so don't emulate it. It won't help. That guy won in spite of the energy he wasted on his breathing, not because of it. In a funny way, he out-psyched me because he sounded so bad. I thought I had him beaten, but I lost my rhythm, and he kept pulling away.

You will help yourself by including some specific breathing drills in your training. These could include the following:

- Keep talking without gasping during your steady runs—and especially when you're running uphill. (If you're suffering, don't show it. Just ask your training partner a difficult question at the bottom of a hill and see how he responds!)

- Occasionally, see how long you can maintain a pattern of breathing in for four steps and out for four steps while running at a good pace.

The benefits of learning the skill of breathing correctly are manifold. It allows your lungs to absorb more oxygen and lets you relax more as you run, too, saving your energy. It also gives no encouragement to your rivals.

The effect on you should be like a car coming down from altitude to sea level—and taking the brakes off. It's a double whammy if ever I saw one!

KEY POINTS TO REMEMBER

- Run tall and relaxed so your chest has room to expand.
- Strengthen your upper body and increase the flexibility of your chest and shoulders by swimming front and back crawl and lifting weights.
- If you're running with a group, talk a lot.
- Do your steady runs while inhaling for three steps and exhaling for three steps for as long as you can maintain it.
- Sometimes, try to run while breathing in for four steps and out for four steps for limited periods.
- Improve your lung capacity by doing short repetitions with very short recovery times.

Chapter **7**

Going Clubbing

I was out recently on a bright April day. The sun had chased away the winter's chill, the days were growing longer, and the London Marathon was approaching. I saw a lot of people out running, getting ready. And all of them were running alone.

Then it struck me: I almost never see runners training together in packs these days. They're nearly always on their own. And they've always got their earphones in. It looks lonely and boring and very uninspiring.

When I was running, we often used to train in groups. We'd chat, laugh and joke, the miles would tick by, and the whole thing was a sociable activity. Now running has become quite *un*sociable in many respects, and I think that's a shame.

I joined a running club when I was 13, virtually as soon as I'd started running at school. There are many benefits to joining a club—not only the coaching and races but also the camaraderie and training partners. But there are drawbacks too—for example, training runs that are not what you personally need or that cater to the lowest common denominator. However running alone is not always much fun, and it's definitely not the best way to reach your full potential.

‘ I strongly recommend you join a running club for fun and camaraderie! Just remember not to risk injury by being coerced into inappropriate sessions and too many races. ’

I began running at school, Haberdashers' Aske's in Elstree, northwest of London, where my dad taught biology and looked after the cross country team. Having been a good middle-distance runner himself, once winning the RAF 880-yard title in his National Service days, he knew something about interval training, and he had plenty of success with the school teams he coached. Although I don't remember doing many hill repeats, we did run hard up hills—and often did a paarlauf, a two-man relay—round a circuit on the school grounds. And we practiced running over ploughed fields, vaulting over fences, and that sort of thing because they happened to be on our school course.

He also organised pre-season training camps in Snowdonia, a beautiful mountainous area in North Wales. We'd camp there for a week, running before breakfast and then walking in the mountains all day. The whole experience was great pre-season conditioning, not only for the training but for building team spirit, as well.

The school had close ties with the local club, Shaftesbury Harriers, one of England's oldest running clubs, having been founded in 1890 when Queen Victoria was still on the throne. I joined the club just after my 13th birthday and soon had plenty of club races as well as school races.

Train—don't race—in a group. That way everyone can benefit.

But for the next three years, I trained only at school. And it soon became clear that natural ability and my dad's sessions weren't enough. I was improving but still having difficulty keeping up with the top boys. At 16, I could still barely get under 4:50 for the mile. And many boys I could beat at cross country would be faster than me on the track. Yes, I was a bit of a plodder!

Enter Bob Parker, one of our top club coaches, who was already having success with Dave Bedford, and had a group of kids developing into a good team. He immediately put me on a schedule of 40 miles per week, including a hill session, a track session, and a long run of 10 miles each week. Within three months, I was down to 4:20 for a mile—but still not quite good enough to make the English Schools 1,500-metre final that year.

That fall, I increased my mileage to 70 per week. I regularly trained twice a day, and I increased my long run to 12, 13, and even 15 miles sometimes, and I did two speed sessions each week. Suddenly, I was winning nearly every race I entered. The following summer, I reduced my mile time to 4:10, set a world 17-year-old age group best for 3,000 metres (8:14) and won the English Schools 5,000 metres.

Not only was Bob Parker's coaching superb, the guys organizing the club's teams were also really switched on. They didn't just let us drift along. They looked after us—making sure we were organised, that we were at the start on time, and that we got our kit back at the end of the race.

I remember getting ready before the start of my first English Cross Country Championships, at Blackpool, a seaside resort town in northwest England. There was quite a chilly wind blowing and while I was warming up I could

© Human Kinetics

feel a stitch coming on—something to which I was susceptible, especially in cold weather.

Desperately looking for something to keep my midriff warm, my dad and Bob found a newspaper, which they wanted me to tuck down inside my vest. That's an old cycling trick, where riders put newspaper inside their jerseys to protect them from the cold on the descents.

I was just a kid, and I have to say I wasn't too keen on the idea. I really didn't want to run the race with a newspaper stuffed down my front. But it worked a treat. I ran really well, coming fourth despite being tripped soon after the start and having to pick myself up from virtually last place.

I know, we were just kids, so perhaps you'd expect the club officials to look after us. But they created a feeling of excitement and team solidarity, and the sense that it *mattered* to them. They gave us a reason for running ourselves into the ground. It was nothing like doing a fun run, where you just turn up to see whether you can complete the course. It was a *race*! A *battle*! There were scores of other teams! You could feel and taste an atmosphere and sense of expectancy. It was *exciting*!

' Whatever your level, running as part of a team gives you far more motivation than just running on your own, and helps you realise your potential. '

Look, there's no doubt—the jogging boom has been good for people's general health and fitness. But something's been lost, too. So many people enter races nowadays as individuals. The kids may shout, 'Go on, Mum!' But it really doesn't matter to anyone how any particular person finishes. Not even, probably, to Mum herself. The aim just seems to be to finish.

It's a big change. And I think at the bottom of it all is a psychological change—a feeling now that the challenges we set ourselves are just about completing rather than competing.

The 'Go on, Mum' fun run is not a bad thing. It gets people off the sofa and into the fresh air. But it's not the same as a proper race where every second counts, where people run for themselves *and* their teammates. Then, you're competing for someone. You're part of a team, and that's a huge incentive. If you push harder and overtake just one more person, that can help your team's standing at the end of the race. Your mates are relying on you to try as hard as you can, which is all anyone can ask. You're not playing for matchsticks anymore. It matters. And then afterwards you compare notes about what went right and what went wrong, have a laugh or two, and either bask in the glow of achievement or vow to do better next time.

Clubs offer benefits beyond just racing, of course. They're a great source of training partners. And training with others is much better, and more effective, than trying to do it all on your own. I'd recommend running in smallish groups—maybe half a dozen runners—rather than larger, unwieldy groups. Just one partner is often better still. Ideally, you should find someone a bit better than you for your hard sessions to motivate and pull you along. And you might try to find someone not quite up to your standard for your easier runs (and their harder ones), because it's important to include easy workouts in your program, and it helps to sometimes have nobody pushing you harder than you want to go. Even though you might feel quite good that day, you don't want to get tempted into a semi-race.

Clubs usually have a regular pattern of sessions, which can give structure to your week. Rather than drifting along, you'll know that on Sunday morning all your mates will be there for a long run, for example. Tuesday evening they'll be doing hills or interval training, and Thursdays might be a fartlek or a fast, sustained run.

You'll also find yourself immersed in the world of running, privy to all kinds of information and gossip you otherwise wouldn't get. You'll hear from your running friends—now that you have some—where the best running shops are (preferably staffed by runners), what kind of kit seems to work the best, what they do about chafing, what training has helped them, where the best races are, and more.

Of course, you can find all this on the Internet or via runners' chat rooms, but you can't beat the camaraderie of chatting with your mates while you run, and back in the locker room as well.

Having said all that, there can be drawbacks to club membership that you should beware of—and compensate for, if need be. Some clubs don't have anyone who really takes charge and organises the training sessions in an effective way.

Ideally, a club should have someone who not only knows what sessions to do, but also knows how and when to do them—and how to adapt them for each person in the group and for different times of year. Because people are different, not all of them are capable of running the same session. Or the same session might not be right for them because their aims are different. Perhaps some are aiming for a marathon, while others may have just had a hard race or are just coming back from injury.

But many clubs don't have anyone like that. Instead of adapting the sessions, the coach just says, like it or lump it. Or no one takes charge at all. And some clubs don't add much structure to your week. Instead of a night for speedwork and another for hills—hopefully designed to accommodate runners of different abilities—the danger is that everyone just gathers in a big mass and comes up with their excuses for not doing a hard session that night.

'Oh, I'm a bit injured', they say—or ill, or tired, or whatever.

'OK, guys', someone will say, 'let's just go for a steady run.'

And after a time they set off in a group of 30 or so, which is far too large, and trundle along on a medium-length, medium-speed run without any specific training purpose in mind. That might be sociable, even fun, and it's certainly better than not running at all. But that sort of run can easily develop into a bit of a race, which can be fun, but not ideal for those who are hanging on for dear life, and not particularly useful for the better runners either. Whatever your standard, you really need more specific and structured sessions to help you progress. Too many nice, sociable club runs like that can hold you back unless you take charge of your own training.

❛ If your club tends not to organise sessions with specific aims in mind, then pick and choose what's best for you and organise the rest yourself. The club's long run on Sunday might fit into your plans very well. But you will want to find training partners for your speed sessions, hill repeats or fartleks, and quite possibly do them outside the club. ❜

Of course, having done those sessions, it's really good to join in the club's steady runs. The social side of running clubs is great, but in proper measure. It used to be—and at some clubs it still is—that people arrived in street clothes, changed at the club, did a session, showered and changed afterward, then maybe had a cuppa or even went out for a beer.

But now it's more common for people to arrive already changed into in their running kit, then stand around forever before actually setting off. That's not a great start, because it's nice to have a sense of urgency and a sense of purpose as you start your session. You want to feel a little bit of time pressure—I've got to get it done. I've got sixteen 400s to do, and I'm going to run them in such and such a time. I'm going to warm up for two miles, and I'm going to get at it. Or, I've got 10 miles to do, and I have to be back by a certain time.

You should feel a bit of excitement and maybe even some nervous anticipation because quite possibly the session is going to be difficult. You—or better still your coach—have got it written down: You have a task ahead of you, and it's not going to just happen by itself. You can chat while you're running, no problem. But don't spend a lot of time beforehand thinking about what you should do and waiting for someone else to turn up. You'll go flat mentally.

When it's all done, then it's time to relax. But not to stand around again for ages in your wet kit, chatting and getting cold and stiff. That's just not good for your muscles. It's not a good way to take care of your body, which is really the point of the whole exercise. It's better to shower and put on dry clothes, and then have a cuppa. At least put on some warm, dry kit and do some stretching while you're chatting.

Another problem with clubs can be the pressure to race every week. *Don't race every week!* You'll get stale and stuck in a rut.

You need to be mentally fresh for races. Racing is, after all, a performance; It's something special and not just another run. Not only that, you also need to keep some weekends free so you can fit in some of your harder sessions. Pick and choose your races—and stick to your plan. Remember, you're racing for yourself, too, not just for your club. Your club's job should be to help you progress, not race you to death.

I liked racing. I used to race a lot—too much for my own good, in many ways. I often ran 40 or 50 races a year, mainly voluntarily but sometimes because of club pressure. Obviously, some races are harder than others. And sometimes I ran two or even three races in an afternoon, either to help my club or the team or to help with my own preparation. I found doubling up at the 1,500 and the 5,000 in the same afternoon with just 20 minutes rest particularly useful preparation for a 10,000-metre race. I regularly did it for Shaftesbury Harriers, for Oxford University in the varsity match against Cambridge, and for the RAF in the Inter-Services Championships. And twice, when my club needed me to, I ran both the 5,000 and the 10,000 in the national interclub cup final—fortunately with several hours rest between them.

I enjoyed these challenges—especially when the team won—and willingly made the sacrifices. But naturally I would be less happy to do this if the rest of the team didn't respond or my efforts made no difference to our chances of winning.

Team managers always ask for more, of course, but it was clearly not possible to give this level of commitment every week. So, obviously, I had to say no sometimes. And when certain team managers (often, unfortunately, in the RAF) wouldn't take no for an answer, that was when things sometimes got difficult. And I somehow earned, in certain quarters, a reputation for being a non-team person and a bit of a prima donna.

Outrageous! Well, you just can't please all of the people all of the time!

Of course you will have even more problems if you get ill or injured and your club still pressurises you to race. Resistance is the best advice, although it's easier said than done. When I was 20, I succumbed to this pressure, being forced to run in a cross country match for the RAF against the Civil Service when I was clearly unwell.

'Oh, you'll still do better than our reserve', was our team manager's argument.

That was true, but it wasn't the point. He should have been looking after his young athlete, not risking his health and well-being.

Sure enough, I managed to stumble round and finish fourth. But I ended up in bed for two weeks with glandular fever, and I was out for the rest of the season. Bob Parker was furious. I learned the hard way and tried never to make the same mistake again. And I urge you to avoid it, as well. Don't race when you're ill. You'll just set yourself back.

Your relationship with your club should of course be mutually beneficial. Contribute all you can. But also, take from your club what works for you. Avoid the pitfalls. Don't compromise or sacrifice your own progress just for the benefit of the club. You have to find a happy medium.

I am sure I would not have become the runner I did had I not joined Shaftesbury Harriers. It was through the club that I hooked up with Bob Parker, whose coaching helped me so much in the early stages of my career. It was the club and Bob's training group—and Dave Bedford in particular—who inspired a whole generation, both in the club and outside, to run fast and aggressively, with joy and passion.

I was three years younger than Dave, and we were regular training partners for several years. What a fabulous opportunity it was for a young runner to talk to, learn from, and train with one of the best distance runners of the day. He was a brash trailblazer and pied piper who chased records and brought the crowds and excitement back to British athletics. I could see at first hand what kind of training regimen he followed. I could try to keep up with him in workouts. And I could be in on the behind-the-scenes build-up as he prepared for his world record. What a time!

Mind you, he wasn't entirely a good influence. In those days, he was the George Best of athletics, always burning the candle at both ends. But however much he drank and however little sleep he'd had, he would still be out training the next day. He certainly made the hard training, and life in general, a lot of fun.

Shaftesbury Harriers was an excellent club to be part of, with high standards and even higher aspirations. As a young athlete I was once asked by an athletics

Mark Shearman, Athletics Images

'I did it for you, Bob.' Dave Bedford with coach Bob Parker immediately after breaking the 10,000-metre world record at Crystal Palace in 1973.

magazine what my aims were. And I didn't come up with the usual answer—Olympic gold. I just said I wanted to get the club 5,000 metre and 10,000 metre records. Which to my mind meant virtually the same thing, as they were both faster than the Olympic records at the time: 27:30 for the 10,000 and 13:17 for the 5,000!

There's no denying the motivation that records—even just club records—can give you. In my first year at Oxford, my aim wasn't just to win the varsity match 5,000 metres, but also to break the previous record, held by former European champion Bruce Tulloh. Likewise, throughout my RAF career, my aim was to set RAF records for 1,500 metres, 5,000 metres, and 10,000 metres.

I'm proud to say that I broke all of those, setting records that still stand today. But, really, I hope that they can inspire current and future generations of Oxford, RAF, and Shaftesbury athletes. That's what records are there for—to be broken!

As for Shaftesbury Harriers, I did get the club record for the 5,000, running 13:15. But, regrettably, I never did get the record for the 10,000, managing only 27:34—still, not too shabby when the club record had been the world record at the time. We're the only club that has, as of this writing, 2 people in the top 12 on Britain's all-time list for the 5,000—I'm 10th; Bedford's 12th. Not to mention 2 people in the top 8 in the 10,000—Bedford's 6th; I'm 8th. Thirty years later, that's not bad.

And in all these clubs, of course I enjoyed the camaraderie, the repartee, the laughs, and the fun and excitement of being with people who helped me to achieve the best I could. In clubs, I found people who understood what I did, why I did it, and what it took. Not to mention the partners for the long runs, the inspiration they gave me, the mutual respect—and the friendship.

All that's available to you as well. You've heard of the loneliness of the long-distance runner? Avoid it! Join a club!

KEY POINTS TO REMEMBER

- The benefits of joining a club—coaching, motivation, inside information, camaraderie—far outweigh the drawbacks. Joining a club will help your running.

- Running as part of a club team, whatever your level, gives you more motivation and inspiration than running on your own, and that helps you dig deep and discover your potential.

- Run for your club's benefit, but also your own: Don't race every week, despite the pressure. And don't race when you're injured or ill.

- If your club is not good at organizing structured sessions, pick and choose what's best for you, or start organizing some sessions yourself. Go on the club's long Sunday runs, for example. And use the club as a source of training partners.

PART

II

SHARPENING THE KNIFE

Now you've established a base you can build on—one that includes running correctly and running fast. You're doing several different kinds of sessions every week, each with a specific aim in mind. The task now is to put it all together and perform better in a race than you've ever done before.

This will require the introduction of some speedwork sessions that are more structured than fartleks. These will involve timed repeats, carried out in a progressive way over a period of time. It will involve some hill reps and cross-country running which will help you develop strength and resilience, and some faster timed sessions either run on road, grass or possibly even better, a running track. It will involve training differently at different times of year. It will also involve learning to taper off your training in a way that leaves you rested but not sluggish on race day.

And a lot of it is going to involve getting the most out of yourself psychologically. That's going be different for every runner. But there are ways to train your mind, to discover that you can do more than you thought, to believe beyond doubt that you can turn in a performance far better than anything you've done in training. And that belief may be the most vital ingredient of all.

So here's to that race you never thought you could run. Because I know it's in you.

Chapter 8

The Ups and Downs of Running

Runners are by nature very competitive. Whether they've reached county, national, or even international standard, they all tend to know where they stand in the pecking order.

When I was at my best, in the late 1970s and early 1980s, there were several guys like Charlie Spedding, whom we respected as great blokes and good runners but didn't consider to be a major threat. They weren't quite in our class. And I think Charlie would agree—he wasn't getting the results he wanted, and he was not fast enough to trouble the likes of Mike McLeod, Dave Moorcroft, Steve Jones, Nick Rose, Barry Smith, or me. We beat him time and again.

Charlie was a pharmacist's son from County Durham, a coal mining area in northeast England. As he details in his autobiography, *From Last to First*—an excellent book, for non-runners and runners alike—he was a poor student, had trouble with his eyes, and wasn't generally near the top at anything he tried.

Even though he discovered almost by accident that he was good at distance running, he was still not really in the upper echelon. In 1977, when his Gateshead Harriers team-mate Brendan Foster won the English National Cross Country Championship at Parliament Hill, Charlie finished 39th. Four years later, in March 1981, when I won the National on the same course, Charlie finished 56th, five minutes after I crossed the line. It must be said that he didn't like running in the mud—he preferred the unyielding surface of the roads—but still, that's not even close.

But at the Los Angeles Olympic Games in 1984, Charlie beat some of the fastest runners in the world, including the Australian Rob de Castella, the world record holder, to win bronze in the marathon.

However we might have rated him, Charlie's the one with the Olympic medal. And richly deserved, too: He ran the race of his life on the day it counted, and it wasn't a fluke. He'd won the London Marathon earlier that year, as well. And he finished second at London the following year behind my good friend and running rival, Steve Jones (a proud Welshman), posting a lifetime best of

2:08:33. A quarter of a century later, Charlie remains the English record-holder in the marathon.

Charlie's remarkable improvement after years of running below the top echelon is a testament to his determination and self-belief. He was able to change his psychological approach, to get rid of thoughts that limited him and substitute ones that allowed him to release the potential he'd always believed was inside him. It's an inspiring story.

But there was another important factor, as well—hills.

HILLS ARE YOUR FRIENDS

This quote by Lance Armstrong is just as true for runners as it is for cyclists. When Charlie decided in 1980, despite years of not doing as well as he hoped, to double down and get even more serious, he moved to Boston. He fell in with a group of runners that included Greg Meyer, who went on to win both the Chicago and Boston marathons. This group did hill sessions. Charlie was part of the group, so almost by default, hills became part of his routine. The group regularly went out to a place called Pump House Hill. It took a minute and a half to race up it, and these guys would charge up it six or eight times in a row. Week after week.

Charlie didn't like hills and so, like many runners, he tended to avoid them. As he admits, his technique wasn't good. His stride was too long to carry him up the hill with any speed. But he learned to shorten it up—in effect, to downshift a gear—for more power. Crucially, he got stronger—both physically and mentally. His fitness improved, as did his confidence.

After spending the summer of 1981 training and racing in the United States, he returned to England again, and that fall he entered the Paris-to-Versailles road race in France. The 17K course begins in the shadow of the Eiffel Tower and runs along the banks of the Seine on its way toward Versailles, the grand palace built in the 1600s by Louis XIV.

I had won that race the year before. The palace is all very nice, but I can tell you from personal experience that the race has one

Mark Shearman, Athletics Images

Record breakers! British record holder Steve Jones (2) and English record holder Charlie Spedding running in the 1985 London Marathon. Twenty-seven years later their records still stand.

mother of a hill to climb as it leaves Paris. When Charlie got to that point in the course, he remembered all the hill training he'd done in the United States. Mr. Hill, he knew, was now his friend. He pushed on hard—and won the race. Pump House Hill had worked its magic.

What worked for Charlie Spedding can help you improve, as well, whatever your level. Not that running hills will necessarily get you an Olympic medal—I ran plenty of them, and a Commonwealth bronze was the closest I came. But all the top runners in the world do hill repeats, not because they guarantee a medal but because they build specific strength and endurance. That, in the end, was what Charlie wanted for himself, and it applies just as much to a 50-minute 10K runner as it did to him.

You want to get your time down from 48 minutes to 46? Get under 45 or run your first sub-40? Make hill repeats part of your weekly schedule for most of the year. It's possible you'll put in less mileage than if you did another steady run that day, but your times will drop.

'Hills are speedwork in disguise', the American runner Frank Shorter said once. Like Charlie, he's known primarily for his marathoning, having won Olympic gold in Munich in 1972 and silver in Montreal in 1976. But he did know a thing or two about speed: He was an American 5,000-metre champion once, with a lifetime best of 13:26, and five times the American 10,000-metre champion, with a personal best of 27:45. I agree about hills helping with *speed*. To me, it's obvious: To run fast for long, sustained periods, you have to have the strength to keep your tempo quick, even when you are severely fatigued.

‘ Hill training can be used to target all of the five Ss—speed, strength, stamina, skill, and suppleness—which are the key components of fitness. Hills toughen you mentally, too, and build vital confidence. The last thing you want as a hill approaches is to be frightened of it! By working on all these limiting factors, hill training can improve your performance significantly.   ’

It only stands to reason that hill repeats will increase your *strength*. Hill training creates an overload on your legs. You're pushing yourself upward with each step whilst maintaining a fast pace, lifting your body weight from the bottom of the hill to the top, and then going back down and doing it again. It's just like weightlifting: You're repeatedly pushing against resistance—gravity. It makes you stronger, and you get better at coping with the effects of severe muscle fatigue.

The benefits don't end there. If you're charging up a hill, you're going to be forced to lift your knees and drive off your toes, stretching your legs and using good technique that many runners find harder to do on the flat. So hill running also helps improve both *skill* and *suppleness*—two more of the critical Ss.

And hill repeats will specifically build leg strength, while also increasing your *stamina* in three distinct ways.

First, they will raise your anaerobic threshold level—the effort you can maintain without going into oxygen debt. If your sustainable cruising speed is faster, you'll run better times. Second, they will improve your recovery rate—and in races, you're going to need to recover quickly after every hill even while continuing to go fast. And, third, they improve your lactate-tolerance level, meaning you can still function at a good level even after lactic acid starts to build up and make your muscles burn.

Hills are good for endurance, particularly speed endurance, because they force you to work harder than you might otherwise think you're capable of. It's a funny thing, but novice or intermediate runners are often not able to work as hard as they ought to on the flat. It's a common feeling—five minutes after completing a 10K race, for example—for runners to feel quite well recovered and to wonder why they hadn't been able to go faster in the race.

In a way, they are not strong enough to push themselves to the limit on flat ground. But send them charging up a hill for 90 seconds or more and they'll feel—and react—very differently. The hill helps them to discover how hard they can run once they start to feel tired, especially if the session requires them to repeat the effort five or six times. They learn how deep they can dig. It forces them to work harder than they thought possible. Because of that, they're improving their ability to run in oxygen debt and tolerate the build-up of lactic acid, and to recover, as well. So the training effect is that much better. Having discovered how hard they can work on the hills, they should have the confidence to run equally hard on the flat. But it's not so easy. On the flat, without so much gravity to work against, you have to run quite fast before you're working at your maximum intensity. And other limiting factors such as core strength, leg strength, and running technique can often come into play before you reach this intensity.

And as I mentioned in chapter 1, when we talked about limiting factors, *speed* is limited by all the other Ss. Because running hill repeats improves them all, it will improve your speed. In that sense, Frank Shorter was right on target.

I realize that many runners are reluctant to start doing hill repeats. They think that kind of training is too intense or too boring. Maybe, having run up a hill, they're disinclined to turn around and go back down: They're trying to get somewhere and it seems alien to them to stop and do it all again and again. Or maybe having reached the top, they'd rather just keep going and savour the view.

'Doing steady runs around an undulating circuit is quite enough hill training for me, thank you very much!' they say.

But useful as that type of training is, it's not specific enough to really produce all of the benefits I've just described. You need more structured sessions with a set number of timed repetitions over set distances and with set recoveries.

There's no doubt that hill training can be demanding and tiring. You don't want to overdose on it. Your legs can be sore afterwards and it might take your body a while to recover, so you shouldn't do a massive hill session shortly before a race. You want to be sensible about it.

But if hills are demanding, they can be exhilarating, as well. There's a sense of accomplishment in doing what you set out to do, in finding you're capable of more than you thought, and in being able to power through a race more strongly than before. Hills will give you confidence and mental strength, helping push back the other limiting factor—*psychology*.

So I recommend them very strongly. The benefits are enormous.

Start gradually, as you would with any new activity, such as weight training or running on the track. Work into it slowly; get a feel for it before you put yourself under any real stress. This is one situation where a heart-rate monitor might be helpful. You can use it to keep yourself from running harder than you want to during that initial stage.

If you've never run hills in a structured way, the best way to get started is to run lots of short ones, perhaps 10 or 12 times for 30 seconds up a gradient that's not too steep, jogging back down in between.

Also, get used to running hilly courses: Stride out and attack each hill and then run easily to the next one. A very good idea would be to try some cross country races. This kind of running, perhaps including rough terrain or sticky mud, can give you the strength and stamina you need to get into serious hill training.

I remember the mud and hills of cross country races, particularly at Parliament Hill, in North London. Running on terrain like that would strengthen you all over—or at least you sure hoped that was the effect, considering the way you felt during the race and for a long time afterwards. All the parts of your legs would be sore—your hamstrings from pulling your feet out of the mud, as well as your calves and your adductors, along the insides of your thighs. Even your arms would feel drained and heavy. And your insides? Well, they felt like they'd been put through a wringer! This kind of running is terrific for your abdominal muscles and core strength, the vital links through which the movements of your arms are transmitted to your legs. The ground's uneven; you have to keep your balance; you might stumble a bit; you have ditches to jump here and there, maybe one foot sticks in the mud more than the other, and you're working to keep yourself stable and to keep your rhythm and momentum.

That core strength will help you as a runner in general. It will help you as you move on to hill repeats, where you really do have to pick your knees up—and use your abdominal muscles and core to do it.

Training on this sort of terrain, whether with steady runs or fartleks, will get you used to running up and down hills while staying relaxed, and recovering off the tops of the hills without needing to stop for a rest—which, of course, mimics the experience you'll have in races.

But pretty soon you're going to want to do more structured hill sessions, which is to say timed repeats. And timing them is very important. It motivates you and it gives you feedback. You can see if your 10th rep was as fast as your first—which is the goal—or if you misjudged your pace. You might be surprised: There's a chance that, even though you felt horrible, you did the last rep as quickly as you were aiming to. And then you think, 'Considering the way I felt, that was really *good!*'

It's also useful to know if you *were* actually as slow as you felt. You can modify your workout next time, adjusting your pace so you can maintain it for the desired number of repetitions.

Timing the repetitions also allows you to see your improvement. Keep a diary. If you look back and see that you're doing the same hill four seconds faster than a year ago, that boosts your confidence. It's a way of working on your mental strength, which can carry you to greater heights, as it did for Charlie Spedding.

' Some sort of hill training is appropriate almost all the year round, as it can easily be adapted to produce different and very specific training effects, by varying the distance, the gradient, the intensity and number of repetitions, and the recovery periods. So hills can be used for strength and conditioning, stamina, short recovery training, style and technique training, and sprinting. '

Here are some workouts to get you started, though the possible variations are endless. Hill reps are often best on fast surfaces, such as roads: You need a good surface to run really fast and maintain good technique.

As you do your steady runs, be on the lookout for different hills, terrains, and gradients. Vary your hill sessions to add as many strings to your bow as possible—to work on your weaknesses, and to suit the events you're planning and the time of year. Generally speaking, for stamina you want to run a mixture of long, steady efforts and many more efforts with short recoveries. For strength, run faster efforts up longer or steeper hills with various recovery periods. And for power, do fewer short but very fast—and sometimes steep—efforts at maximum speed. It depends on the season, but at certain times of year, by way of variety, you might want to concentrate specifically on strength by doing hill repeats up steps, maybe in a stadium or on sand dunes.

HILL SESSIONS FOR STRENGTH AND STAMINA

These strength and stamina sessions are generally appropriate for early winter to midwinter if you plan to do a lot of your racing in the summer.

- Short hills: many repetitions over short distances, with jog-back recoveries. One example: two sets of ten 30-second hills, running quite fast up the hill and jogging down quickly, as well.
- Medium to long hills: fewer reps with longer recoveries. One example of medium hills: Six to eight 90-second reps up the hill with jog back recovery. One example of long hills: Four to six three-minute reps, which get very hard toward the end. Again, jog-back recoveries for nice long rests.

- Long repetitions over a short, hilly circuit that includes two or three uphills and downhills, perhaps doing four by four-minute efforts around the circuit, with three minutes rest in between.
- Continuous uphill and downhill running around a small circuit on the side of a very steep hill. Each circuit might take only 20 to 30 seconds. The aim is to do as many circuits as possible in a given time—four minutes, for example, or even up to 10 minutes. Speed is not important in this session. The hill should be so steep that your goal is simply to avoid walking. This is also a good session to try on sand dunes.

Strength and stamina aren't the only components of fitness you will need to run your best. Fortunately, hill training is versatile enough to help you with other aspects of your conditioning, as well.

HILL SESSIONS FOR SPEED AND POWER

In spring, as the summer racing season approaches, you can use hill training to sharpen up and increase your speed.

- Fewer short or medium hills, run faster than before. As you do these reps, make sure you emphasize your arm action, driving forward with high knees, fully extending your rear leg, and getting right up on your toes. (Note that the long hills discussed earlier are less appropriate to speed-oriented sessions, unless you adapt them, perhaps by changing pace and sprinting the last 30 seconds—either before you reach the top or after you've gone past the top.)
- An example of short hills for speed and power: four sets of four 30-second hills, run fast. Recover by jogging or walking back. Take three minutes rest between sets.
- An example of medium hills for speed and power: two sets of three 90-second hills, run fast with jog-back recoveries. Three minutes rest between sets.

Hills create serious overload. That's what gives you the training effect. You might see sprinters on the track running with a harness, dragging heavy tyres behind them, or even straining against the resistance of another person. On a hill, the resistance comes from overcoming gravity. And that overload allows you to improve your fitness far beyond what you can do in your friendly and chatty steady runs—no matter how many of them you do or how many miles they add up to.

VARIATIONS ON A THEME

But that overload also makes it easy to overdo it. Select the gradient, length, and surface of your hill carefully for the session you have in mind. You'll likely want a recovery day afterwards. That means an easy run, walk, or swim, not a day doing nothing. And keep in mind that one of the goals of any training session is to leave yourself fit and ready to train again. You want to work very hard but you don't want to become jaded. So you've read somewhere that the New Zealander Peter Snell ran two-minute reps up a hill with (allegedly) a gradient of one in three—which, take it from me, is quite steep. Yes, he won three Olympic golds and set five world records. But that doesn't mean you should try the same thing. Snell was an unusually powerful runner. You need to make the sessions manageable for *you*.

You can run some longer hill reps, though, and they'll benefit you if you're trying to get ready for a longer race, like a marathon. The trouble with longer reps is that it takes so long to jog back to the bottom that you get more rest than is optimal. But there's a way to get around that. Find a hill that's Peter Snell's length or even longer, and run it in segments.

Sebastian Coe, for all his exploits, was not a great cross country runner. His world records were all on the flat, of course—on the track—but he ran some serious hills on his way to setting them. Famously, he used the Rivelin Valley Road, a three-mile hill just west of Sheffield, to do long hill repeats.

One of his sessions was six times half a mile. His dad would follow him up this three-mile hill in the car, because everything was timed and measured. Seb would run 800 metres fast and then, instead of jogging back down, he'd have a timed rest right where he was, and then run another half mile up the hill, until he'd run the six half-mile efforts.

That's a good way to approach it: Don't think, 'I've got a three-mile hill, so I've got to go from the bottom to the top all in one go.' You can be a little more imaginative, and come up with a pattern that suits your abilities and requirements.

Here's an effective variation on long hill repeats: Find a 90-second or two-minute hill. Run hard to the top, jog back only 45 seconds or so, then turn around and sprint back to the top, probably in about 20 seconds. That's one set. Then jog all the way back down to the bottom and do five more sets of one long and one

Medals are won in the winter—they are just collected in the summer. Sebastian Coe illustrates this with an intense hill session in the winter in Richmond Park.

Mark Shearman, Athletics Images

short hill. You might develop the session further over time by doing just four sets but having each set made up of one long and two short hills.

There are a couple of benefits to this sort of pattern. You do a long hill but give yourself only a short rest before starting up again on your sprint. You replicate feelings you get in a race—you're feeling tired, and you're going to have to sprint. But the sprint is much shorter than the full effort, and you're likely to find out you had a lot more left than you thought.

'Wow', you think, 'that's not so bad.' You can still sprint—even when you're tired! The reason being that you're using a different energy system, and you *can*—especially if it's just for a short time.

That gets you pumped up, and then you get a long rest as you jog all the way down to the bottom. When you get there and start the 90-second run again, you'll probably feel the pace is quite slow. And so you start to gain confidence that you can actually go a bit faster and still feel it's a sustainable speed.

There are many possible variations on hill repeats, so experiment. I think you need one structured hill session per week, pretty much year round. But don't hammer out the same session again and again. Make sure the sessions are appropriate to your training aims at that particular time of year. And use them to develop as many training effects as you can. In other words, don't just do the ones you find most comfortable. Bear a couple of things in mind as you explore variations: Design your sessions to achieve particular aims. And try as often as you can to replicate situations you'll encounter in a race.

' One very effective way to practice for a race situation: Don't stop when you get to the top. Keep going! Run strongly off the brow of the hill for another 20 seconds or so. At certain times of year, especially in the pre-competition phase, actually change pace and sprint off the top of the hill. '

This allows you to practice changing pace. You're going to have to change from the shorter stride you've used to power up the hill to the longer stride you need to run faster.

It also allows you to practice recovering without stopping, since there's no stopping in a race. You have to overcome that feeling of wanting to stop to get your breath back. You *will* recover as the terrain levels off, but not immediately. It's a delayed reaction. Go with the flow, and you'll learn not to let the hill knock you, and how to get back into your stride quickly. It comes down to pace judgement and gear selection—in other words, your cadence.

It's important that you choose hills that are *manageable for you,* not just the steepest hills you can find, and that you learn to judge your effort, based on breathing rate rather than heart rate, so that you are running up the hill at a sustainable rate. If your breathing starts to feel unsustainable, you're going too fast, so slow down slightly, keeping the same cadence, just as you would if cycling up a hill. But don't be frightened of being out of breath—as long as it feels controlled and sustainable, there's nothing wrong, and you're not going to die of asphyxiation!

Running strongly off the brow of hills is a great tactic for opening up a gap in cross country and road races. Often, there is little difference between the speeds at which different competitors run up hills. It takes a lot of extra effort for someone to open up even a small gap.

But at the top, with practice and a bit of determination, you can often convert a 10-metre gap into a 50-metre gap, or even more. Practicing running strongly off the top of the hill can help enormously in developing this skill for races.

Another effective variation on hill reps is to change pace midway up. You might run partway up at 80 percent effort, then go flat-out for the final third. Apart from the excellent physical and mental training effects, this particularly helps with pace judgment. And of course it helps keep your feet nice and quick, even when you're running up a hill.

I can't say it often enough: Don't plod! No matter how long or steep the hill may be. I'm always trying to get people to run with quick feet, even if they're training for the marathon. The main thing is to keep your feet light and maintain good cadence. It's your *arms*, not your legs, which control this. These reps will teach you to cope with being in oxygen debt and having heavy legs. And one way to cope is by shortening your stride—in cycling terms, changing down a gear or two. Can't make it up the hill with long strides? Don't try. You want to be zippy all the way up and ensure that you can run strongly off the top. Move your arms quickly and your legs will follow.

HILL SESSIONS CAN BE SOCIABLE

Sometimes people avoid hill reps because they like the social aspect of running, and they think they have to do hills only with people of the same ability. Not so. It might take a little organizing, but hill sessions can be an excellent way for runners of different abilities to train together.

Here's one way to organize a hill session for runners of different abilities: Starting together, everyone runs up the hill until the fastest one reaches the top. At that point the fastest runner signals and everyone stops. They mark how far up the hill they got, and that point becomes their target for the remainder of the session. Everybody regroups on the jog back down, and everybody starts the next rep together, so the times of the efforts and the recoveries remain the same for the whole group.

Another way is to run the hill as a handicap, where the fastest runner starts at the bottom of the hill, and less-strong runners start at various points up it. They all start at the same time and, hopefully, they all reach the top very close together. This session has enormous benefits for stronger and weaker runners alike; the stronger runners have people to chase the whole way up, while the weaker runners enjoy the feeling of being ahead for most if not all of the rep. By the time they do get overtaken, they've got a good chance of matching the faster runners' speed for the last few metres.

If you have a group of runners who aren't so quick, and one guy who's really fast, you might have everyone run to the top of the hill—but the fast guy has to sprint off the top another 50 or 100 metres.

There are lots of ways of extending the faster runners while still keeping a group of different abilities together. And everyone can learn from and encourage each other while enjoying a bit of banter, which is one of the great aspects of doing any repetitions in a group, whether on the hills or on the flat. These sessions are so much harder to do on your own, so it is important to find ways of making them sociable.

Although hills are hard work, hill training is not *all* about effort. You should always be trying to run with good technique. This means running tall, relaxed and balanced, with loose shoulders, high knee lift and a powerful drive off the ball of the rear foot. The power and attack of your running action will vary depending on the gradient and distance. But if you feel your form has gone completely, that means you're doing too hard a session. You're doing too many reps, or the reps are too long, or the gradient is too steep, or you're not taking enough rest time between reps. Adjust your session accordingly. You want to train hard, sometimes very hard, but you want to always practice good form as well.

Hill work helps increase suppleness, too. If you're maintaining good form at speed, you'll be working toward the limits of your range of movement and helping increase your suppleness. And the reverse is even more true: If you stretch regularly and work on your suppleness, you'll find it easier to run faster while keeping relaxed—even up a good long hill.

As with any activity, it's possible to pick up an injury running hills. But actually I think the bigger risk with hill training is the possibility of jarring yourself jogging back down between reps. It's quite hard to relax and patter down the hill. You might think it's easier to jog down with slow legs. Resist the urge. Crashing down like that on slow legs, you'll be hurting your knees, your hips, your back, and your quads. Try to patter, with quick feet and light landings, not so your pace is fast but so your legs are springy and the impact of each step is minimal.

Charging up hills again and again does create overload, and that, too, entails some risk of injury. But the risk comes primarily when your body is not adapted to the overload. The answer is to start hill training gradually, allowing your body time to get used to these sessions, and then stay adapted.

One of the best ways to minimize any detrimental effects of hill work is to practice it regularly. It doesn't always have to be intense. But hill sessions can be appropriate throughout almost the entire year. By doing them year-round, you'll benefit from a whole range of training effects, and also make the transition to more intensive hill sessions more manageable when the time comes.

So that pretty much wraps it up as far as hill work goes, right? Well, most people would think so. And I certainly thought so myself at one time.

But as an up-and-coming athlete, I remember comparing notes with one of my rivals, a guy named Dave Black. He was a strong, tough competitor with a short stride and a very fast cadence, who went on to win two national titles and two Commonwealth medals. On one of our trips, I remember asking him if he did any hill training.

'No, not really hill training', he said. 'But I do sometimes run downhill repetitions.'

I can remember thinking that Dave was either being very cagey or else he was a little soft in the head. I thought, *'Downhill?* How's that going to help you?' You've got to run uphill to get stronger—and usually the steeper the hill the better.

But, looking back, Dave knew something I didn't. Uphill reps are great for stamina, strength, and power. But none of them really helps develop leg speed because you're always fighting against gravity.

Downhill running, though, encourages the feeling of falling, which forces you to move your legs quicker. It allows you to run faster and, more importantly, with greater leg speed. In many ways it's similar to when a cyclist drafts behind a pace car. Instead of working on the drive phase, as in uphill running, running downhill develops the leg strength you need to keep you from buckling, even when you're running at higher speeds than usual.

And even though you're working with gravity instead of against it, downhill running improves your strength, too. Think of fell runners. For those of you who live in places where there's no such thing, fell running is cross country running up and down mountains—very popular in the hilly regions of northern England and Scotland. Fell runners are extremely good at running downhill. In fact, that's where the races are generally won and lost. The best runners don't just patter down—they *launch* themselves off the hilltops. They're extremely strong, and it's that strength that allows them to race down the hills without jarring themselves and putting on the brakes.

Try running fast down a hill and you'll soon realize you need even more strength in your quads than you do to run uphill. One of my RAF team-mates, John Wild, turned to fell running and, after a year or two during which he became British champion, his quads developed so much he needed a complete set of new trousers.

If you're not very fit or your legs are stiff when you start running down a hill, you feel you have to put the brakes on with every stride. But, maybe three-quarters of the way down, as the gradient levels off a bit, you'll feel able to take the brakes off and let yourself go. Suddenly, you're running faster and feeling easier at the same time.

The fitter you get, the higher up the hill you can do that, and the steeper the downhill gradient you'll be able to cope with. When you're really strong, you can take the brakes off and really fly down the hill, totally relaxed, letting gravity work with you for once. To my mind, when you're able to run downhill like that, it's a big indicator that you're very fit, strong, and ready to race well.

Knowing how to run downhill fast in races can give you a big advantage. We've already seen that people who push hard uphill are likely to gain only a slight advantage. The downhills are just the reverse, as the fell runners demonstrate. Other people will be just shuffling carefully down the hills, running at a normal sort of pace. But, having practiced it, you can relax and flow down the hill and quickly open up large gaps. Practice doing this whenever you can on downhill sections of your steady runs and fartleks.

‘ **The things to remember when you run down a hill are to relax, avoid jarring, and keep your legs moving quickly. Try not to land on your heels.** ’

This is difficult when you're tired or it's steep. But try not to brake—don't lean back, and don't land stiffly with straight legs—and relax your arms and shoulders, using your arms for balance rather than power.

SPECIFIC DOWNHILL SESSIONS

For specific downhill sessions, pick a gentle gradient on a soft, forgiving surface: You want to be able to handle the extra speed without crashing down on your heels and jarring your legs, hips, and back. You want to feel that you're running fast and relaxed. It's almost a drill—you *have* to move your legs quicker than usual to avoid falling on your face.

If you hear your feet landing heavily or feel you have to lean back, you know you're fighting gravity and putting on the brakes. Try not to do that. Either adjust your technique or find a shallower descent.

When you're running down a slight gradient you should be able to maintain a strong running style, using a vigorous, rangy arm action and attacking each step with a bent knee and a strong push off the toes of your rear foot. You're driving forward, not holding back. Down steeper gradients, just let gravity do the work—all you have to do is avoid putting the brakes on!

Practice relaxing and running fast downhill on your steady runs and fartleks all year round. I wouldn't generally suggest doing specific downhill sessions, except for the following two *to be done on a very shallow gradient.*

Sharpening Session for the Pre-Competition Phase

For a week without a race, when you want a harder sharpening session that still includes some downhill try 6 sets of 40 seconds fast and relaxed downhill at 95 percent effort, followed by 20 seconds rest, then a sprint back up the hill to your start point at 100 percent effort, trying (but probably just failing) to match the 40-second time. Recover for a full 3 or 4 minutes between each set.

Tapering Session

For a fairly easy downhill session that would be ideal three or four days before a race try 8 to 10 times 30 seconds fast and relaxed down a slight gradient with a jog back recovery.

However, as with all your tapering sessions before a big race, remember that the times you record in your sessions are less important than feelings. The only times that matter are your race times. Your sessions should be designed to enable you to produce good performances on race day. It's better to run them slightly slower but with good technique rather than faster and out of control.

Yes, the idea of hills can be daunting. Yes, they require effort. And maybe I've given you a lot to digest here. But remember, most of these sessions will take up less of your time than one of your steady runs yet give you far greater benefits. And they can leave you more invigorated (and less in need of a nap) than all those longer runs you thought you needed. Really the only daunting thing about hills is the idea of getting started. As Franklin Roosevelt said, 'The only thing we have to fear is fear itself!'

So remember these key things: less time, fewer miles, more strength, better technique, greater fitness, more variety, and more challenges. Besting rivals who practice only the art of plodding. You're going to be smarter than they are and practice the art of *running fast*. It all adds up to more fun! Get started, and you'll learn, as Charlie Spedding did, that Mr. Hill can be your friend.

KEY POINTS TO REMEMBER

- Include some form of hill repeats in your schedule for two-thirds to three-quarters of the year. You might do less mileage than with another steady run, but you'll race faster.

- Hill training can target all of the five Ss—speed, strength, stamina, skill and suppleness. It helps with psychology, too. Which means it can improve your performance significantly.

- If you've never run hill repeats, start by running over hilly terrain. Enter some cross country races. This kind of running gives you the strength and stamina you need to get into some serious hill training.

- Run long, steady efforts uphill for stamina; many more shorter but faster efforts for strength; and fewer short but very steep efforts at maximum speed for power.

- Sometimes run downhill reps on a gentle gradient to improve your leg speed.

9

Strength in the Fields

February 1970. Parliament Hill Fields.

Dave Bedford had just won the Southern Counties Senior Cross Country Championships when a buzz went through the crowd.

I'd won the youth division earlier in the afternoon, then stayed around to watch Dave run the seniors. After his victory—by nearly a minute—a rumour started spreading like wildfire: Bedford's going to run the junior race, as well! He's going for the double!

'Cocky sod', some people said, 'Serves him right if he comes unstuck.'

Actually, Bedford was going for the treble to make it three wins for our coach, Bob Parker, and also the overall team championship for our club, Shaftesbury Harriers.

Dave was only 20, so he was still technically a junior. But he'd already raced nine miles over the demanding, gut-wrenching terrain of Parliament Hill—the same venue where I would win the English National some years later. The junior race would be another six miles. And there were only 20 minutes between the end of one race and the start of the next—barely time enough for him to grab his new number and line up at the start.

He did it, though. And won it. In his autobiography, he attributed his victory in that second race largely to his fearsome reputation and a bit of bluff—kidology, as we called it. Had anyone really challenged him, he wrote, he might have buckled. Instead, he said, even the best of the other runners stayed a respectful distance behind.

Well, there's probably something to that. Dave did like to psych people out. And he was good at kidology. I remember him showing up at races abroad, when all the runners would meet up at the hotel, mingle and ask each other how they were getting on and how their training was going.

And Dave would say, 'Oh, I'm in great shape. I eased down a bit last week and just did 140.' He meant miles, and it was probably true. But he said it in such a way that it made the other runners lose heart even before the race had begun.

And in the Southern juniors that day, the other runners were intimidated by him, that's for sure. But, though he didn't put it in his book, he *was* challenged, at least a bit. He wasn't in the lead going up that long first hill for which Parliament Hill is famous. I don't think he was even in the top 50 for the first mile or so. The other guys were giving it a go.

But Dave was soon back in the groove, churning out his remorseless rhythm while the others were slipping, tripping, and stumbling through the mud and over the ditches. By the end of the first lap, the halfway point in the race, he was already in front and pulling away. And in the end, his victory wasn't close. He won—again—by over a minute.

So kidology is all very good. But Dave had a lot more than that going for him. He was just outstanding in those days, because he would grind relentlessly over whatever was in his way: hills, mud, jumps, or anything.

That toughness—both mental and physical—helped him in cross country. But I think a lot of it also *came* from cross country.

> **6** The best time to introduce runners to cross country is when they're young. Kids love the mud and puddles, the jumps over ditches, and the switchbacks. They're enthusiastic cross country runners. That is a crucial time to make running fun, and cross country is one of the best ways of developing strong kids. Basically, you build strength while just having a good time. **9**

We all know kids are not as strong today as they were a generation ago. There's not enough tree climbing, not enough jumping around outside, and most certainly not enough cross country running, especially at schools. This may be partly for health and safety reasons—the course would probably involve going outside the school gates (horror of horrors!). And partly because schools almost kill the kids with kindness by offering a wide range of other usually far less strenuous sports, which, human nature being what it is, sound far more attractive. Not many kids are going to choose a three-mile cross country run over a game of netball, rounders, volleyball, or basketball—let alone sailing, archery or shooting, or even a spot of dance. Nothing against these excellent sports and activities, but they aren't in themselves going to burn many calories or do much for the kids' aerobic fitness. Wouldn't it be better to run for 10 or 15 minutes as well, either beforehand or afterwards?

But how do you make this run fun? Too often the perception is that cross country is too tough or too boring—or worse still, a punishment.

To make cross country fun, kids need to be given good reasons for doing the sport, which involves excitement, speed, overtaking, jumping ditches and puddles, and *racing*! Kids are competitive, but it does get boring if the races always have the same result, with the same people winning all the time. The answer lies in designing training sessions with lots of short races, team relay races, handicap races, races where slower kids are given a chance, and a reason to try their best, sometimes by giving them shortcuts and sometimes by putting them in relay teams with faster runners. From this base, the more able kids need to be introduced to proper races—but again, they need to be *shown* how to prepare, not just chucked in the deep end. They need to know what kit and shoes to wear, how to warm up, how fast to start, how to judge their pace, and how to cope with the feeling of being out of breath. They need to be confident they can work hard, get out of breath, and still keep racing.

Too often, I see kids thrown into races at the last minute, totally unprepared and wearing inappropriate kit. Of course, they're nervous; they start off too fast, come nearly to a halt after a minute or two, and have a really unpleasant experience that puts them off cross country for life.

Would the schools throw someone into the swimming pool and tell them to race before they'd even taught them how to swim? Of course not. It's no different with cross country running.

Show these kids the basic skills of the sport and they will find it a lot of fun. Not only that, but it will also help build the fitness and stamina required for almost any other sport they care to do and start to develop the mental toughness and stickability that will stand them in good stead for the numerous challenges they will encounter in life.

Kids who aren't strong grow up to be adults who aren't strong. You see it in athletics: Just look at the declining performances of most developed countries' top endurance runners over the past 15-20 years. You also see it in everyday life, for example in declining entry standards of fitness for the police or the army.

One British newspaper recently reported under the headline, 'Blobbies on the beat' that police trainers were reporting 'repeated and pathetic failures' from recruits undergoing basic fitness tests.

And it's not limited to Britain. As a paper in the United States reported, 'The waistlines of America's youth are expanding, shrinking the pool of those eligible to join the U.S. military.' So guess what? The U.S. Army has introduced a waiver program for overweight people who want to enlist on the theory they can shape up after they join.

Better late than never, though.

And that applies to cross country, too. It's certainly easier to run cross country as a kid, when you're younger and lighter. But that's no reason to shy away from it when you're an adult, especially if you're trying to improve your running overall. I hope I've convinced you that a bit of cross country will be good for you. And I hope, too, I've convinced you it will be fun.

And not only training—there's no reason to shy away from cross country racing, either. It's much more fun than racing on the track and probably the roads, too. Racing on the track, certainly, and to a lesser extent on the roads, it's all uniform. The surface doesn't vary, your rhythm hardly varies—it's almost like running on a treadmill. And if someone gets a lead on you, it's a heck of a job to catch them up.

But with cross country, it's often a case of horses for courses. You have to adapt to the terrain and the conditions, sometimes slipping and sliding, sometimes having to lift your legs out of sticky, heavy mud, and sometimes having to jump streams and ditches. Some people can cope with the mud better than others, some prefer the uphills, some prefer the downhill sections. Admittedly, some courses are a bit flat and boring, but in proper cross country races the terrain is always varied, interesting, and challenging. Often you have a choice of how to pick your line. You can go through the puddle or around the edge. You can jump a ditch this way or that way. You can slog through the mud on a straighter line or try to find a way to avoid it. Some people manage to find a better grip than others. Then there's the scenery, the sounds, the conditions, and the atmosphere. It's just nice to be away from roads and cars, either in peaceful surroundings or surrounded by the noise of supporters encouraging you and urging you on.

So discover your inner kid and get out there!

‘ Racing cross country can help you become a better runner on any surface by pushing against your limiting factors: It is enormously effective in developing strength, skill, stamina, and psychology—mental toughness and stickability are improved, too. And that will help you on the roads or the track much more than you might imagine. ’

That was a remarkable day, when Bedford won the double. And it inspired me to copy that effort—albeit to a lesser extent—a number of times. If you were fit enough, doubling up could be an exciting challenge. And it was a way for me to help my team, too.

Later that year, in the Southern Counties Junior Athletics Championships, I won the 1,500 and the 3,000 on the same weekend.

And the following year I was still a junior, and this time both races were scheduled for the same afternoon. Could I still win them both with just a couple of hours between them? I'm pleased to say I managed to do it again, but it would actually have been easier had there been only 20 or 30 minutes between the events. Having a two-hour gap entailed warming up a second time, and on the second warm-up I can remember feeling pretty rough and not at all sure that it was a good idea!

As an undergraduate at Oxford, I started doing a similar double—the 1,500 and the 5,000—at the annual varsity match against Cambridge, and then often continued doing this when representing the RAF in the Inter Services Championships. With only 20 minutes between, it was much easier, and I found this double proved excellent 10,000-metre preparation. Dave had shown me that all you needed to do was line up for the second race and the opposition could be psyched out and would only run for second place.

And twice in finals of the GRE Cup—the athletics equivalent to soccer's FA Cup—I ran the 10,000 and the 5,000 on the same day. No one else had attempted that before, and I'm not sure if anyone has since. Both times, I managed to win the 10,000, which was first, but not the 5,000. It's hard, after the longer race, to quicken your pace for the shorter one. But I think I finished third in the 5,000, which still meant good points for the club.

Those doubles were on the track, of course. And that's really the point: One way you get the kind of strength necessary to run those doubles—and to run well on the track in general—is from cross country.

Cross country may involve slogging through the mud and running a bit slower than you otherwise would. But it gives you all-over, full-body fitness and resilience that will help you enormously when you run on quicker surfaces.

‘ The best way to prepare for cross country racing is to train off-road whenever possible. Don't just run at a steady pace. Cross country, with its ups, downs, mud, and jumps, isn't like that. Do fartleks, varying your pace as you run on a woodland path. Do off-road hill sessions. And it's especially important to get used to your racing spikes by doing some speedwork in them before you use them in a race. ’

You'll likely be doing these speed sessions in the winter, when it's colder—not the best time for sprinting. And cross country is not the fastest running surface, by any means. So for your sessions in spikes, it's best to concentrate not on faster reps but on longer ones—perhaps six times 1K or four times a mile or maybe 16 times one-minute efforts.

Of course you'll want to do these sessions on terrain that's suitable for spikes, because spikes give so much better grip in muddy conditions. Playing fields are ideal, as are forest trails and parkland. Of course, if it's not muddy and slippery, normal training shoes are fine.

Another skill of cross country running involves the ability to read the course, take the right line, and find the gaps through a heaving mass of runners. There are all sorts of little parts of a cross country race where you can gain ground on someone else, not by working harder but just by taking a jump better, by getting to a gate or a corner ahead of a group, by avoiding a muddy patch by running further, or by daring to go straight through a puddle rather than round it. Often, you can close a gap without any extra effort, just because the other guy's got stuck in the mud or had a bad jump in a ditch—or even slipped over! You can do better than someone else by being clever, by planning ahead and putting your feet in exactly the right places. It adds an extra dimension that you don't get when you race on the roads.

Having said that, you do want the course to be runnable. You don't want a course so difficult that all you can do is plod. Running over frozen plough, where you're more likely to break an ankle than run fast, is worse still, and something to be avoided at all costs. But in most races, you should be able to run fast at least in some places along the course. And if there's a hundred metres of quagmire along the way—no problem. Just go with the flow!

If you're going to do some cross country races, you're going to need a few additional items of kit, particularly shoes. The best racing shoes are undoubtedly specialist cross country spikes, which usually come with a studded and slightly cushioned rear sole. But spikes are no good if the course includes sections of road. In that case, you're better off in a pair of studded fell-running shoes.

Either way, your regular trainers will be too clumpy and won't give you enough grip. So warm up in them and then put on your racing shoes for the event itself.

Other kit you'll need will depend on the conditions. Generally speaking, a snug-fitting, long-sleeved thermal top will be useful under your singlet. A pair of gloves and a hat can be useful, too, especially to warm up in.

And always have warm, dry clothes to put on afterwards, and get a warm drink down you as soon as possible after you've finished the race.

It's easy enough to find cross country races over the winter, at least in Britain. There are numerous league races around the country, involving perhaps one race a month, usually over about 8K. The best thing is to join your local running club so you can run the races as part of a team.

Travelling together and running as a team makes it much more fun than just going on your own. And running for a team motivates you to do your best. It's a very different experience to just entering a fun run and running for yourself, or even for a charity. This is a proper team competition, sometimes even with team prizes at stake!

And, as with all races, you'll have friends to share the experience with afterwards: 'How'd you get through that slippy part near the end?'

'Oh, man, I couldn't *believe* that! I was on my hands and knees!'

And you share a laugh, congratulate each other, change into some dry kit, and bask in the knowledge that your friends were out there facing the same challenges as you. You might very well find out that other people had a tougher time of it than you did. That's a lot better than thinking you were the only one who had to work to adapt to the conditions.

There are plenty of open races and championship races you can run in too. In England, the structure of the cross country season revolves around the County Championships in early January; the Area Championships (the Northern, Southern, Midland, Welsh, and Scottish Championships), which are usually held at the end of January; and the National Championships at the end of February.

Most of these races are about 12K, although the Southern is still run over its traditional and more demanding distance of 15K.

None of these events is any more elitist than, say, the Great North Run or the London Marathon. Enter, and you'll find a complete cross section of runners taking part, from international to club runners, from novices to veterans, from lean-and-hungry speedsters to rather portly slowpokes.

So give it a try!

'Cross country running is excellent for developing strength. The terrain forces you to run with your whole body. Your leg strength will improve. Your stomach muscles will get stronger. Your core strength will be enhanced. You'll be compelled to pump your arms. And increasing your strength—one of the critical five Ss—will help you run faster on the roads or on the track.'

Often on the roads you see runners who are barely moving their arms at all. They don't lift their knees very much, either. They don't develop much strength that way. But at times, cross country can be like running with a weight on your back. You really have to work with your legs. They can feel like they're about to buckle underneath you! Whereas on the road you can usually just patter along. Your legs might start to feel dead, but they don't buckle.

Sometimes in cross country, you do a jump or you're running up a hill, and you're not sure if you're going to stumble. Or maybe you've picked up a lot of mud on your shoes and they feel as heavy as rocks. Either way, you're building enormous *strength:* The hills and mud develop power and resilience in your calves, hamstrings, and quads. The uneven ground strengthens your feet and ankles.

Keeping your balance through all the twists and turns and dips is tremendous for your core strength. The challenging terrain makes you

Neil Tingle/Action Plus/Icon SMI

Strength in the fields: There's no better way for distance runners like Paula Radcliffe to build strength.

lift your knees, and that works your abdominal muscles and improves your technique, or your *skill*—another of the five S's. And the remorseless cycle of stress and recovery as the hills roll by will do wonders for your *stamina*—yet another of the Ss.

Beyond that, the soft, forgiving, even sticky surfaces, not only increase resistance, making you stronger, they also reduce the jarring effect on your body. When something makes you work harder yet reduces your risk of injury, that's a good workout.

Because you're forced to work much harder in cross country, you get more out of breath than you do on the roads. Your heart rate goes up more, too. And that's a huge benefit. Off-road racing is a very effective way to develop your cardiovascular system, producing a powerful heart, an efficient set of lungs, and a dense network of capillaries to transport oxygen to the muscle fibres.

And it makes you stronger upstairs, too.

‘ Cross country racing is a superb way to develop determination and stickability, pushing back against that final limiting factor—psychology. The mental strength that cross country develops will help you in any kind of race you try. ’

Just as the physical stresses are tougher in cross country racing, so are the mental stresses. Many's the time you'll say to yourself, 'If I can just get up this hill without stopping!' At this stage you're not even thinking about whether you can finish the race. Maybe you'll think about that when you get to the top of the hill. For now, you're just seeing if you can make it up this one hill without walking. That's really quite tough—you don't usually get that feeling in a road race!

But you adapt to psychological stresses just as you do to physical ones—by getting stronger. When you *do* make it to the top of that god-awful endless hill, you will have reinforced and improved your toughness. With every success you'll become more confident. When you experience those feelings where it all hangs in the balance and you're in danger of losing heart, but in the end overcome that nagging voice urging you to give up, your self-esteem gains a real boost. The battle's against yourself and the conditions, not just your rivals: It's good character-building stuff!

I think runners who've done cross country have the sort of strength necessary to cope when the going gets tough on the roads or the track. Because endurance running is largely about how you cope with these feelings. Mental strength is not about being fitter than the other guy; it's about stickability and learning to suffer and dig deeper. When you overcome these hardships, you develop the confidence, the drive, the fierceness, and the aggression to really get the most out of all the physical training you've done.

And I think that's brilliant! The sense of achievement and the satisfaction you get from having strained sinews and limbs to the limit is fantastic.

In all those ways and more, cross country helps you improve, whatever your goals. Unfortunately, there are people—some of them, I'm sorry to say, involved in British athletics—who don't seem to recognise the enormous value of cross country, and consider it to be a bit of a sideline to 'real' athletics. Britain used to have a great cross country heritage: After all, splashing through the mud is a very English sort of sport. But unfortunately, over the last 25 years or so, the sport's administrators and coaches seem to have conspired to devalue its importance.

A lot of the coaching has been done by people who never ran cross country themselves. And the perceived wisdom has been that cross country running develops plodders, not track runners. 'To beat the best runners and run fast on the track', they say, 'you shouldn't practice running on slippery, soft, slow surfaces.'

And they'd point to people like Dave Bedford, Dave Black, Steve Jones, Bernie Ford, and me and say we were all plodders. Well, that's quite a put-down. If we were plodders, we were extremely fast plodders!

Part of the problem was the hectic schedule of races, which delayed our preparations for the track season. The National Cross Country Championships, then held in the first week of March, was a very important race—one most runners couldn't afford to miss. It was the race used to select the team for the World Cross Country Championships three weeks later.

And getting to the World Cross was a big deal. It was arguably the hardest title of all to win. Because among the entrants you had all the 5,000-metre runners, all the 10,000-metre runners, all the marathon runners, all the steeplechasers, and all the cross country specialists—all competing in that one race. In the Olympics, they're spread out between five events. So the World Cross was absolutely *the* world championship of distance running.

But if you got to the World Cross, it probably did distract you and delay your preparations for the track. It really entailed trying to peak twice, once in March and then again in June or July. And to fight your way onto the British track team, which was very difficult in those days, meant you had to be pretty fit by the end of May, as well. That left a quite a short time to make the transition.

However, the World Cross is generally run on a smooth, fast course and the answer, really, was to train for it like a track race.

But of course Britain has a bit of a problem with its weather, and even if we hadn't been preoccupied with cross country races, it would have been too cold here to do hard, fast speedwork. Preparing for a track-type race in March is difficult if you're in Britain. Warm-weather training camps can be very beneficial. I know they were for us. Otherwise, it can be hard to compete with the Kenyans and the other Africans. They're undoubtedly training in warm weather, and they might be finding it easier to get that speed in their legs.

But it's not that cross country slows you down, it's just that British weather and British cross country courses tend to conspire against fast running—or

Press Association

Nine miles over hills and through mud—great for club runners and Olympic stars alike. Steve Ovett (322) and Brendan Foster (304) to the fore in the 1977 National at Parliament Hill Fields.

so some people think! But I think the evidence points otherwise. Numerous winners of the nine-mile National Cross Country Championships were sub-13.25-minute 5,000-metre or sub-28-minute 10,000-metre runners. The year I won the National on a particularly muddy course, not only was I the fastest 5,000-metre runner in that field, but the England team that was selected from that race included five sub-13:30 track runners! And that same year, I went on to post my fastest-ever 5,000—13:15. In 2009, by contrast, I think only one Brit ran under 13:30 the whole summer.

As you can see from the Kenyans' excellent results, they can reach quite a major peak for the World Cross in March, and that doesn't prevent them from setting records and winning Olympic medals in August.

And consider the Ethiopian runner Kenenisa Bekele. He's the most successful athlete ever in the World Cross Country Championships with six long-course titles, over 12K, and five victories in the short course, run over 4K. Yet he's won Olympic gold in the 5,000 and the 10,000, and holds the world record for both. Cross country doesn't seem to slow him down. I think it probably helps him.

And what about those of us who were good at cross country but supposedly plodders? Well, Bedford set a 10,000-metre world record on the track, and

Jones a world best for the marathon, and the rest of us were pretty quick, too. Check out the list of Britain's sub-28:00 men for the 10,000. Eamonn Martin, Dave Bedford, Brendan Foster, Nick Rose, Tony Simmons, Dave Clarke, Bernie Ford, Mike McLeod, Richard Nerurkar, Dave Black, and me—we all won the National Cross Country Championship. And Ian Stewart, although he never won the National, did win the World Cross Country Championship. Nearly all of this country's sub-28:00 runners were very good at cross country.

If you look at the times we ran 30 years ago, they would welcome any of us on the British team today with open arms. So de-emphasizing cross country doesn't seem to have made people faster. And, while you can argue that cross country diverted us from our track preparations, you certainly can't argue that runners who've done less cross country—running instead over shorter, flatter courses—have run faster. They haven't.

No, cross country didn't slow us down. And it won't slow you down, either. It will speed you up.

As the heat fades and winter approaches, you don't want to go back to square one with your training. On the contrary, winter is the best time to build strength and stamina, and getting in some of those miles off-road will really help. The different terrain will do you good. A change is as good as a rest, we used to say. You'll be doing something different than pounding the roads. Your risk of injury will be reduced by the change and by the softer terrain.

Look, all sorts of people these days enjoy these tough-guy races and adventure challenges where they run through icy ponds and slither under barbed wire through frigid mud. Compared to that, cross country is a stroll in the park. Enjoy it—get muddy, get stronger, and get mentally tough.

And you'll reap the rewards in the summer.

KEY POINTS TO REMEMBER

- Racing cross country can help you become a better runner on any surface because it's very effective at developing strength, skill, stamina, and psychology (mental toughness).
- In muddy conditions, the best shoes are specialist cross country spikes. But if the course contains sections of road or stony ground, you're better off in a pair of studded fell-running shoes.
- Prepare for cross country racing by training off-road. Do fartleks. Do off-road hill sessions. And if you're going to race in spikes, remember to try them out a few times in your off-road speed sessions. In fact, whatever shoes you plan to race in, try them out in speed sessions first.

Chapter

10

Running Round in Circles

Mention speedwork to many runners—perhaps even most of them—and the reaction tends to be lukewarm at best, and sometimes downright antagonistic.

'Too much like hard work!' they say. 'Takes the enjoyment out of running!' Or, 'Too much risk of injury!'

'I can't run fast, anyway', others tell me. 'That's why I do long distance running.'

'I can't afford to do speed sessions. If I did, my mileage would go right down', many say. 'I run marathons so I don't *need* to do speedwork.'

Even runners who recognise that speedwork does have some benefits tend to offer explanations of why they don't do more of it. 'Yes,' they'll tell me, 'I do a bit of speedwork just to sharpen up before a race—after I've done all my stamina work.'

But stamina is exactly the point. For distance runners, speedwork is *not* sprint training. Because it involves running fast—often considerably faster than race pace—*many times with limited rest periods*, it *is* endurance training. It enhances your speed endurance and strength endurance. And far from being relevant only as a bit of sharpening just prior to a race, speedwork in one form or another is beneficial throughout most of the year.

‘ Without speedwork, endurance running will:

- Build stamina—but not strength.
- Build aerobic efficiency—but not raise your anaerobic threshold.
- Extend your range—but not your fast cruising speed.
- Improve your recovery rate—but not your ability to recover whilst still running at speed. ’

But with speedwork, endurance running will build strength, speed endurance, lactate tolerance, and your ability to recover quickly while still running.

I recognize that many people—primarily those who've never tried it—think of speedwork as something unpleasant, because clearly it takes you out of your comfort zone. But I certainly enjoyed it, and wouldn't have missed it for anything.

For one thing, it gives your training structure, variety, and focus. It gets you away from the boredom factor, the where-shall-I-go-for-a-run-today syndrome. For another, it is actually quite a sociable thing to do. You and your partners gather at the track—or the fields, woodland or parkland—roll your eyes a little at the thought of the session to come, banter during the recoveries, and maybe give each other a bit of stick as you cool down.

If the session is organised properly, you can all keep together, even if the group includes people of different abilities. Maybe the faster guys will run longer repetitions, or the slower runners will do only every other rep. But, by doing speed sessions together, you can learn from each other, motivate each other, and try to match each other. I think it's a much more social experience than many club runs, which tend to turn into a bit of a race, leaving runners strung out along the route, running at their own pace—and on their own.

I would have certainly found it boring to just run steady all the time. The whole pattern of training would have become tedious, week after week, and month after month. I think a change is as good as a rest, both mentally and physically. It keeps your outlook fresh. And it keeps your feet lively: I've said it before, don't practice plodding.

Beyond that, you simply cannot get much better at running without doing regular speedwork. Steady runs ad infinitum are not going to bring significant improvement, even if you get your mileage up.

When you first get up off the couch and start running, of course you'll see improvement with steady runs. You'll almost certainly lose some weight, which will allow you to go faster. Your stamina will quickly improve as your cardiovascular system gets more efficient, which will allow you to go further at the same pace.

But then the improvement will gradually stop. The law of diminishing returns will set in. Once you've attained a basic level of fitness, I think the effect of steady running on your anaerobic threshold level—the level of effort you can maintain without going into oxygen debt—is minimal. And that level limits your cruising speed, almost like a speed governor on a truck. If you don't do speedwork, the effort you can sustain over the course of a race isn't likely to change much.

Speedwork elevates your pulse, so your heart starts to get bigger and stronger. Speedwork gets you out of breath, so your lung capacity grows. It makes your legs stronger over a greater range of movement, so your power-to-weight ratio improves. It enhances your ability to cope with lactic acid in your system while continuing to run hard. It improves your ability to recover more quickly. And you can piece together successive speed sessions in such a way as to train yourself to go further at the same speed or cover the same distance faster.

How many of those benefits do medium-paced runs provide? None of them, really, certainly not to any great extent. And a balanced training program doesn't leave huge amounts of time for steady runs.

Let's say you're running seven times a week and already have a good base level of fitness. My advice would be to do one hill session, one interval session either on the track or the grass, and one fartlek. This leaves you one day for your long run, one day for an easy recovery run—and just two for steady runs.

Piling one steady run on top of another so you can increase your weekly mileage may be useful at certain times of year—say in the three months before Christmas, if you're aiming for a major race in the spring or summer. Chasing the miles can become addictive, but it shouldn't be done at the expense of including some speed sessions.

'I've always felt that long, slow distance produces long, slow runners,' Sebastian Coe said, as quoted in the 2003 book, *Running for Fitness*.

I'm sure some of you have already discovered that for yourselves, which may be why you're reading this book.

During my career, I rarely ran more than 100 miles in a week, and I never got above 120. But considering the effort I put in, sometimes I'd be as tired as if I'd done 160. And I certainly *could* have run 160 miles in a week, if I'd done them slower (and not had a full-time job!). But I don't believe it would have been so effective, and I wouldn't have had as much fun.

Speedwork, broadly defined, is any running that's faster than your race pace. If your 10K time is 45 minutes and you'd like to improve it, you need to do a significant amount of your training faster than 4:30 per kilometre. Of course your speed will vary depending on the sessions you design. But that means that, for you, a session of 10 times 1K in four minutes with two minutes recovery between each would qualify as speedwork—and that's *not* sprinting.

But while that is a useful session, I think that's still too similar to a pace you know you can hold for 10K without stopping at all. It's much better to do just six repeats, but at 3:30-per-kilometre pace. That's still not sprinting, but it is significantly faster than race pace.

And don't stop there in your quest for speed! Why not also go to the other end of the spectrum and design some sessions that, while they're not flat-out sprints, are nevertheless quite fast—200-metre repetitions for example?

Well, as soon as you start talking about 200-metre reps, a lot of people say, 'Crikey, that sounds too fast for me! Look, I'm an endurance runner, I do one-kilometre reps.'

Well, maybe. At certain times of year, one-kilometre reps over an undulating cross country circuit are excellent. But on the track, I'd be less enthusiastic. A kilometre is a long way: The danger is that you'll be unable to run the reps significantly faster than race pace and that you'll end up plodding and discouraged as your time for each rep gets slower and slower.

And that's the real mental block many people have: They think they won't be able to go fast enough. But the truth is they *can*. And they'll find it exhilarating, if only they give themselves a chance to discover it.

How? Skip the one-kilometre reps. Instead, do sets of five 200s with short recoveries—and there are your one-kilometre reps, but in a format that allows you to run considerably faster than race pace.

Let's say your plan had been to do four times one kilometre. Doing 20 times 200 gives you the same distance, and you definitely won't be sprinting. The key is to allow yourself only short recoveries between the 200s: half a minute preferably. Then take a longer rest between each set of five—in other words, between each kilometre. Three minutes should be ample. You'll run faster than if you were doing one-kilometre reps, and you'll have more rests, even if most of them are short.

This kind of workout offers lots of benefits. You get used to the feeling of running fast. You flow better. Your technique is better. You're not plodding. Your balance is better, and your timing's better, too. After a while you will be able to do the session you originally desired—four times one kilometre—but, crucially, *at a good speed!*

And I think your risk of injury will be reduced too. If you always run slowly, at the same cadence with the same stride length and the same landing, then you may get overuse injuries. It will make you more resilient if you train at *different* speeds, on *different* surfaces, and on *various* gradients.

Because speedwork doesn't have to be done on the track. It can be done on hills, sand dunes, parkland, playing fields, and woodland trails. The only requirement is that you run faster than your race pace at times, while at other times you walk or jog and generally ensure that you get the recovery you need.

GETTING USED TO SPEED

As with any new activity, you must use common sense as you ease your way into speedwork. If you've never done any faster-paced training at all, and you lace on some spikes, head off to a track and try to hammer out a dozen fast 400-metre reps with very little rest in between, they're going haul you out of there on a gurney. That's not the goal at all.

As I mentioned in chapter 2, the best way to get used to running different speeds is to begin with some fartleks, literally speed play—steady runs with a few faster bits thrown in when you feel like it. Challenge yourself! Experiment! Choose a target—a tree, a lamppost, or a hilltop—and run faster than a sustainable race pace until you get there. Then jog until you feel ready to go faster again.

Vary the distances and the speeds at which you run your efforts. Vary the recoveries, too, sometimes taking longer than you think you need, and sometimes starting your next effort before you feel you've recovered. Start to discover what you're capable of—and if you're in a group, what effect the efforts have on your training partners. Maybe some of them are faster than you, but maybe, too, they take longer to recover than you do.

If you're doing this sort of session with a group, take it in turns to lead and to decide how much rest the group gets. Fartleks may be unstructured, but they're excellent training: They help you develop speed, pace judgement, and the confidence to run faster than you thought possible. And it's basically just play—a game with a slight edge!

To start with, do eight to ten efforts, each between 30 seconds and 3 minutes, in a five-mile run. It's best if you can do your fartleks off-road on forgiving ground that won't pound your legs too much before they develop the strength to cope with it.

Once you've done some fartlek running to get used to striding out and running faster, a good first step toward more structured speedwork is to do track-type repetitions on the grass. Keep your efforts short and your rests long—say 10 times 200-metres with two-minutes recovery in between.

The distances will be only estimates, of course, and that's fine. You're just trying to get used to the speed while still wearing your normal shoes. At first, doing these sessions on a softer surface like grass or trails covered with pine needles can be a good thing, because the surface of the track can take some getting used to. If you begin on grass, you don't have to adapt to both the speed and the surface at the same time.

As you do these 200-metre efforts, remember—you're not meant to be sprinting! In this workout you're not interested in *pure* speed, as in how fast you can run 200 metres flat out, just one time. You're interested in *repeatable* speed—in running close to your best while keeping the pace consistent from first repetition to last.

If you're aiming for 10 reps, the first two or three should feel fairly comfortable, even at just three or four seconds slower than your flat-out speed. But by the sixth or seventh rep, you'll start to understand that this is not a pure speed workout. You've limited your recovery times, so the session is going to start to bite. And what's going to limit you, even with reps as short as 200 metres, isn't primarily your *speed*. You're going to be limited instead by your *stamina, strength, and endurance*—in other words, your ability to recover and repeat the efforts at the same speed.

Even though it's called speedwork, this session really won't do much to improve your pure speed. Instead, it will increase your strength and endurance—exactly what you need to run faster times in the 10K.

MOVING FORWARD:
THE IDEA OF PROGRESSION

Now, having got used to running fast on the grass, you may want to run on a track, perhaps even—eventually—in spikes.

A good way to start doing speedwork on a track is to just simply jog the bends and stride the straights. Try eight laps of the track. Use your regular running shoes or the shoes you run road races in. Don't *sprint* the straights, as if you were trying to catch Usain Bolt. *Stride* them, with high knees, rangy steps, and a quick cadence. You're just trying to go fast-ish, to get used to the track surface and to being out of breath. Then jog the bends slowly to recover. You must get your breath back. The session is like a gentle, structured fartlek.

After you've got used to jogging the bends and striding the straights, try to extend it a bit. Instead of striding out for 100 metres at time, try striding for 200 metres at that same speed, then jogging 200 metres to recover. And do it for ten laps instead of eight. That will give you 10 times 200 metres with about two-minute recoveries.

It's a logical progression. Each 400-metre lap will be run in about the same time as before: You're just putting your two 100-metre striding bits together into one 200-metre effort. And then you're giving yourself twice as long a jog to recover, as well.

But in the process you're teaching yourself to maintain your faster pace for twice as long. You'll be developing the art of sustained speed, which is what distance racing is all about. And you will have added a couple more laps to the session, as well, for a little more work on endurance.

You can build up gradually from there. You might try your track sessions with spikes. When I was competing, it was second nature for us to wear spikes: They were nice and light, and they helped us get a grip and maintain a fast and powerful stride. Bear in mind that tracks get slippery in the rain, and your usual trainers may not be ideal. To limit the risk of sore calves and Achilles tendons, you can get spikes with light, cushioned soles.

Whether you decide to use spikes depends on you and your goals. For a middle-aged guy who's aiming for the half-marathon and has never worn spikes in his life, it will almost certainly be asking for trouble: calf injuries in particular. He'd be much better off running in the same shoes as he's going to race in on the road. If the track is wet, just be careful—or do the session on the road or a cinder path instead.

Over time, you want the kind of progression I described when I talked about extending the 100-metre efforts to 200 metres. You don't want to hammer out the exact same session again and again. I know people who've read somewhere that to run a marathon in a certain time they have to run ten 800-metre efforts, each in that many minutes. They want to run the marathon in three and a half hours, so they go to the track and pound out ten 800s in 3:30—week after week after week. That's not progress. It's stasis.

6 **The idea behind your speedwork should be to design successive sessions to build on the previous ones.** 9

You can hold the same speed a bit longer, even if you take longer rests, so you're working on your speed endurance. Or you can keep the efforts the same speed and distance but, perhaps three or four weeks later, shrink the rest periods slightly, teaching your body to recover more quickly—and mimicking the experience of a race, when you have to recover from a hill or a surge without stopping at all.

To design your sessions to build on each other this way, you need to time your efforts and your recoveries. Timing your efforts gives you instant feedback, not only on how well you are running and how well you are recovering between efforts but also on your pace judgment. All of which is invaluable, not just at the time of the session, but also months and years later.

When you get home, record your times in your training diary. Don't just think you'll remember them. Recording these details will, in time, give you proof of your progress, which in turn will give you a great sense of achievement. It's nice to know you're running faster sessions, without having to run a whole race to prove it. And it's also nice to know that all your hard work is producing results. You need to have confidence in your training, knowing that it is working and paying measurable dividends. There's no substitute for confidence, both in your training and in a race.

Perhaps the traditional way of doing speed work sessions is to run all your repetitions in the same time—your tenth 400 in the same time as your first. And that's the way I did many of mine. But although this is a very motivational and effective way of training, I think it needs varying from time to time. Dave Bedford and I were very good at time-trial-type running. We could sustain a very fast pace for quite a long time. In Dave's case, that got him a world record in the 10,000; in my case, pretty close but no cigar.

But neither of us could change pace well, and for that reason neither of us was all that great at winning the big international races on the track. When he and I were training with Bob Parker, our coach, we realized that was a problem, and Bob tried to work on it with us. We often used to run 600s where we had to run the first 400 in 65 seconds, for example, and the last 200 in 30 seconds or less. So we had to change speed at the end of the rep.

These sessions helped us, but they didn't address our basic lack of pure speed, so we were never able to develop a devastating, race-winning change of pace. I found it quite hard to run much under 30 seconds for the last 200 metres of a race. I did run some final laps in 58 or 59 seconds—pretty good, considering that my fastest 400 metres ever was only 54 seconds. But it was terrible when I was up against people who were running the last lap of a 10k in 53 seconds! Clearly, if these runners managed to hang onto me until the last lap began, I was liable to have some trouble. It was the same for Dave—and unfortunately, we never quite cracked that problem.

On the one hand some people would tell me, 'Well, you're that sort of runner. You've got slow-twitch fibres—in fact, I'm amazed you're able to run as fast as you do!'

But on the other hand, looking back, maybe we should have trained differently. Maybe we did too much mileage. Maybe we didn't do enough weights. And—just maybe—we did too many of those sessions with all the reps paced exactly evenly.

For his part, Dave didn't seem all that interested in developing a serious change of pace. He would argue that, if he could improve one second per lap by doing even more miles and getting even stronger, he would cut his 10,000-metre time by 25 seconds. But if he worked really hard on his kick, he might improve his last lap by just two seconds. His feeling was that he'd rather have the 25. But that ignores how easy you make it for the other runners. If your tactics are predictable, and your opponents can just find a way to hang onto you, their race in essence becomes one lap shorter: If they're with you with one lap to go, they've won. And beyond that, front-running is harder on the leader, so he or she is quite likely to under-perform while helping his or her rivals to over-perform. Paula Radcliffe is another classic example of a front-runner with this sort of problem.

For those people too young to remember Dave's competitive days, think of the two moustachioed runners in the 118 118 television adverts. Those guys looked like him—too much like him, in fact, to be legal. Dave filed a complaint saying his image was being used without his permission, and Ofcom, the British communications regulator, upheld it. 'The adverts', Ofcom said, 'caricature David Bedford by way of a comically exaggerated representation of him looking like he did in the 1970s, sporting a hairstyle and facial hair like his at the time, and wearing running kit almost identical to the running kit that was distinctively worn by him at the time, including red socks, sky-blue shorts with gold braiding, and a vest with two hoops.'

Dave certainly was distinctive. There weren't many other world-class runners competing in red socks. And he was a great runner, one of the best in the world, no doubt about it. Remarkable, considering the enormous number of miles he ran, not to mention the number of pints he quaffed.

But he could easily have won a lot more races—and some Olympic medals, to boot—if he had figured out how to inject a decisive change of pace in the middle of a race. As with the Australian Ron Clarke, who set 17 world records but won zero Olympic golds, all Dave's best races involved him out in front, running against the clock with no need for tactics. The problem for him wasn't leading; it was getting clear in the first place. That was fairly easy for him against domestic opposition in the 1970s, but much more difficult in the major international championships.

In the 1970s, the master of the mid-race surge was the British runner Brendan Foster, who often injected a brutal two-minute 800-metre burst in the middle of a 5,000. He won a lot of races that way.

I, too, tried this tactic many times, usually decimating the field—but not quite managing to shake off every single runner. I regularly ended up second, third, or fourth. Again, not quite good enough!

If I had it to do over again, instead of running twelve times 400 all within a second of each other the way Dave and I used to do, I'd experiment with running the repetitions in different times. That's what I've done with runners I've coached since I retired, with good effect.

Don't be a slave to always running each of your reps in the exact same time. Run some faster than others in a pattern. Alternate reps that are fairly fast with ones that are quite fast, or design pyramids where the reps get faster and faster.

Brendan Foster—the master of the mid-race surge—about to make his move against Bernie Ford, Dave Black, and Ian Stewart.

This will develop your ability to run at different speeds even when you're tired. You'll develop more gears to use at the end of a race. It's another way of adding more strings to your bow.

If you're a top-class runner, instead of doing all 12 of your 400s in 60 seconds, you might try just 10, alternately doing 62, 56, 62, and 56.

Or you could try doing this 12 times 400 metres session as a pyramid: Run three 400s in 60 seconds each, with 200-metres jog recoveries; the next two in 58, with 400-metre jog recoveries and the next one in 56. Take an extra 400-metre jog recovery between each set and a full 800-metre jog recovery before repeating these same six 400s—but in reverse, one in 56 seconds with an 800-metre jog, two in 58 with 400-metre recoveries, and the last three in 60 seconds with 200-metre recoveries.

Obviously, you need to adjust the times to suit your ability, but the pattern and structure of the session can be followed by anybody. If your starting point is 90 seconds for 400 metres, so be it. The principle is the same. Experiment; mix it up; don't work on developing one speed only. Teach yourself to kick it up a notch even when you're tired. That will help you in races no matter what level of runner you are. But also allow yourself sometimes to go slower than your maximum speed so you can experience the feeling of fast, strong running that you could maintain for longer. In other words, do sessions where you're building yourself up rather than tearing yourself apart.

Beyond mixing up your speeds within each session, you should also structure successive speed sessions so there's progression. Remember, though, the training effect takes time to come through, so you should only try to toughen up a particular session every three or four weeks—and definitely ease back down just before an important race.

' There are four ways to achieve progression in a particular workout. Take as an example the initial session we discussed earlier—10 times 200 metres with two-minute recoveries between reps. Once your feel comfortable with that workout, you can try the one of the following:

- Increase the number of repetitions, moving to 14, 16, and eventually even 20.
- Cut the recovery time. Instead of taking two-minute recoveries between reps, try taking only 90 seconds, and then only one minute. Eventually, when you're comfortable with that, you may even be able to cut it down to 30 seconds.
- Increase the distance. Stretch the reps to 300 metres, and then even 400—each time maintaining the same speed at which you were doing the 200s.
- Increase the speed of the reps, while keeping all the other factors the same. **'**

A word of advice: Introduce only *one* of these adjustments at a time. The aim of these workouts, like all others, is to build yourself up, not tear yourself down. Be smart.

Compare how you feel doing these sessions with how you feel on a steady run with your club-mates. Do you get as severely out of breath on your long run? Does your heart rate climb up so close to its maximum? Do your legs get so heavy? Of course not. And that means that these sorts of progressive speed-work sessions have the desired training effect, building *strength* and *stamina* as you push against all these limiting factors that your steady runs never come close to extending.

GOING FASTER FOR LONGER

I talked earlier about *repeatable* speed, doing quite a number of 200s at not far from your top speed. But as a distance runner, you should also be also concerned with *sustainable* speed—how well, for example, you can maintain your repeatable speed over longer distances, like 400 metres, 600 metres, or even 800 metres. You can think of it as finally shrinking the rests between your short-recovery 200-metre sessions all the way to zero.

Obviously, in a session like this with longer efforts, your recoveries need to be much longer, too. As a rule, you should wait until your heart rate has fallen below 120 beats per minute before setting off again. After a really hard, sustained effort, or a series of shorter efforts with only short rests between—for example, four times 200 metres with 20-second rests—it should take at least three minutes before you feel ready to repeat the effort, possibly even longer.

But that can expose a problem: Many runners have trouble running hard enough to *need* that much rest. They can run at what they think is their flat-out speed for 600 metres, get to the end, and be ready to go again just a minute later. They feel fully recovered. Their heart rate has already come back down below 120.

In this session, they're not being hampered by an inability to recover quickly, nor are they unable to repeat the same effort several times. Here, the limiting factor is not just speed, it's *strength*. The work rate, and therefore the pace these runners can sustain for as long as 600 metres, is not much faster than the speed they can sustain for a whole 10K race.

These runners should construct sessions with the long efforts split into shorter segments, with very short mini-recoveries. I'll set out examples of such sessions in just a moment. Doing them enables these people to run much faster, thereby improving the limiting factors of speed and strength endurance.

And during the winter months, they should incorporate more strength training into their schedules—more hill sessions, more work with weights, and more cross country running.

For those new to interval training, pace judgment becomes an issue as soon as you start introducing repetitions longer than 400 metres. The danger is that each repetition will become slower, until it is barely above race pace. This won't achieve the desired training effects and—worse still—it can make the runner feel disheartened. We don't want this—we want these sessions to produce a feel-good factor instead! That's vitally important to your training!

One way to address this problem is to adapt the session so you can maintain your original speed and form.

Let's say your intended session is six times 600 metres with three-minute recovery times. You run the first one at a speed you think you can repeat five more times. But even after three minutes rest, and even though your heart rate is back below 120, you may well find it hard to match your original speed on your second repetition.

Don't give up! And, unless you've run the first repetition ridiculously fast, don't be satisfied with completing the session at ever slower speeds. Instead, adapt the session this way:

- Run 600 metres hard, and record your time. This is now your target time for the rest of the session.
- Take three minutes rest.

- Run 400 metres at the same speed, take a 30-second rest, then run 200 metres more. The time for your 400- and 200-metre efforts combined should add up to your 600-metre target time.
- Take three minutes rest.
- Run 200 metres, rest 20 seconds, run 200 metres, rest 20 seconds, then run a final 200. Again, the times for your three 200-metre efforts should add up to your 600-metre target time.
- Take three minutes rest.
- Repeat all those steps a second time.

There are a lot of rests in that session. And I think some people shy away from speedwork because they don't want to be seen to stop, and that probably goes double for stopping to catch their breath in the middle of their supposed 600-metre effort.

But in speedwork, you're *allowed* to take rests. And you've designed this session with a particular purpose in mind. What you're doing, in essence, is refusing to compromise by slowing down. You're training your body to run the six times 600 metres at the desired pace. If at first you have to throw some mini-rests into the middle of your 600-metre efforts, no problem. That's a heck of a lot better than just getting slower and slower as the session wears on. Slowing down is not what you want to practice. Not even when you're getting tired.

As your body adapts and you start to get stronger, you can progress toward eliminating the mini-rests by taking the session I've described earlier and mixing it up a bit.

For example, you can try running the full, non-stop 600 metres every other time instead of every third time: First 600 metres—then 400 plus 200—then 600 again—then 300 plus 300—then 600 again, and finally 200 plus 200 plus 200, with the same three minutes rest in between.

As you get stronger still, you might run two of the full 600-metre efforts in a row, then one of the broken-up 600 metres, then two of the full 600s again, then another broken-up effort, and you'll have done your six.

There are numerous permutations: Adapt the session to suit yourself. But be strict regarding the mini-recovery periods—they're not intended to give you a full recovery, just to give you the minimum recovery necessary to maintain your original speed and form.

Sooner or later, you will be able to eliminate all of the mini-rests. How much is 20 seconds rest worth, anyway? In some ways, you'll find it's easier *not* to stop for 20 seconds and then have to get started again. You'll find it simpler to just keep running! Then you'll be doing the desired session—six times the full 600 metres at your target pace.

Training this way will significantly increase your sustainable speed. Without speedwork, you'd be missing out.

DESIGNING SESSIONS
THAT ARE FAST ENOUGH

How much of your training should be speedwork? And how fast should your speedwork be?

I said earlier that speedwork could be defined as any training that's faster than your race pace. So if your event is the 10K, anything faster than your 10K race pace would qualify. I certainly maintain that a good portion of your training *should* be faster than your race pace.

But perhaps you've read in a running magazine that most, if not all, of your training should be *slower* than race pace. Well, I agree with that, too! Ideally, at least 80 percent of your running should be done at a comfortable cruising pace—but not just jogging, though.

But clearly, if you're doing 10 sessions a week, a far lower proportion of your running will be above race pace than if you just run three times a week. If you're training less often, the proportion of speedwork will be higher: It just wouldn't work if you decided to do one speed session every three weeks to ensure your slower running sessions amounted to 80 percent of your total training.

Also, running *at* race pace does not qualify as speedwork. I know several running clubs that do a track session of 10 times 1K at 10K race pace. I'm sorry, but what is the point of this? It's just no good! This type of session won't extend any limiting factors at all. They already know they can run 10K at that pace without stopping. They're just taking rests when they don't need to. It's a nothing sort of session, hard enough to tire you out but not hard enough or specific enough to be of any real benefit. They might describe this as a threshold pace session, but there are too many rests.

Real threshold pace runs are somewhat different, and can bring your fitness level up considerably. They are fast, sustained runs, at or just above race pace (but just below your anaerobic threshold level), over distances shorter than the race distance. For example, if you're aiming to race 5,000 metres, a 3,000-metre time trial could be considered a threshold run. If you are running 5- or 6-mile cross country races, a fast 3- or 4-mile sustained effort on the roads would also be a threshold run.

Now I'm going to toughen up the definition of effective speedwork a bit. For one thing, the optimum pace depends on the length of the repetitions. Doing 200-metre reps just a hair faster than your 10K pace won't really do anything for you, either.

To be effective, even your *slowest* speedwork should be done faster than your best pace for the distance *below* the one you are aiming for. If you're training for 10K, run your long, sustained-speed repetitions at a faster pace than you can sustain for 5K. Much of your speedwork will be at pace that's faster still, of course, depending on the structure of the session, the length of the efforts, and the rest periods.

As you design your program from week to week, bear in mind that you should be using speedwork in a two-pronged attack to achieve speed endurance. Some sessions need to consist of a high number of short repetitions with short rests, to build repeatable speed. Others should be made up of longer repetitions, but fewer of them, with ample recovery periods, aimed at building sustainable speed. And between those extremes, there are any number of permutations and variations.

KEEPING YOURSELF IN CHECK

From time to time, you might want to do speed sessions in which you're not striving for every second. Sometimes it's extremely beneficial, physically and mentally, to do speed sessions at a slightly slower pace you're capable of. You can use below-max sessions to build confidence and anticipation as a big race approaches. Many runners consider tapering before a race to be simply running less fast, less often, and less far than usual. But speedwork can play a useful role in the tapering process and should not be ignored. Also, you can use below-max sessions to help yourself recover in the week or two following a hard race.

I remember a session I did just a few days after my National Cross Country victory. It was intended as a recovery session, just to stretch the legs out and get them moving again.

'I want you to get out on the track and just do some 400s to blow the cobwebs out after the race, but I don't want you going too fast', my coach, Harry Wilson, told me. 'I know you feel good and you've recovered, but I just want you to stride out for the first 300, then do the last 100 fast.'

That was a fabulous session. I followed Harry's instructions and I still couldn't go any slower than 60 or 61 seconds for each 400—even though it was a cold winter evening. I was flying, and it felt great. Mentally, it's a wonderful feeling to be going so fast, yet still feeling you're holding plenty back. Never underestimate the psychological benefits—the feel-good factor—of *not* going as fast as you can, of knowing you could step on the accelerator and go faster any time you felt like it. But it's still important to time the session; otherwise you'll never know how well you're doing. Remember, you can't always trust how you feel as an indicator of your speed.

Looking back, I think it's a mistake to *always* try to do personal bests in your interval training. It's nice to run fast, but it's good to experiment, too. Experiment with the speed, experiment with the rest, and experiment with changing pace without any rest. Sometimes you want to feel, 'Wow! I had a good workout today! Hardly breathing! I was just ticking over—I've got plenty in reserve!'

That kind of session stretches your legs out and freshens you up mentally.

RECOVERY—IT'S A VITAL PART OF YOUR TRAINING

It is important to remember that your training in general, and speed sessions in particular, will only work if you allow your body to recover. Of course, that means having suitable food and drink and the proper amount of sleep. But it also means ensuring you have easy days between hard sessions.

To judge what is actually easy on these recovery days is quite an art. Sometimes you do a hard session and you feel fantastic and fully recovered the next day. Other times it can take several days to recover. And it doesn't just depend on how hard you've been training. Other factors come into play, too—travelling, the late nights, the parties, the kids, the stress at work, and a host of other things.

Similarly, you can never predict how long it will take for the training effect of a session to come through. You can never say *today's* session will make you stronger *tomorrow*. There's no recipe that says it takes exactly 20 minutes to cook. It just doesn't work that way. There's always a time delay, of course, but you never really know how long that delay will be.

In any event, you're only going to be a better athlete when you've recovered. No training takes effect in a day, but neither can you say it will take two weeks to feel the benefit of a particular session. It might be much less. Some sessions and races bring you on significantly and rapidly. Others only have an infinitesimal effect, and it's the whole block of training that produces the desired training effect. It's like recovering from jet lag: Sometimes you feel fully recovered quite quickly; other times it seems to take ages to recover, and you just feel tired all the time.

This is when you really need to listen to your body and judge what you need to do. It's not as simple as following a pre-determined program—it's a skill and an art. You need to be smart in order to give yourself every chance. It's a terrible thing to run PBs in your session on Wednesday, then feel listless in that weekend's race because you still haven't recovered.

Or worse still, you could hurt yourself. Leading up to the 1997 World Championships in Athens, the British runner Kelly Holmes was in the best shape of her life. After setting new British and Commonwealth records for 1,500 metres, she had gone on to wins in the European Cup in Munich and the Bislett Games in Oslo. She then lifted the 800-metre title at the British Championships, and victory in Athens was starting to look a distinct possibility.

Then, shortly before the World Championships—the race that meant more to her than any other that year—she finished off a fast session by sprinting 200 metres in 23.7 seconds, an excellent time. But she picked up a slight injury to her heel. Soon afterwards, she did another very tough session, 800-metre repeats with a pacemaker, each effort run in 2:03—until her heel injury flared up.

Then at the championships in Athens, in the heats of the 1,500, her leg blew up. She'd ruptured her Achilles and torn her calf. Her meet was over on the very first morning of the championships.

What did she stand to gain by doing that sort of session so close to the big race? Maybe it would have given her a psychological boost—but physically, almost nothing. She was already five seconds faster than anyone else in the world. So why risk it?

She was flown to Zurich to see a specialist, wound up with her leg in plaster, and watched the final on TV.

Fortunately, at the Athens Olympics in 2004, she got it right and won gold in both the 800 and 1,500.

So listen to your body. Work hard but don't be foolhardy. Plan your sessions so that you progress rather than set yourself back. As I've said before, the primary aim of every training session should be to leave you fit to train again tomorrow.

AS THE SEASONS CHANGE

I would encourage you to rid yourself of the idea that speedwork is just for sharpening, something to be done only in the few weeks leading up to a major race. But of course, after the racing season you will want to ease down and reduce the intensity of your sessions.

Brendan Foster, who won Olympic bronze in the 10,000 in Montreal in 1976, used to allow himself a long fallow period when he would run very little and actually put on some weight—either on purpose or because he enjoyed a beer or two. His club-mates relished running with him when he started training again, because they could regularly beat the great man on training runs. Big Bren, as he came to be known, didn't mind: He knew what he was doing—he was allowing his body to recover—and he had an outstanding record of getting himself into shape for the day that mattered.

While Brendan had a knack of using this fallow period to his advantage, a mistake a lot of athletes make is to lose—almost throw away—most of what they've gained over the summer. After a rest period, they go back to their steady training in the winter, do some speedwork in the spring, and run some races in the summer. Then they have a rest, after which they start back in with the steady stuff again. OK, they tell themselves, I'll ease back and just get the miles in.

But you don't want to advance during the course of a year only to start again all the way back at square one. You want to progress year on year. My advice is to still do fartleks, still do hill sessions, and still do some sort of reps even when you're just ticking over. Just change the emphasis from speed to strength and stamina, and mentally reduce the urgency and intensity of your training. Aim for mental recovery rather than physical rest, and just let the fitness come to you. But do try to ensure that this November you are going better than you were last November.

True, the balance of your training will change with the seasons. In the winter you'll want to concentrate more on longer and hillier repetitions, running them somewhat slower, with shorter recoveries. This will build strength and endurance. Then, before the racing season, and during it, you'll want to focus on flatter, faster reps with longer recoveries.

But you should incorporate speed sessions into your training at least 10 months of the year.

‘ Even if you're only able to run three times a week, don't opt for mileage at the expense of speedwork. One steady run of seven to ten miles would be ample. Another session should be a fartlek of five to seven miles. And the third workout would be a more structured speed session.   ’

Not the same speed session every week, of course. Over six weeks, you could include each of the following speed sessions:

- Week one: Short recovery session (e.g., 4 sets of 4 × 200 metres with 1 min rests. Take 3 minutes rest between sets.)
- Week two: Short hill session (e.g., 12 × 45 sec fast uphill with [short] jog back recoveries)
- Week three: Track session (e.g., 6 × 600 metre broken sets, as described earlier [600, 400/200, 200/200/200]. And repeat.)
- Week four: Three-mile time trial (threshold run at fast cruising speed)
- Week five: Long hill session (e.g., 6 × 90 sec fast uphill, with [long] jog back recoveries)
- Week six: Pyramid session:
    - *1 minute fast* followed by 1 minute jog recovery
    - *2 minutes fast* followed by 90 seconds jog recovery
    - *3 minutes fast* followed by 2 minutes jog recovery
    - *4 minutes fast* followed by 3 minutes jog recovery
    - And back down again.
- Or try this pyramid, with three-minute rests between sets:
    - 4 × 200 metres with 1 minute rest
    - 3 × 400 metres with 2 minutes rest
    - 2 × 600 metres with 3 minutes rest
    - 1 × 800 metres
    - And back down again

After which I'm sure you'll be happy to return to a short recovery session the following week and repeat the six-week cycle, progressing along the lines described on page 124.

DISCOVERING WHAT'S INSIDE

I know a lot of people say they run only for the social aspects, and they're not even interested in trying to win a race. But I'm sure that, secretly, many of them would still like to run faster. And I'm sure a lot of people who say they're not interested in racing actually do race a little bit—perhaps as much in training as in real races.

And most runners know the feeling that comes from reaching a critical point in a race—maybe up a hill—when you're getting tired, the race is getting tough, and the elastic breaks. You know: 'I'm just behind. I'm just behind', and then, 'Aw, they got away.' And it's a feeling they'd rather avoid.

The point is to understand what happens at this critical point that makes the elastic break, and how to stop that from happening. Or conversely, they'd like to learn, when they're in front, how they can break the elastic and get away from their pursuer. It might well require a positive move rather than just hoping the other guy will fade. It's hard, but it feels really good if you can pull it off.

Well, you can acquire those skills. Doing so requires mimicking the race experience in training, particularly the difficult parts. Let's say you're the guy who just got dropped, and it was on a hill. You want to re-create the feeling of that hill, and practice running it well instead of poorly.

But don't just do one hard run. It's not beneficial going out for a 10-mile run and saying after eight miles, 'OK, this is the point where I had difficulty. I'm going to practice changing pace halfway up the hill.' Because in a run like that, if you just charge up one hill at the eight-mile mark, you only get one bite at the cherry. You want to re-create that feeling more than once. How? Warm up and run a three- or four-mile fartlek, so you're fairly tired. Then do perhaps half a dozen repetitions up a hill—with, of course, sufficient recoveries in between. Sometimes experiment so you run each repeat slightly differently. Get to know how to pace yourself up the hill, what cadence is most effective, and maybe practice changing pace half way up or as you run over the top. Then run home at a comfortable pace, throwing in just two or three easy strides to cool down.

Then the next time you reach that point in a race, you can say to yourself, 'OK, I've been here before. I've practiced this—and not just once, but many times. I know the feelings to expect, and I know I can cope with them: I will recover.' And, as you develop this fitness and mental strength, you learn to hang on in there.

Or, better still, you're going to have the confidence to say, 'This guy thinks he can beat me but this time I'm going to pre-empt him.' *Vroom!* Make your move first—put *him* under pressure! See how he likes it, and whether he responds—or crumples! There's nothing like it. It's games, it's poker, it's friendly rivalry, and best of all, it's a lot of fun.

Look, I'm a competitive guy. I find it hard to understand people who don't respond that way, and say instead, 'OK, I'll just go at my own pace. I'll see you at the top of the hill. Just wait for me there.' I think that by taking the easy option, these runners deny themselves the chance to discover what they're really capable of. Sometimes you have to discover what you're capable of in training before you can attempt to do it in a race.

They're saying, in essence, 'I don't want to play.' But that leaves them with only part of the sport. They're playing poker for matchsticks rather than real money. 'It doesn't matter if I lose', they say. 'You can win as many matchsticks as you like!'

Of course it doesn't matter if you lose. But perhaps it does matter if you don't even try! Raise the stakes and—figuratively—play for real money.

In the end, of course, it's not about the money or the matchsticks. And it's not just about getting fitter and faster and feeling fantastic. It's about you being improved and giving your best. Even more than that, it's a means of building character, of reaching deep. It's about the journey, discovering the depths of courage and bravery you have in your soul, and enjoying the fulfilment of a well run race.

Enjoying the sport more fully doesn't start with just showing up on the start line and telling yourself, 'Alright, now race.' You have to prepare yourself first. Don't just throw yourself in at the deep end.

It starts with taking part in these rep sessions and experiencing what they feel like while, learning to cope with the discomfort and enjoying the results, which make your efforts so worthwhile. It's like anything in life—the more you put in to something, the more you take out.

But first, you have to be prepared to make that investment.

You'll also find that the more of your heart and soul you invest and the greater the commitment you make, the more emotional the experience will be. It's not at all unusual—just look at the medal winners on the podium or at Roger Federer, who has a tendency to cry, not only when he loses major championships but when he wins, as well. Or look at the British cyclist Mark Cavendish. When he won the fifth stage of the Tour de France—his first victory in the 2010 race—he broke down in tears of joy. Clearly, these guys aren't playing for matchsticks. But it's not about the money either. It's about the physical courage and commitment that they have invested in their effort.

If you don't do speedwork, you're missing out on so much—greater fitness, the thrill of learning to run fast, and the satisfaction of discovering your real potential.

Yes, some people might assume it's unpleasant. But they don't know, because they've never really given it a go. Take it from me—it feels *great*. It leaves you pumped up and exhilarated. Afterwards you walk around feeling excited—not just about what you have achieved with your running but also about what you can accomplish in general if you just give it a real good shot.

And, for most people, it's a whole lot more than they expect.

KEY POINTS TO REMEMBER

- When you first start speedwork, begin on a forgiving surface, like grass, and just get used to running fast, perhaps 200 metres at a time, with plenty of rest. After that, you can move to the track if you want.

- Don't hammer out the same session week after week. Structure your speedwork so there's variety and progression—the recoveries between repetitions get a little shorter, your speed gets a little faster, or the reps get a bit longer. (But only make one of these adjustments at a time.)

- Do speedwork virtually year-round, not just for springtime sharpening.

- Don't go back to months of steady running only and wind up back at square one. Include some form of speedwork in your weekly schedule at least 10 months a year.

Ouch, That Hurts!

Ask most people what they think causes runners to get injured and they're likely to reply that it's too much running. It seems obvious: Runners suffer most often from overuse injuries—in other words, from running too much.

Although it's undeniably true that running often brings on, and certainly exacerbates, injuries, I think it's wrong to blame all running injuries, in a rather simplistic way, on just too much running. So many other factors are involved. As we've seen earlier in the book, running with good technique in a way that cushions the impact of each footstep can minimise the risk of injury. So too can being supple, warming up correctly, running relaxed, wearing the right shoes, and avoiding hard surfaces and cambers.

‘ Running should be a completely balanced activity. Everyday activities that stress you more on one side than the other leave you unbalanced—and it's imbalances that lie at the root of most injuries. ’

Furthermore, many so-called running injuries have their roots in non-running activities that have already strained or unbalanced the body—like carrying a heavy briefcase, sitting at a computer or digging the garden—rather than in running itself. Even the genuine running injuries that do crop up from time to time often come more from running too little than from running too much or too fast. More often, it's not speedwork that causes injuries: It's layoffs.

I would say I spent three-quarters of my training time trying to get fit, strong, and resilient enough to train properly, without aching and feeling stiff.

But when I reached the promised land and attained the fitness needed to train at that level, I very rarely got injured. And that wasn't because I was training lightly. I would often be doing 80 to 100 miles a week, with plenty of fast, hard sessions—and races, too. But, once fit, I would recover quickly, and I wouldn't get hurt unless I did something silly like falling over, wearing the wrong shoes, running on a camber, or failing to warm up and stretch properly.

That's the opposite of the accepted wisdom, which holds that overtraining causes overuse injuries. To the contrary, my injuries usually came not from doing too many miles or too much speedwork but instead from coming back from a period of enforced rest—particularly after I had to take a week or so off because of an illness. I was careful not to come back too fast. But the problem was that, during the illness, I would stiffen up from sitting or lying down too much, and I found I would lose suppleness, muscle tone, coordination, balance, timing, and so on as a result. Running even steadily after these setbacks often seemed to result in minor aches and pains, which could easily lead to injuries.

And that's true of many athletes. Maybe during the layoff they didn't continue with their normal stretching routine. Almost certainly, they've lost a bit of muscle tone. They're still in very good shape, though, and they come back and say to themselves, 'Wow, I'm flying! I'll try and make up for the training I've missed.' But somehow it goes wrong: They are still fit enough to hurt themselves.

Training, you see, is like being on a treadmill: If you have to get off for any reason, it's hard to get back on.

It's been said that it's easy to look after yourself when you're healthy and training well, but what makes a true champion is how you look after yourself when you're injured. I would go further, and say the real key to training consistently is how you look after yourself to prevent injuries happening in the first place.

Listen to what Mark Allen, six-time winner of the Hawaii Ironman says about it: 'The most successful athlete will be the one that trains most consistently without getting injured or ill.'

‘ **The key to running well is training consistently. So the main thing to bear in mind about injuries is that prevention is better than cure. If you're dedicated to preventing injuries, pay just as much attention to what you do when you're not running as when you are running.** ’

You're much better off if you train consistently than if you train really well for a while, get injured, and have to start again. You want to adapt to your training and get resilient enough to train harder. It's consistent training that leads to breakthroughs.

Fortunately, there are ways you can help yourself. If you're a regular runner, you've probably been injured at some point. And it may well be that you can pinpoint what you did to trigger the injury: Perhaps you didn't warm up properly, or you rushed back into full training too soon after a layoff. And you think to yourself with the benefit of hindsight and more than a tinge of regret that you could have avoided the injury.

INJURY PREVENTION

My opinion is that most injuries are preventable. Unless you trip and twist an ankle or a knee—and, granted, that does happen—most distance runners' injuries, as opposed to those of sprinters, do not happen suddenly. They come on over a period of time and give us plenty of warning. If you learn to recognize the early signs, and how to figure out what's causing the problem, you'll get hurt a lot less often.

Like all of running, injury prevention is a skill, even an art. When you're feeling good, it's easy to blithely go along without ever giving a thought to prevention. But mastering injury prevention is part of becoming a successful runner. A smart runner pays attention to his or her body, recognises the first sign of trouble, and takes action to prevent it from developing into a full-blown injury.

Also, looking after yourself when you're not injured is the key. Run correctly—tall, relaxed, and balanced. And run on soft surfaces whenever possible.

I've alluded to running correctly throughout most of this book and dwelt extensively on it in chapter 3. Technique is not an optional extra: It's an integral part of running well, conserving energy, making the most of your fitness, and avoiding injury. Here are some steps you can take to reduce your chances of getting hurt.

Try not to run on your heels, as this can jar your knees, hips, and back. Remember, your heel is *not* a shock absorber. Instead, use your entire foot as a shock absorber, just as you would if you were running on the spot.

All your movements should be backwards and forwards, not side to side. Balance is especially important, because it is imbalance—whether in running or in everyday life—that leads to most injuries. Even limping because you have a small blister means your movements are unbalanced, and that can lead to more serious injuries.

❛ Get friends to watch you closely to see whether you're evenly balanced when you run. ❜

It's easy to run lopsided without knowing it. I often see runners holding their heads to one side or running with one shoulder or arm higher than the other. Although they feel perfectly balanced, they are not, and they need another pair of eyes to identify these imbalances, and show them how to make the necessary corrections. If they are used to running round left-hand bends on a track, they often find themselves leaning slightly to the left even when running straight. But this kind of imbalance can just as easily be due to constantly sitting at an angle in front of a computer or carrying a bag over one shoulder. Very few people are equally strong, supple, and balanced on each side, and running can soon exacerbate these imbalances to such an extent that injuries occur.

I had hip problems early on in my career, probably as a result of cycling to school with a heavy bag across my left shoulder (it never felt comfortable on the right), and maybe from running around left-hand bends on the track. And my coach, Bob Parker, noticed that I carried my left arm low. He'd tell me to lift it or drop my right arm. But by that stage I'd lost my sense of balance, my arms still wouldn't be level, and my shoulders wouldn't be level either.

So I used to get friends help me. 'I know I'm running all over the place', I'd say, 'but I can't tell whether I'm leaning to one side or one shoulder's higher than the other or my arms are level. Can you go behind me when I'm running and tell me what I need to do to balance up?'

And they'd say, 'Up a bit, down a bit.' And it wouldn't feel right to me but they'd say, 'No, that's it!' And I would feel that I was running better, but I still wouldn't *feel* balanced. It took time and concentration to get my sense of balance back.

Beyond good technique, another way to minimize impact is to avoid running on roads—especially on a camber—whenever you can. Run on forest trails, dirt tracks, and playing fields. This can be harder work than running on hard surfaces, so in addition to avoiding injuries you'll get fitter and stronger, too.

RUNNING SHOES

Choosing the right running shoes can be difficult. There are so many to choose from, and you should be aware that most of them *won't* be right for you.

As your foot lands it should act as a shock absorber, and as it leaves the ground it should act as a spring. It takes timing and coordination to do this, and considerable strength if you're going to do it two or three times a second for an hour or more. Some shoes actually prevent your feet from working properly, and this can lead to many injuries, particularly to your Achilles tendons and calves, but also to your knees, hips, and back.

‘ **Run in shoes that are right for you. They should allow your feet to work properly, while still giving you sufficient stability, cushioning, and grip.** ’

You want shoes that allow, and even encourage, your feet to work properly. They should provide some cushioning, but beware of too much of a good thing. As you get tired, you'll find it harder to keep the spring in your step, so you'll rely more and more on your shoes to cushion the impact of landing. And that's important. But if your feet are too cushioned, you'll lose the feel of the ground. And the thicker the heel, the higher your feet are off the ground and the more unstable they become. You'll be more susceptible to turning your ankles.

Some shoes have heel cushioning so thick that, unless you're going uphill, it's nearly impossible to avoid landing heel first. This might feel comfy, but it actually prevents your feet from working as they are designed to do, making them weaker in the process. Running on your heels prevents you from using your foot as a spring or a lever. That limits your stride length and makes your quads do more than their share of the work while your calves are taking it easy, and your hips and pelvis take the impact of every footfall.

The same applies to stability—yes, you need some, but beware of too much. You don't want your shoes to be too rigid. They need to be flexible enough to allow you to get up on your toes when you're running fast or going uphill.

To work properly and get power off the balls of your feet, your feet *need* to pronate to a certain extent. But even if you tend to over-pronate—if your foot and ankle collapse inward as your weight goes over the foot—you'd be ill-advised to choose shoes so rigid that they force you to run on the outsides of your feet. Granted, this would control your over-pronation, but it would almost certainly transfer the problem to your knees, hips, or lower back. It's much better to concentrate on strengthening your feet (doing foot exercises and using a wobble board) and using shoes to gently support them, rather than rigidly holding them in place and forcing your weight onto the outsides of your feet.

So how to choose the proper shoes?

Well, it's difficult. It's not just a question of size and fit. There is a bewildering array of factors to be considered, including weight, stability, grip, and width—and that's just for starters.

Do you need shoes that are straight-lasted or curved? Do they offer a good, snug arch support? Do they have cushioning under the forefoot as well as the heel? Do they have mild motion-control devices or extreme ones?

First of all, *don't* buy shoes just because a running buddy has recommended them. Runners' bodies, weights, and mechanics are different; their feet are different; their running styles are different. What's good for them may well not be good for you. And *don't* buy a particular brand just because that company produced a different model—or even an earlier version of the same model—that worked for you before. Shoe companies produce different models to cater to different feet, which is a good thing, so take advantage of it. But they also are always trying to steal a march on their competitors and come out with something new. And often they upgrade popular models by introducing gimmicky variations so that the new shoe bears little resemblance to the original model.

If a new pair of shoes alters the motion of your feet, it's very possible that it will provoke injuries.

The best thing to do is to seek the advice of experienced staff (who are often runners themselves) at specialist running shops. Some shops may even ask you to bring your old shoes so they can look at how they've worn down to see how you land on your feet. Many now also have facilities for recording and analysing your foot motion on a treadmill, which can help them recommend a certain shoe. Their help is often invaluable—but remember it's you who has to wear the shoes, and you have to feel comfortable in them. Not just one shoe, but the pair. And that doesn't mean just walking around the shop in them, it means jogging in them, or better still running on the shop's treadmill in them. I have seen countless runners who have been sold inappropriate shoes that affected their running style and comfort and led to unnecessary injuries.

Having found a suitable pair of shoes, don't keep using them after they've lost their cushioning and support. Buy a new pair before your old pair has worn out so you can alternate and get used to the new ones gradually. It's always best to have several pairs on the go at any one time. A change of shoe is as good as a rest, not only for your body, but for your feet as well. It's always useful—and sometimes vital—to have different shoes for different surfaces and conditions.

You may also hear recommendations to replace your shoes after a certain number of miles' worth of wear. Again, this type of hard-and-fast guideline is misleading. How your trainers show wear depends on the type of shoe, the composition and thickness of the sole, the cushioning system (whether gel, air, wave, etc.), and your weight. It's very hard to generalise. But use your fingers to feel whether the sole has any resilience left, and check for uneven wear patterns. It's like a car tyre: If it's bald or misshapen in one place, it needs replacing.

RUNNING KIT

It is very important, whether you're injury-free or have a little niggle, to keep your limbs warm, and keep yourself warm generally. Sometimes I see runners out in the cold wearing as little as they possibly can. I suppose they tell themselves they're going for a long run, so they'd better not wear too much. They'll generate their own heat. But I don't think they ever warm up—not the way you should. Their core is warm, but those poor old legs: Wrap them up! Look after them!

My advice would be to err on the side of wearing too much rather than too little—especially in the British climate. Warmth is good for your muscles and joints, and it does a lot to prevent injuries. I used to see sprinters wearing two or three track suits to warm up in, even when the weather was quite warm. That's because they didn't want to get hurt.

> ' To help prevent injuries, wear the right kit. Have a care for your muscles and joints and keep them warm before, during, and after your sessions. '

Distance runners aren't sprinters, and they're less vulnerable to sudden muscle pulls. But muscles that are warm and elastic work better than ones that are cold and stiff. I nearly always did my steady runs in a track suit. Sure, there were some steady runs in the summer when I'd just be in shorts and a singlet. But I'd always wear a track suit to warm up in before doing reps and then, very importantly, for the warm down. And if I were competing today, I would even do my reps wearing compression tights unless it was warm. They enable you to run fast and keep warm—just what you want. And then when you come to a race and strip off, you feel the added benefit of being lighter, cooler, and looser. Many muscle injuries are triggered by getting cold and stiff after a run, not by the strenuous activity during the run itself. Make sure to warm up and stretch before your run or your reps, and jog a bit and stretch to cool down afterwards.

Don't be afraid to stop and stretch during a run, either, if you feel the need. One of the biggest myths among everyday runners is that once you've started a run you mustn't stop—and certainly mustn't be *seen* to stop. Don't think that stopping in training is a defeat of some kind! On the contrary, if you've got a good reason to stop, by all means do so—guilt-free.

Stopping for a quick stretch certainly qualifies: You want to run loose and free.

And after you warm down, put some warm, dry clothes on! Don't stand around chatting while your muscles get cold and tense. Look how the trainers of horses—and even dogs—look after their charges after a race, immediately wrapping them in blankets to keep them warm and prevent them catching a chill or stiffening up. Sometimes we're better at looking after our animals than ourselves!

LISTEN TO YOUR BODY

When something goes wrong, if you're overtired, or unwell, or feel a slight twinge—STOP! Don't be foolish. If in doubt, do less than you meant to. If in doubt, miss a session. If in doubt, pull out of a session halfway through.

If you persist when you shouldn't, you're cutting your own throat. You're not making yourself faster with your bull-headed determination. You're setting yourself back.

Having said that, I think a lot of people are *too* cautious, or as my good friend and long-time training partner Peter Barratt would say, 'overprecautious!' You don't need to go to the extent of saying, 'Oh, dear, my heart rate's up a little today. That must mean I'm tired, so I'll skip today's training.' You know there's nothing wrong with you. You're not injured. Get out there and train!

Of course, as with so much of running, there's an art to it. You don't want to be too bold, but you don't want to be too wimpy. You've got to go with how you feel. But if you're still in doubt after warming up, pull out. Rest to train again another day.

VARY YOUR PACE

Perhaps three of the most common mistakes made by middle-of-the pack runners are: They avoid running fast when they train. None of their training sessions are easy, either—everything's medium. And they think running involves only their legs. All of these mistakes increase their risk of injury—and these often are genuine over-use injuries.

I said earlier that the idea the most running ailments are overuse injuries was largely a myth. And I stick by that. Nevertheless, overuse injures do occur—and the surest way to get them is to fail to vary your pace.

Want to avoid getting hurt? Don't always run at the same pace on the same surface with the same range of movement and the same style. Running at different speeds has a more beneficial training effect—and it also helps prevent injuries. And when you try to sprint at the end of a race when you're tired, you don't want it to be something you've never really tried before. For injury prevention, make sure to include some fast sessions in your training.

Don't get carried away with going harder and further each day, either, with each week a step up from the one before, just building and building and building. You need easy days, and you need easy weeks. The best way to ensure progression is to overload—*and recover.* Without the recovery, you'll just get stale, ill, and injured. Athletes should not think of planned down time as non-training, but as a part of the training itself. It's only non-training if it's enforced downtime caused by injuries.

And upper-body strength? You don't run with just your legs: Your back, shoulders, arms, and stomach play vital roles in maintaining posture and stability, and in channelling power to your legs. Weight training, circuit training, cross country running, and hill running should all be included in your training at certain times of year. They help develop the strength needed to run fast. And they help make you resilient enough to withstand the stresses of training.

I'm convinced that everyday life can be more hazardous than running. It is very often the things you do when you're not training—which is the vast majority of your life—that trigger injuries that become apparent only when you run.

If you always carry a bag on the same shoulder or in the same hand, that can make one side of your back tighter than the other. And what about driving, constantly working the clutch with your left leg? An imbalance in your back almost invariably leads to leg problems when you try to run.

It's the same for women who always carry their babies on their left hips because they're right-handed, or for people who sit at an angle from the computer all day, or who spend a lot of time holding the phone to their ears with their shoulders, or stand on one leg and lean against the bar.

The list is endless. It even includes some sports. Tennis is a one-sided, one-armed game, and probably isn't really compatible with running. So's cricket. People get stiff backs from sweeping snow off the driveway or digging in the garden, or painting the ceiling with one arm reaching overhead. And perhaps the absolute worst movement of all is lifting kids in and out of rear car seats. It's hard to avoid, but be careful!

People are often quite tense without being aware of it. If you asked everybody to just stop what they were doing and relax, would their hands be relaxed? Their elbows? Their shoulders?

'Oh, no', they'll exclaim, 'I didn't realize I was still tense there!'

That's just normal life. Just try to be aware of it, and every now and then take a deep breath, heave a sigh, and see if you can relax yourself.

And small things when you're running can throw you out of balance and lead to big problems. Even a tiny blister or a broken toenail can make you limp and land differently on that foot.

Same with cambers: Don't always run on the same side of the road. Switch sides now and then, at the very least. Better still: Try to run in the middle of the road, if it's a country lane with not much traffic. I used to run on the roads a lot in the evenings around the various RAF stations where I was based. It would be so dark I couldn't even see the verge. But if a car was coming, I could easily see its lights. So it was perfectly safe running in the middle of the road, where I'd be on the flat, not on the camber. And I figured I was probably less likely to step in a pothole, as well.

The thing about being unbalanced is that it creates problems elsewhere, especially when you run. In my experience a great many leg injuries, like knee, calf, and Achilles problems, have their origins elsewhere—either above or below the site of the actual pain. Unless you've banged your leg or wrenched it, the problems almost always come from the back, hips, and glutes down, or from the feet and ankles up, which in turn is often due to the way you land on each foot. And that's largely controlled by the strength and suppleness of your back, the balance of your hips and pelvis—and, of course, the shoes you're wearing.

I'm not implying that athletes are such highly-tuned thoroughbreds that they haven't got the resilience to cope with the slightest thing that knocks them off balance. But be aware of what you're doing. Switch the bag from shoulder to shoulder. Switch the baby from hip to hip. Maintain good posture, whether standing, sitting, walking, or working. Don't always cross your legs the same way. And stop holding the phone to your ear with your shoulder. Being aware of balance in all of these everyday activities can help you avoid running injuries.

WHEN INJURIES DO OCCUR

Despite our best efforts, we runners do get injured from time to time. Sometimes there are freak accidents. You can trip on a kerb or twist an ankle. I hurt myself falling a couple of times. Steve Cram famously tripped over a can of Coke once and twisted an ankle. Steve Ovett never seemed to get injured until he got tangled up with some church railings—and from then on he was never quite the same again.

Other injuries aren't due to accidents so much as laziness or lack of awareness. Perhaps you think a tight calf muscle will just ease off on its own, but instead it gradually leads to an inflamed and swollen Achilles tendon. Or you might try to squeeze the last miles out of a favorite pair of trainers that have lost their shape and cushioning, and end up with a calf or knee injury.

Clearly running is not risk free. You cannot always avoid cambers. Cross country, for all its benefits, can lead to twists and strains—not to mention bruised heels—as I know only too well! Your hamstrings may protest, especially the day after a race, if you were having to yank your feet out of the mire with every step.

When an injury does strike, the most important thing is to remain positive. Don't lose heart. It's easy to say of course, and I know from personal experience how tempting it is to throw your toys out of the cot and sulk, thinking, 'If I can't run, I don't want to do anything. I'll cheer myself up with a few beers and watch rugby, cricket, cycling, or whatever.'

But if you start worrying and telling yourself you're not as fit as you were and you're losing more of your fitness with each passing day, that's pretty negative. You're just focusing on things you can't do much about.

Instead, focus on what you *can* do. That's the challenge. There's nearly always something you can do yourself to aid and speed your recovery.

Caring for yourself when you're injured is a full-time job. It's funny; it's like discovering that being unemployed is a full-time job. You probably need to work harder when you're out of a job than when you have one, searching, applying, interviewing, and so on.

And so it is with running. If you're fit and training twice a day, you might be spending an hour and a half, maybe two, on your running every day. And everything's hunky dory.

But when you're hurt, don't just leave it all to somebody else. You need to spend time treating the injury yourself, applying ice, stretching rigorously, doing specific strengthening exercises, maybe driving yourself to the therapist, and perhaps travelling to the pool or the gym so you can maintain your overall fitness. All that can take more time than your regular daily workouts do when you're healthy. But it might well be the measure of whether you end up becoming a good runner or staying a mediocre one.

❛ Treat your injures—even the minor ones—rather than just ignoring them and hoping they'll go away. ❜

A running injury is not like a cold or the flu, where you just hang around and rest and wait for things to get better. Just because you think *overuse* caused it, which may not be the case at all, don't think *underuse* is going to put it right. Getting back to fitness takes work.

Even if you've just got a niggle and you're planning to run through it, still treat it. Ice it regularly, maybe even two or three times a day. Massage it and knead it to stimulate the blood flow. And for goodness sake, wrap it up, and keep it warm—both when you're running and when you're not.

It can be hard to tell whether or not to run through an injury. When you've overdone it a bit, maybe in a cross country or a tough road race, you're bound to get some stiffness. When that happens, a lot of people will tell you to just run it off. Well, sometimes that works and sometimes it doesn't. Often after a hard race, both of my calves would be stiff. Nice steady runs would often ease one calf and make the other worse. So what do you do? Like so much of running, caring for yourself and getting yourself back to full strength is a matter of feel and judgment and often comes down to experience and knowing your own body.

One rule of thumb would be: Don't limp. Limping will do you no good at all, and will only cause secondary problems. But if your niggle feels better as the run goes on and you're able to run without limping, that's good. Just go a mile or two, and stop before you overdo it. If it doesn't feel good, stop and walk back. There's no point in forcing it; you'll just make it worse. Either way, keep treating it with ice, self-massage, stretching, compression, and by keeping it warm.

'If the injury gives you any real trouble, see a sport massage therapist or physiotherapist. Go sooner rather than later; don't let it linger for months. And you'd also be very wise to visit a sport massage therapist regularly while you're healthy, as one of the steps you take to ward off injury.'

A sport massage therapist can identify imbalances and treat them before you're aware of them and before they develop into injuries. And anyway massage loosens you and relaxes you so you can run more freely.

I found this was really useful when I was competing. Usually before every big race, say four or five times a summer, I would get a massage on my back and legs. It would be part of the build-up; it had nothing to do with being injured. It was to help me feel looser and run faster and prevent injuries. I found it most helpful to have a massage two or three days before the race. And I'd often have one a few days after the race as well, because I found that really helped me recover.

I am now a sport massage therapist myself, and almost invariably when people come to me for treatment, whatever their pain or injury, the cause stems from their back. Most people have a lot of tension in their shoulders, sometimes unevenly. And the back also takes a huge amount of strain, not only from the impact of landing, but also from the exertion of lifting the knees. You can't really avoid that in running.

Despite this, runners' backs are often weak and stiff. That often means the lower back is arched, and the stomach is going to 'hang out' a little more. This will make it harder to tuck and pick the knees up, which in turn makes it harder to run correctly, flowing along with a cycling motion. This results in their footfalls becoming heavier, leading to jarring and sometimes even stress fractures.

This is an area where a sport massage therapist can be very helpful. Because if you get rid of the tenseness in the shoulders and the stiffness in the back, that relaxation can spread through the whole body. You'll feel better, you'll be able to breathe more easily, and you'll have much more spring in your step when you run. Even standing still will feel more comfortable.

If it's important to see a sport massage therapist when you're well, it's even more important to see one—or else a physiotherapist—when you're hurt. As I've said, a great many leg injuries have their roots elsewhere, quite possibly in a part of your body that doesn't appear to hurt at all.

I've treated many runners who have come to me saying they've got Achilles trouble—but nearly always they've had calf trouble first, and they think the calf has got better. But the calf hasn't been working properly and maybe has lost some of its elasticity, causing the Achilles to take extra strain. Also, the calf problem will almost certainly have caused the balance and movement of the foot to change, and running exacerbates the problem and can start to affect the Achilles tendon, causing the sheath around it to swell—nature's way of protecting it. Once the Achilles tendon gets swollen it can be very painful, and it takes a long time to heal due to its very poor blood supply, and the fact that it's very difficult to rest it. Standing, walking—even driving—can aggravate the tenderness.

Achilles pain is what these runners have become aware of. But the initial cause can often be traced back to the calf, and that is the root problem that needs to be treated. And often that can be traced to how the foot has been landing. And that in turn goes back to the back, hips, and misalignment in the pelvis, often making one leg appear longer than the other, thus causing a slight limp, or a similar effect to running on a camber.

Or let's say your knee is killing you and unbeknownst to you the cause is tightness in the ITB—the iliotibial band, down the outside of your thigh—which is pulling the kneecap slightly off-centre, causing it not to track properly. If that's the case, you can ice you knees from now until kingdom come, but unless you identify the source of the problem you won't find any lasting relief from just treating the symptoms. Of course identifying the problem isn't enough: Sometimes you need an expert to treat it. It might be something you just can't treat yourself.

Let's take tightness in the ITB again; it's a common cause of knee pain. Well, tightness is easy to fix, right? Just do some stretches. Yes, there are stretches you can to for the ITBs: You'll find a couple of good ones in chapter 5. But often the problem is a knot or spasm in the middle of the muscle. When you do your stretches along the length of the muscle, you'll often succeed in stretching the parts that are already loose and elastic while the knot in the middle remains.

You need someone with expertise to find the spot and give it a good, firm kneading, maybe getting the thumbs in there a bit and breaking the knot down. You may soon find the knee feeling a lot better.

Some parts that get injured have poor blood circulation. As massage therapists, we try to increase the blood flow, to encourage regeneration and promote healing where there might be knots, muscle spasms, or torn muscle fibres.

Essentially, massage therapists try to relax the muscles, squeeze them, and loosen them. It's a bit like gently tenderizing a steak. The muscle tone, elasticity, and circulation are a lot better when the muscle has been softened up.

> ❛ There are other experts to see when you are hurt, as well. Often, a good osteopath or acupuncturist can help fix persistent injuries. ❜

Skeletal imbalance is another example of a condition that causes injuries elsewhere. The imbalance might be because of your posture, or it might be that the spine and the bony structure of the body is a little bit out of alignment. The bones can move slightly, especially in the feet and—particularly after a fall—in the pelvis and back.

If the spine is realigned correctly, the muscles can often relax and loosen themselves up. The tension they've had from been held in the wrong position has been relaxed. Suddenly you can hold yourself properly and your body can work efficiently again. So sport massage and osteopathy are very complimentary.

And you can sometimes get the same sort of effects—in terms of relaxation, rebalancing, and perhaps even re-energising—through acupuncture. I know people tend to be sceptical of it. And I was, too.

The first time I went to see an acupuncturist was almost by accident. He had been trained as a physiotherapist, and John, my regular physio, had recommended I go to him, as I had been posted up to Lincoln with the RAF.

'He's a great physio, but he's gone off the rails a bit', John told me. 'He does acupuncture now. Just don't let him stick any needles in you!'

Well, within two minutes of going through the door, I had needles in me! I can remember thinking, 'Oh, no, what have I done?' But it turned out to be a brilliant treatment and not painful at all, and I've benefitted from regular treatments ever since.

Many massage therapists give very effective treatments working on acupressure points with their hands, but hands cannot always be as precise as a needle.

That's one of the beauties of acupuncture—how precise it is. It's the pattern of the needles that makes it so effective. You can have 10 or 15 needles in you and then the acupuncturist puts that last one in and you just *know* it's in exactly the right spot. You can feel the relaxing effect. It's like the relief of finally reaching an itch and giving it a scratch: 'Oh, yes, *that's* the place!'

As with all these treatments, it's not just the therapy, it's the therapist that makes the difference. Anyone can give you a massage. Anyone can crack your bones about. Anyone can stick needles in you. What matters is how well they've been trained and whether they make the correct diagnosis and give the right treatment. You can go on a two-week acupuncture course to learn needling techniques for pain relief, or you can go on a full three-year course. There's a slight difference.

Get recommendations, whether from fellow runners or from other professionals. And if the people you're going to see are runners themselves, so much the better. They'll know exactly what runners need, which is definitely *not* the usual doctor's advice to rest and come back in three weeks if it's not better.

SURGERY—A LAST RESORT

There's no doubt that surgery has saved many careers, from Kelly Holmes, the double Olympic gold medal winner, to Paula Radcliffe, the women's world record-holder in the marathon, and countless other athletes, as well.

I remember a wonderful place just outside Slough, near London, called the Farnham Park Rehabilitation Centre. It was a residential facility where you would go after a serious injury—often involving an operation—and follow a full-time rehabilitation programme. Absolutely fantastic. The main man there, Dr. John G.P. Williams, was a sport injuries specialist and a pioneer of Achilles tendon operations.

In 1975, I had badly sprained an ankle which had been put in a plaster cast for three weeks. And I was lucky enough to get into Farnham Park for my rehabilitation. I couldn't run at all for three weeks after getting out of the cast. The ankle had stiffened up so much that at first it was difficult even to walk. But the place had a terrific full-time programme that, over a period of several weeks, took you from beginner to advanced level as your rehab progressed, finishing with extremely demanding circuit training. By the time you came out, you were super-fit. Although running was difficult for several weeks, I found I *could* do other activities—doing specific foot and ankle exercises, working on a foot-driven lathe, cycling a jigsaw, and getting physio treatments twice a day.

By the end, I was able to jump, play volleyball, and of course run. It was a good example of how a return to full fitness requires work—a concerted effort—not just treatment and rest. Six weeks after leaving Farnham Park, I was on the England cross country team and really flying again.

I know from what I saw there that surgery can fix people who thought they'd never be able to compete again. But it carries risks and it shouldn't be done lightly.

One of the other patients who was there at the time was a girl who had won the English Schools 1,500 metres in 1970, the same year I won the 5,000. We had both gone on to compete in the Schools International in Dublin, but I hadn't seen her since then. Although she'd run quite well in the meantime, she had picked up an Achilles injury and had just been to Dr. Williams for surgery. It had been a fantastic success.

She was so pleased with the result that she reasoned it would save her time and hassle to have the other one operated on there and then, rather than returning to training, getting fit, and then needing a second operation (which she thought would be inevitable) in a few months time. So even though there was no problem, she went straight in for a second operation, hoping she'd then be guaranteed a future without Achilles problems.

Well, who knows what kind of logic that was, or why Dr. Williams agreed to do it. But the second operation did not go so well, got infected, and led to all manner of complications. And I don't think she ever really ran properly again. What a waste of talent!

So operations are fine as a last resort. But *only* if necessary. Stay away from the knife if at all possible!

FIND OTHER WAYS TO KEEP IN SHAPE

When you can't run because of injury, work out anyway. If you want to be as good a runner as you can, don't lose all your hard-earned gains. Stay fit by other means. Nearly always, you can still swim. I've had runners tell me they hate it, they can't swim, and so on. But it gets you out of breath, it pumps the blood round, and it's very therapeutic. You don't have to be *good* at it. In fact, the worse you are, the more you'll get out of breath. And that should be one of your main goals—finding something that raises your heart rate and gets you breathing hard.

I'd stay away from doing the breast stroke too much, because that gets your neck and shoulders very tense, and the kick can aggravate your groin and knees. But front crawl or back crawl are really good for you. And if you can't do them, learn! There are plenty of swim classes out there.

Personally, I would say that swimming is far better than just doing aqua-jogging, where you're trying to run without your feet hitting the ground. Aqua-jogging is OK, I suppose, but it strikes me as pretty demoralizing. It's hard work, and you're not going anywhere. But swimming can be fun; you can measure improvement. It helps you stretch out. And it will get you working just as hard as, if not harder than, aqua-jogging.

Often if you've got leg problems, you can still do upper body work in the gym to keep your strength up without aggravating your injury.

Also, you might still be able to cycle. I obviously couldn't swim while my ankle was in plaster, so I tried a bit of biking in an effort to keep the aerobic fitness that I had.

I managed to borrow a bike from a friend. I'd wrap a plastic bag round the cast to keep it dry, and off I'd go. Not for long rides, just a series of one- or two-minute efforts, so that it was similar to the reps I might have been doing had I been able to run.

And this was in the dark, up at RAF Cranwell. Looking back, I must have been a bit mad—it was not a good idea. My ankle didn't work too well when it was in a cast! I could easily have come off the bike and done further damage to myself. A stationary bike in the gym would have been a much better idea. But my aim was to keep my blood pumping round and to keep getting out of breath so as to lose as little aerobic fitness as possible, and that's what I did.

You don't have to be as crazy as I was, but at all costs, don't just sit there and mope. Do something to keep yourself moving. Walk, swim, or go to the gym. Even table tennis can help keep you active.

One word of caution: After you've been injured, don't try to come back into full training too quickly. Ease gradually back into running again to avoid further setbacks.

Generally speaking, I would suggest you get back to steady running for a week or 10 days before you start doing anything harder. But obviously if you are trying to get fit for a race, you might have to accelerate this timetable. It depends on how long you've been off running and how much fitness you've lost.

If you master the art of avoiding injuries insofar as possible, and of caring for yourself well when you do get hurt, you'll lose less time to injuries and be a better athlete for it. In what seems like no time, you'll again have that sense of well-being—that feel-good factor—that running injury-free can give you in such great measure.

KEY POINTS TO REMEMBER

- Running well requires consistent training. When you're healthy, make it your business to prevent injuries and proactively treat the niggles.
- Run in shoes that provide support, stability, and cushioning—and that are right for the way you run.
- Run correctly—tall, relaxed, and balanced. And run on soft surfaces whenever possible.
- Wear the right kit. Keep your muscles and joints warm, before, during, and after your sessions.
- Always warm up and always warm down. And stretch before and after your sessions.
- Don't be foolish. If in doubt, do less than you meant to. If in doubt, miss a session. If in doubt, pull out of a session halfway through.
- Don't think faster running is more likely to cause injuries. Vary your training speed. Don't just jog; run fast sometimes. But be sure to build easy days and easy weeks into your schedule.
- Pay attention to what you do when you're not running. Everyday activities that stress you more on one side than the other leave you unbalanced, and imbalances lie at the root of most injuries.
- Treat even your minor injuries rather than just hoping they'll go away.
- If an injury gives you real trouble, don't let it linger. See a qualified a sport massage therapist, physiotherapist, osteopath, or acupuncturist.
- When you can't run because of injury still keep active if you can. Swim, cycle, walk, or go to the gym—do anything to work your heart and lungs. Maintain your fitness for when you are able to run again.

Chapter 12

All in Your Head

Running is an art in so many ways. You must tune into your body, pushing it hard yet heeding its warnings. You need to master momentum and balance, timing and tempo. You must be able to exert maximum effort while staying fully relaxed.

And yet to some extent it's easy to get yourself physically ready to run your best. As we've discussed, there are plenty of ways to develop the five Ss—speed, strength, stamina, suppleness, and skill—even though not everyone will become an artist as great as Ovett, Gebrselassie, or Bekele.

But we come now to the sixth factor—psychology—a component perhaps more important than any of the others. Here the need for artistry is greater still: No one gets it right all the time. But the best sportsmen have the knack and skill of focusing, concentrating, and getting it right on the day that matters.

To some extent, strange as it may seem, I don't think your absolute peak psychological performance can be achieved intentionally. The best we can do is to learn about ourselves as individuals and try to create the conditions that will allow our motivation, relaxation, concentration, and determination to fully emerge on the day it matters most.

Certainly, the power of the mind is extraordinary. When I won the English National Cross Country Championship, I was fit and running well—that's obvious. But for me to win by two minutes, running 13 seconds per mile faster than some of the most accomplished runners in the world, something else had to be at play. Or was I just consistently underperforming the rest of the time?

On another level, think of the phenomenal long jump by the American Bob Beamon at the Mexico City Olympics in 1968. Throughout the 20th century, the world record in the long jump had been broken, on average, by two and a half inches. On that magical day, Beamon broke it by nearly two feet—far beyond what he thought himself capable of and beyond even the limit of the measuring equipment officials had on hand.

And we hear about similar events in daily life. In December 2009, a 5-foot-7, 185-pound guy in Kansas saw an 8-year-old girl trapped under a Mercury sedan and lifted the car off her. The guy told the Associated Press that he tried lifting cars after that to see what would happen. Surprise, surprise—it didn't work. The psychological conditions weren't there for him to perform at that level.

The point is that *all of us* are physically capable of far greater feats than we think, if only we can harness the power of the mind. What makes this happen can be difficult to say. When I won the National, my focus may have been enhanced by anger at having been excluded from the Olympic team and relief at being able to run again after I'd injured my heel. The thoughts of the guy in Kansas were clearly focused by a life-or-death situation. And heaven only knows what was going through Bob Beamon's mind.

But there are a number of things we can do to make ourselves mentally stronger, and to give ourselves the best chances of being psychologically fit and aggressive on the day of the race.

> ❝ Make your training targets demanding but achievable. And once you've set them, don't disappoint yourself. Just get out there and do it! ❞

Psychological training takes place in every session you do. Each session you miss or fail to complete undermines your self-belief and accustoms you to not achieving your goals. Over time this can be extremely damaging.

On the other hand, every session you complete, every little challenge you rise to, adds to your self-esteem and confidence. That's particularly true of the tough cross country runs where perhaps half way up a hill you may be not be sure you can make it all the way up without walking—but in the end you do. Every time you train, you're rehearsing either quitting or pushing on through. It's much better to practice the latter. If you've said you're going to do it, then do it. If it's written on your schedule, get it done.

It's easy to start feeling guilty about family and work. You might think you're being seen as too focused or too selfish. But you've got to have it in your mind that you're prepared to do all the other things you should, but you will still do the things you promised yourself. And that's an end to it.

It's easy to listen to friends at work who urge you to have a beer at lunchtime, when you had planned to get in a session. It's easy, as well, to look outside at the elements and wonder if it's worth it. But if you start missing your training, psychologically it's a small thing that grows and grows. You don't want to get used to giving up or taking the easy option.

Instead, you want to think: *'I'm an athlete.* I'm stronger than that. If it's raining, it doesn't matter. If it's snowing, it doesn't matter. I'm going to get out there and train.'

Of course, if you're not feeling well or the conditions are awful, you don't have to stick to exactly what the session was going to be. Adapt it. Your main aim is to do something that's good for you. But at least by getting out there you're being tough and mentally disciplined. Your self-esteem and belief will be enhanced, not diminished. Go for it!

6 Be organised before the race and give yourself plenty of time to avoid last-minute hassles that detract from your focus. 9

As a big race approaches, you may find your focus narrowing in, especially on the morning of race day. I remember right from my earliest days at school, if I had a race on Saturday, I'd start to feel excited, even a little nervous, on the Friday afternoon. And a bit of nervousness is good.

I'm not talking about being so nervous you can't perform. But being slightly nervous means the race matters to you, and to some extent that's what the sport is all about. You *want* the stakes to be a little bit high. If you have butterflies because the team is depending on you or because you think you have a chance to do something special—something better than you've ever done before—that's great.

But being nervous and being frazzled are two different things. I think we've all had races where things went wrong—maybe there was too much traffic or the train was late. Maybe the car broke down on the way to the race. Maybe you had trouble parking, and when you finally got where you needed to be, you couldn't find the loo or figure out where to pick up your number.

I know I've had some race days like that. And worrying about whether you'll make the start takes something out of you. It uses up energy, detracts from your focus, and knocks your confidence.

Sometimes these things can't be helped. But to get the best out of yourself physically, you really have to be organised and relaxed mentally, but also up for the race. Cool, calm, collected, and confident—that's the Steve Cram combination. If you go in disorganised, you can find yourself feeling tense and shaky. It's a shame to put in all that training and then be unable to perform to your potential.

Go over in your mind what you want to accomplish. As you find the nerves kicking in, ensure you keep cool. Take a deep breath and concentrate on keeping relaxed. And be flexible enough not to be thrown off-stride if for some reason you're unable to follow your normal pre-race routine.

It is very important to go into a race in the proper frame of mind. And it doesn't just happen by itself: You do need to work at it. But I question the mental visualization approach suggested by many sports psychologists. If you're getting ready to run the London Marathon, I don't think it particularly helps to visualise yourself running across the finish line in first place, as though it's a dream and you're trying to make it come true. I just don't think that's relevant or realistic.

But I think you *do* need to visualise what you're going to do before the race and what you're going to do during it. Plan when, and what, you're going to eat. Visualise where you're going to warm up and when and where you're going to do your stretching and pre-race strides. And plan where you're going to leave your bag and kit. It helps to keep everything relaxed and in order.

As for the race itself, it is important to have a plan, and not just see how it goes. You can visualise where you're going to make a move or how you're going to react if a rival makes a move first. You can visualise what you think your rivals may do, and ways of reacting to, or pre-empting, their moves. It certainly helps to visualise what you plan to do at key points on the course, and to recall previous races where you did things right (repeat those) or wrong (don't make the same mistakes again). Prepare yourself mentally for the race by rehearsing how you expect to feel at certain key points: Think of where you'll have to work to maintain your concentration and not allow yourself to 'fall off the wave.'

Concentration is a big part of mental strength. I used to mentally rehearse how I would respond to what other people might do in a race—or how I would avoid repeating previous mistakes. I'd ask myself, 'How in the world did that guy beat me last time?' I let him get away slightly and thought it didn't matter because he was only two or three metres ahead, and I thought I'd have time to make up the ground. But, as so often happens, the elastic stretched just a bit too much. You have to prepare yourself to react quickly, not just when you feel like it.

So I would tell myself as I concentrated on the race ahead: It's essential to react quickly! Don't hesitate! Don't doubt yourself! Go with him! Close the gap immediately. And *that's* the part I tried to visualise. That's where the race is won or lost. Not as you cross the line waving to the crowd!

Don't focus in on the race to the point of obsession, though. It's well documented in almost every sport from darts to pole vaulting that if you try too hard, your performance goes down.

Some people get too tense and worried, and that inhibits them. For you to do well, things have got to flow. Look at Tom Daley. When he was 13 years old, he won the British 10-metre platform diving championship. Shortly afterwards, he won gold in the European Championships. And later that summer, having achieved the ripe old age of 14, he finished seventh in the Beijing Olympics.

He doesn't have time to think: His performance just has to flow. That's true for runners, as well.

So your mental preparation should be geared toward getting yourself excited but relaxed. Everybody's different in what they need to do to achieve that. Some people talk a lot, some people joke, some don't talk at all. Some people want to be in a crowd, other need to be alone. Some feel they need to walk about while others prefer to lie down.

The art of it is getting to know yourself—how you respond to different situations and what works for *you*. Some of the guys I raced with used to like watching a *Rocky* film before a race to get themselves all pumped up. Seriously. Very often, certain music can help get you in the right frame of mind. For me before the National it was the Dire Straits album 'Making Movies'—especially and very fittingly, as it turned out, the song 'Skateaway'. And the British middle-distance runner Kelly Holmes used to choose a favourite track that would be her theme for a meet and listen to it over and over. For the 2004 Olympics in Athens, she chose 'If I Ain't Got You', by Alicia Keys. It might not have worked for me, but she won gold in both the 800 and the 1,500—becoming only the third woman ever to achieve that double—so it worked for her.

And look at the antics of the incredible sprinter Usain Bolt. Before races, he's manic. He's a talker and a showman. Maybe some of that is meant to psych out other competitors. If I tried acting like that, I'd lose concentration and wouldn't feel comfortable at all. But look at his results: Three Olympic gold medals and a world record in the 100 metres kind of says it all.

But generally distance runners have very different psyches to sprinters. My habit was to be more inwardly focused. Certainly, you should try to ensure you're in your own comfort zone, and not made to feel uncomfortable by the antics of others. As a junior, I'd often be in the company of Dave Bedford. Not as a hanger-on, just that I'd travelled to the race with him and Bob Parker. Looking back, although this helped me in many ways, this was obviously not my preferred option. Instead of being forced to follow him, I learned that I needed to do things my way. I needed my own space.

That's true of a number of athletes. The Russian pole-vaulter Yelena Isinbayeva—a two-time Olympic gold medallist—puts a towel over her head to block out the outside world and gather her thoughts before she competes.

I didn't sit around before a big race with a towel over my head. I tended to be pretty quiet, but in no way did I just relax and switch off. Years ago I used to see an eminent and somewhat eccentric Harley Street doctor who claimed to have healed some patients with inoperable diseases simply by faith, by the power of the mind. He tried to teach me how to tune into this vast, untapped reservoir of power, and control my mental state by relaxing and generating certain kinds of brain waves that could be detected and measured on a machine. If an athlete is able to emit more alpha waves and fewer beta waves he or she can reach an ideal state that is relaxed yet focused. Maybe that's what we call being 'in the zone.'

The science of that is a little beyond me. But this doctor encouraged me to try and find a quiet place where I could lie down and concentrate on completely relaxing every part of my body. When that was accomplished, I could start to focus mentally on the race, on how determined I needed to be, what my tactics were going to be, how I would cope with other runners' tactics, and that sort of thing.

It's hard to say whether that works or not, but when I managed to do it, it seemed to help me. The problem is that it's hard to find a place to do it. It's no good if the only place is out in the rain, or on an uncomfortable wooden bench in the gym where everyone's walking around, or at major championships, in the athletes' reporting room with a lot of nervous people looking at each other.

So, whatever your preferred preparation is, it's quite important not to be thrown if you find yourself unable to follow it. I've known people who think, 'Oh, God, I haven't had my favourite food! I can't run until I've had my muesli!' Sometimes you have to compromise and adapt and keep things in perspective. It's not the end of the world. Go with the flow. Make the best of the situation you are confronted with.

Everyone's different, so there are no hard and fast rules. You have to come to know yourself. Before the race, the state you want to be in is relaxed, focused, thinking clearly, and in control. You should be pleasantly nervous and looking forward not just to a fight, but also a performance.

Body language is important, both before and during a race. If you're suffering during a race, at all costs don't show it. Looking bad encourages your rivals, but looking good can demoralise them. Remember they are probably feeling just as bad as you are. And if you convince them you're feeling OK, they may start to tail off. As soon as that happens, you'll start to feel considerably better.

Anyway, if you run like you're in distress, it's counterproductive. If you're clenching your teeth and your neck's tense and your arms are tight and you can't breathe, you're making it harder for yourself. You'll be much better off if you hold it all in and continue to flow despite the discomfort. All the best athletes make it look so easy, don't they? Believe me, they are usually masters of disguise.

Dave Bedford won the Amateur Athletic Association 10,000-metre title five years in a row, from 1970 to 1974. And for at least one of those titles, he was nowhere near fit. Yet that year he still beat Bernie Ford, an excellent runner and future Olympian. And Bernie was in good shape at the time.

I wasn't at that race but I know Dave. He would have been acting the part beforehand—he was a master of kidology, or bluff. And whatever he was feeling in the race, he would have concealed it. When you have a reputation as fearsome as Dave's was and you don't look like you're hurting, that can dishearten even a runner like Bernie.

Dave said afterward that it was a race he definitely should not have won. Which goes to show you that physical fitness isn't everything: The way you carry yourself during a race matters. Your psychological fitness, your pride—call it arrogance even—is reflected in your body language and can often help you defeat runners who really ought to beat you. And sometimes, running on memory can make up for a lack of fitness. As in poker, it's not always the player with the best hand who wins.

If you can hide your distress from others, you might be able to hide it from yourself, as well. Your outer confidence can seep into your inner thoughts and buck you up. That way, you'll have a better chance of getting through the bad patch until your running starts flowing again. But *always*, when you're suffering, go back to the basics. You're not after more effort, but more *skill*. What you need is to regain your control, balance, and timing. Good technique will help you through a bad patch.

The goal, of course, is to be fit both physically and psychologically: That's when you can achieve something special. So be confident, and encourage yourself. Because you've proved in training and in those tough cross country races that you have stickability and determination, and you can do it. Be certain in the belief that if it's hurting you that's not such a bad thing, because it's hurting everyone else, too. Maybe they're suffering even more than you are.

You can take a lot of encouragement from seeing other people suffering. Not in a sadistic way, but it's nice to know other people are finding the race as hard—or even harder—than you are. There will be times when someone comes past you and you think, God, he's doing really well. But hang in there, because five minutes later, you may be passing him if he's over-reached himself and come unstuck. And that's a lovely feeling that can revitalise you and help speed you on your way.

‘ **Don't drop out of a race unless there's really no other choice. If you don't think you're well enough to race, don't line up at the start.** ’

The problem with dropping out once is that it makes it more likely that you'll drop out again. I've seen that happen a lot, especially with kids, but with adults, too. One year, they'll be great. Then the next year they'll drop out of a race—perhaps for a legitimate reason, like illness, glandular fever, or whatever. But having allowed themselves to drop out once, the danger is that they will do it again and again.

I remember Graham Side, a top junior 800- and 1,500-metre runner, a really nice guy. He was unbeatable one year. But he dropped out of a race or two the following year, and then for a long while it became almost a rarity for him to finish a race.

‘How long do you think he'll last in tonight's race?’ his rivals would joke beforehand.

And after reading Athletics Weekly the following week and not seeing his name in the results, they'd say, ‘I thought Graham was doing that race.’

‘He was’, someone would answer, ‘He must have dropped out again!’

Because for a while Graham completely lost it. Dropping out had become such a habit, his confidence was at rock bottom, and he was expecting the worst as soon as the race got tough.

Now, the first time, he might have had a nasty illness, and he might have had no choice but to drop out. But in that case he shouldn't have been lining up for a race in the first place. Racing became hopeless for him because everybody knew that, with a little bit of pressure, he'd be gone.

That's why you daren't go into a race just thinking, ‘Well, I'll try again and just see if it works out tonight.’ You don't want dropping out to be an option. You want it to be inconceivable—you've never done it before, and you're not going to do it now. As with training, you're rehearsing either quitting or persevering. Just as you want to build psychological strength by completing your workouts, you want to do the same with your races, to prove to yourself you can do it even when things get difficult.

Perhaps if you're going to drop out of a race, doing so in the marathon is the most excusable. The most vivid example of this mental toughness and refusal to quit was my friend Steve Jones's performance in the European Championships marathon in Stuttgart in 1986.

He was the overwhelming pre-race favourite following a series of wins in Chicago (twice) and London. On a hot day, and maybe a bit overconfident, he set off at a fast pace and, at the 20-mile mark, he was more than two minutes clear of the rest of the field. But he had a problem with his drinks, got dehydrated, and finished—bravely but futilely—in 20th place. Not often, but sometimes, especially in the marathon, it might be better to drop out and live to fight another day.

❛ Establishing a rhythm is good but don't let it lull you to sleep. Learn to break out of your rut and run even faster as the race progresses. To learn this skill, practice changing pace in your training sessions. ❜

It's funny: Sometimes the hardest thing isn't going fast, it's breaking out of the rhythm you've been maintaining. You feel that you ought to be able to go faster. But you feel you're stuck in a rut. A slower rhythm can be difficult to get out of.

On occasion, something happens in the race to shake you out of your torpor. Otherwise, you have to find a way to wake yourself up—maybe by getting mad, maybe by just forcing yourself to do it.

It can happen to anybody. I remember once in the RAF Cross Country Championships when I was racing against Steve Jones. It was a six-mile race, and for the first three miles, I was struggling to live with him. In the end I just couldn't: In the next mile, he pulled right away from me. With two miles to go, I was well beaten. He was off in the distance over 100 metres clear, and I was pretty much throwing in the towel.

And then something happened. Quite suddenly I got my rhythm and timing back and started to flow. It was almost like finding the proper gear. More speed with less effort! Fabulous feeling! Steve wasn't faltering but I was closing the gap. And I thought, 'This is getting exciting! I could yet catch him!' It turned out to be a very exciting race. I caught him with a half-mile to go and—for once—managed to out-sprint a rival at the end!

That wasn't tactics. Nobody gets that far behind on purpose. Having let myself get that far adrift, I had no control over the outcome. So in that sense, I didn't deserve to win the race. But it was a case of never say die, and I managed to shake myself out of the rut I'd got locked into and get going again.

It just happens sometimes that you just get into a slower zone, and slower zones can be quite hard work, even though you know you can go faster. And when you do manage to make the change, going faster can almost feel easier.

You'll see that sort of thing sometimes in races when you least expect it, when people suddenly break free of their lethargy and come from a long way back. I remember a guy named Tony Staynings, who wanted to make the British Olympic team in the 3,000-metre steeplechase in 1976.

In the trials, I can remember, he was probably in sixth or seventh place with a lap or a lap and a quarter to go. There was no way you could say that he was running a tactical race. He was completely and utterly beaten. And all of a sudden he woke up and just stormed round. And he won the darn race! It was unbelievable!

And British marathoner Paula Radcliffe let herself get passed by the Ethiopian runner Gete Wami in the final mile of the New York City Marathon in 2007. Wami opened up a gap and normally, if you get passed in the final mile of a marathon, that's the end of it. But Radcliffe seemed to suddenly wake up. She bit down, increased her tempo, sped by Wami—and beat her by 23 seconds.

You often get that feeling in long races, like a marathon or a long cross country: You're in equilibrium. It's almost like you can't be bothered. You think, 'I know I can go faster than this.' But it's so hard to shake yourself out of that rut, especially when you can't see the finish.

Sometimes, a hill helps—either up or down. Sometimes a different surface wakes you up, or you turn a corner and suddenly you're able to get going. Sometimes you get angry, and that shakes you out of it. Seeing the finish obviously also helps a lot. And when you get that momentum—and a lot of it *is* about momentum and gearing—you start running faster, and you find you're really moving your legs again. It's like being in a hydrofoil that can't get the skis out of the water. Once it does, it can really start to motor.

And when you manage this yourself, you'll think, 'What was that all about? It's not so difficult after all—I can *do* this.'

That's what we were trying to train for in those change-of-pace sessions with Harry Wilson. And that's why *you* should include some change-of-pace work in your training. Because it's not just physical training, it's psychological training, too. It's rehearsing what to do when your mind starts to tell you that you can't speed up, or doubts creep in and you hesitate or delay, telling yourself you don't really have to make the effort now; it can wait another lap.

So in training, *make* yourself do it time and time again. That way, when you get that lethargic feeling in a race, you'll be psychologically strong enough to have a chance to shake yourself out of it and do what you know you can do.

Be fierce. Work to develop aggression whether you're training with your mates or digging deep to get up to the top of that impossibly muddy hill in a cross country race. It helps your performance, and it opens up a dimension of the sport that makes it much more fun and rewarding.

Most athletes are competitive people, in the sense that they want to challenge themselves and their peers. Of course very few runners get the opportunity to race fiercely, unless they are in the leading group. However, I do think that you can develop this sort of fierceness in training—especially in change-of-pace sessions.

I think I was quite a fierce sort of runner when I raced, not afraid to throw down the gauntlet and attack. Even if they beat me, my rivals would know they'd been in a heck of a race. I enjoyed a good battle, pitting my mind and body against my rivals. Of course I didn't win every race I entered. But when I lost, that didn't mean I was devastated and wanted to pick up my marbles and go home and not try hard the next time. On the contrary, that was the fun of it—to be in a heck of a race!

If there's one of your rivals you particularly want to beat, and you come up short, well, game on. Go away and plan and scheme and train and get your tactics right and your aggression up. And the next time—or the next or the next—surprise him or her, be fierce and leave your rival behind.

There's no harm in being fierce. Aggression in this sense is not a bad thing. And kids just love it. I was in a number of cross country events as a kid where runners would constantly overtake or be overtaken themselves. To do this all the kids had to be pretty fierce and brave in the sense they were not giving up and were still trying to go by. It was a battle—no tactics except get to the front! And the great thing was, they did it for the fun, excitement, and challenge of it.

Training in a group or running on a team can help you develop that fierceness. You get more confident, more eager to challenge, and more willing to lay it on the line. Tough fartleks and timed reps will help you, as well, because they offer you instant feedback. It's a case of discovering what you can do. You get fiercer if you believe in yourself, if you *know* that, even though you're knackered, you're going to recover. And you know, too, from your training, that you can do that—attack and recover—more than once during a race.

Of course, you can be fierce just hanging on in there no matter what. But I think you've got to be *extra* fierce to dish out the treatment. And my philosophy usually was that it's better to get your retaliation in first, especially as I didn't have that ace up my sleeve, a devastating sprint finish.

6 Tactically, plan to make your move to suit your strengths, and to avoid playing to the strengths of your rivals. 9

That doesn't mean, though, that you have to lead early on in a race or start out ridiculously fast. Being fierce and winning takes skill, pace judgment, and tactics.

You want to have a specific plan for the race, and you want to go over it in your mind as you prepare mentally for the race. On the track this will mean maybe taking off with six laps to go, or in a 10K road race you'll go at the 8K mark, or whatever it is. You want to make a move before someone else does or at least when nobody else is expecting it.

Thinking about your plan focuses you and gets you ready.

But it's worth bearing in mind that the race rarely goes according to plan. Other runners have their own ideas, and you have to think on your feet, concentrate, and respond. Things can wind up quite different from the plans you made before the gun went off.

For example, before the English National Cross Country Championship at Parliament Hill, I definitely had a plan. I knew the course well. It was three laps—a total of nine miles—and I was hoping to be in contention with a lap to go. Then I planned to go really hard for the last three miles, perhaps starting the last lap even faster than I could sustain for the full three miles so I could open up a gap and get rid of the other guys. I didn't want the race to come down to a sprint.

Well, it didn't work out that way. I found myself out front all by myself practically from the first mile. I was never challenged. And I was delighted.

Mark Shearman, Athletics Images

Not the original plan! Julian Goater taking the lead in the 1981 national, almost by mistake.

But it could have worked out the opposite way. What if I'd been in the lead group, as I'd envisioned, and someone had really put in the boot at four miles or five? Would I have stuck to my pre-race plan and waited for mile seven? Not if I could help it.

Normally, in a 5000-metre race or longer, if you want to win the race, your job is to be in the leading group. Otherwise the second part of your plan isn't going to make much difference.

Nearly always, there will come a key point in the race where one runner or another makes a move. Then obviously, you have to go, too. Everybody tries to play to their strengths, and everybody knows the other runners' weaknesses, so there's a lot of strategy going on out there.

With my own lack of a sprint finish, I had to run the race in a certain way, and make a move at some point in the middle of a race. And all the other guys knew that. But that still didn't mean I had to take the lead early.

Even so-called plodders like me don't usually want to take off too early. Because the last thing you want is to make a move and wind up thinking, 'I've gone too soon and they've all followed me. *Now* what do I do?' That's a dodgy situation to be in.

‘ **Make your move at the last possible moment that still suits your strengths. Going too early is dangerous. And leading the whole way almost never works.** ’

I remember a European Cup semi-final where I learned that even in a slow, tactical race, a non-sprinter can do quite well by holding his nerve and not taking off too early.

The day before my race, Geoff Smith ran the 10,000 metres for GB. There were only eight runners in the race, and Smith had the fastest time that season of all eight—probably one of the fastest times in the world that year. He was a fine runner, and he'd go on to win the Boston Marathon and finish second in New York.

For that race, he was very confident. He seemed to expect to win automatically—just because he was the fastest on paper.

At the distance runners team meeting, our coach, who happened to be Harry Wilson, asked him how he planned to run the race.

'I'll probably lead the whole way', Geoff replied.

Harry said that probably wasn't a great idea, but Geoff was not particularly interested in listening. After all, he was the fastest guy in the field.

As promised, Geoff led from the gun, but he was nervous and could not get away from the field. They all just followed him, lap after lap, and overtook him at the end. It was like taking candy from a kid. He had just set them up and done all the work himself, without having any idea how he was going to drop his rivals and open up a gap. He finished last and in tears. He just could not believe it. *How the hell could that have happened?*

So the next day, who did Britain have entered in the 5,000? The old plodder, me. It was same situation: eight runners in the race. We were trying to qualify for the European Cup final, so all the British athletics press were there. They all rightly expected it would be a slow, tactical race, and therefore you needed a fast sprinter.

Several pressmen were trying to influence the team manager: 'Goater's not the right person', they said. 'He's going to come last as well in the 5,000, because it will be a tactical race, and he can't sprint', and so on. The team had Dave Moorcroft standing by, because he had already run the 1,500 the day before. Dave certainly could sprint, and if it was going to be a slow, tactical race—well, he probably would win it.

It would have been an easy option for me to succumb to the pressure and allow Dave to take my place. But I said, no, I've been selected for this race. And I've got to do it. And run a very different race to normal.

Harry and I had long talks about how to run it when all the odds were stacked against me. Leading from the start would never do. But I certainly couldn't wait for the last lap, either. It felt like a no-win situation. Maybe everyone was right: I was up against it and nervous as hell.

My thinking was that the latest I could dare to leave it was three laps to go. If I could run three minutes for the last three laps—that's four-minute mile pace—that would be hard work, not just for me, but for the others, too. It didn't seem to me that I would finish last if I could manage to do that.

So for the first nine laps, I was not going to take the lead no matter what. Didn't matter how slow it was. There were a few little bursts, but mainly it was slow. *Very* slow!

Then, as planned, with three laps to go, I took the lead. Suddenly, I did get a gap of four or five metres on the field, but some of the runners managed to pull me back, and my best wasn't quite good enough to win that particular race. But I did run very close to three minutes for the last three laps, and was very pleased I had managed to keep my nerve and stick to my plan. I thought for a while I might get third place, but I was just edged into fourth in the last few metres.

But fourth was still pretty good for the team. And for me, tactically, it was quite a breakthrough. Though it was the slowest time I'd run since I'd left school, Harry was pleased and said it was the best tactical race I'd run so far.

Obviously, I would have preferred to have won it. But I learned a lot from that race. I realised that with the right tactics a non-sprinter like me could still compete with people with faster finishes—and that there were different tactical options than just having to lead the whole way. Instead of making it easy for everyone else by setting a strong, steady pace, if I could hold my nerve, I could settle down and other runners would struggle more than I would with a change of pace. And that was an invaluable lesson to learn.

> **When you make your move, be decisive. Run hard and *commit*.**

I think a lot of people are fearful of making a move in the latter stages of a race because they're afraid of pain. They think it's going to hurt too much. But I wouldn't say it's *pain*. Real pain—sharp, shooting pain—would mean you'd have to stop running. But to do your best, you have to be prepared to inflict a little suffering on yourself. And to leave rivals behind, you have to be prepared to make a really decisive move. Gradual moves rarely work.

That's how the great ones win races. In the 2008 Olympics in Beijing, Kenenisa Bekele decided to try to control the 5,000-metre final from the start. He'd won the 10,000 a week earlier, and he probably had some of that race still in his legs. And winning the double is one of the most difficult achievements in running: No one had won Olympic gold in both the 5,000 and the 10,000 since 1980—two years before Bekele was born—when another Ethiopian, Miruts Yifter, pulled it off.

On Bekele's shoulder loomed some of the best middle-distance runners in the world. After a slow start, Bekele got serious. He led the field around for a few 63-second laps, which is not a sprint but, let me tell you, it's a hell of a good pace. With 2,000 metres to go, Bekele changed pace and threw in a 59-second lap. That took care of most of the field.

Just three men entered the final lap together—Bekele and two Kenyans: Eliud Kipchoge, who had an Olympic bronze and a gold in the World Championships to his credit, and Edwin Cheruiyot Soi, who had run 12:52 for the 5,000, well under the Olympic record.

As the final lap began, Bekele shifted into an entirely different gear and took off. The increase in speed was almost instantaneous. Soi fell off the pace immediately. Kipchoge tried desperately to hang on, but by the first turn he was already three metres behind. With half a lap to go, Bekele was 10 metres ahead and still pulling away. In the final turn, he raised his finger in the air—he was number one. In the end, the race wasn't even close.

Bekele crossed the line in 12:57, breaking the Olympic record by almost eight seconds. He'd run the final mile in less than 3:59—and the last lap in 53 seconds, a pace that equates to a 3:33 mile.

His victory was a perfect illustration of what's needed to win races. You can have all the endurance in the world, you can have good basic speed and tremendous fitness. But if you can't change pace, you're not going to win that often—or get the better of mid-pack rivals in your running club.

It's the other side of gearing, which I discussed in chapter 4. There, I talked about downshifting, going into a lower gear and keeping a nice, quick cadence to run strongly up a hill, for example. Anyone can learn to do that. And everyone should.

But I'm not going to mislead you. If shifting into high gear at the end of a race were easy, Bekele's rivals would have stayed with him on that last lap. And, for that matter, I would have won more races than I did.

It wasn't just me, either. Dave Bedford, although he set a world record of 27.30 for 10,000, couldn't change gear very well either. Bob Parker was a super coach, and still is. But he never talked to us about the proper way to change pace and, as a result, for both Dave and me it was like trying to accelerate in fourth gear. It doesn't work any better on foot than it does in a car. You have to use a lower gear to get the speed up, then try as hard as you can to push the big gear—quick cadence, long stride. It takes practice, it takes strength—and, to a large extent, inborn talent and fast-twitch muscle fibres.

Bedford at his best. A European record of 27:47 on cinders.

Dave was a superb runner. When he was in full flow, he was magnificent—strong and rangy, with high knees and good drive off the back foot. He had great technique and he would just eat up the ground in front of him with his long remorseless stride.

But the thing was, he had great technique in that one gear, not great technique for changing gears. He was quite quick—you can't argue with a world record—but when he was tired or under pressure, he couldn't produce what he needed: a change of pace. And I fully sympathised, because that was always my problem, too.

Dave did develop ways of trying to compensate for that weakness. One was to take off like a bat out of hell, straight from the gun. Since he had trouble leaving the field behind at the end of races, he often did his best to leave it behind at the beginning. However, on a blistering hot day on a cinder track at Portsmouth, running in the AAA 10,000-metre championships, he decided to be patient for once and let the race settle down. This new-found patience lasted all of one lap. The pace was comfortable but by no means pedestrian (especially in those conditions) as they passed 400 metres in 71 seconds. But it was clearly not quick enough for Dave. His time for the second lap was an outrageous 59 seconds. He still had 23 laps to run, and went on to lap every other runner at least once on his way to a European record of 27:47, an unbelievable time in those conditions, and especially after such a fast early lap.

It was outrageous how fast he ran early on in races. But Dave never won an Olympic medal. He's recognised as one of the great distance runners of the 1970s and often, going into big international races, he'd be considered the favourite. But at the 1972 Olympic Games in Munich, he managed only sixth place in the 10,000 metres, and 12th place in the 5,000. It was Ron Clarke all over again, and it just proved that you can't win a major race on the track without changing pace. Perhaps he should have gone again on lap two!

It was Brendan Foster who developed the tactic of putting in a mid-race burst, since leaving it for the end wasn't going to work, even for someone as good at 1,500 metres as he was. It proved to be a very effective tactic for him, and I knew I had to try to do the same thing, too. Naturally, it's not an easy thing to do, and it takes considerable practice in training.

One way I tried to practice for that was to run 1,200-metre repeats, running the middle 400 quite fast—say, for example, running the first 400 in 65 seconds, the middle 400 in 60 seconds, and the final 400 again in 65. That is the most difficult thing—managing to recover after your mid-race burst so that you don't just end up destroying yourself.

Changing pace decisively—pushing the big gear—takes a lot of strength, and you'll want to think about specific training sessions to gain the necessary power. If you have two runners with equal stamina, the more powerful one will win the race. Running well takes not only endurance but also strength. Develop it. What you're trying to do is increase both your cadence and your stride length. A double whammy.

When the Ethiopian woman Tirunesh Dibaba sped away from the pack on her way to gold medals in Beijing—in both the 5,000 and the 10,000, the same feat Bekele accomplished on the men's side—she didn't just move her legs quickly. She opened up her stride a lot.

Go to YouTube and watch the end of Bekele's gold-medal 5,000-metre run in Beijing. The whole race isn't there, but there are some great close-ups of Bekele running that 53-second final lap. You'll see: His legs are still going at the same cadence as before. But now he's also taking very long strides. He's pushing the big gear like nobody's business.

It's very impressive, and it's very hard to do. You have to get stronger to do it. And if you can't sprint, then try to inject a decisive change of pace in the middle of the race. Yes, there will be a bit of suffering involved. But hopefully, it will be made a lot easier because you know the other guys are suffering even more.

There's clearly more to racing than just going flat-out all the way. Be clever. Plan your tactics. I suppose to be fierce you have to be prepared to suffer. But that is *not* an awful feeling. It's actually an inspiring feeling—especially afterwards, but even during a race, if you're able to execute your plan. You hope you're inflicting even greater suffering on the other guys. And you're competing. You're really experiencing the sport.

So although you can expect to suffer in races, it's not really pain. You shouldn't mind being out of breath and sweaty if you know you're going fast. It's exhilarating! It's fantastic! This is what you're good at! This is what you enjoy doing! It feels good!

So keep pouring it on. You'll find the whole experience of getting the most out of yourself is really fun. Go for it!

KEY POINTS TO REMEMBER

- Build mental strength in training by making your targets demanding but achievable. And once you've set them, don't disappoint yourself. Just get out there and do it!

- Be organised before the race and give yourself plenty of time to avoid last-minute hassles that detract from your focus.

- Go over in your mind what you want to accomplish. You should aim to be keyed up yet relaxed. And be flexible enough not to be thrown off-stride if for some reason you're unable to follow your normal pre-race routine.

- If you're suffering during the race, don't show it. Looking bad encourages other runners—and if you convince them you're feeling OK, you might convince yourself, as well.

- Don't drop out of a race unless there's really no other choice. It can become a habit. If you don't think you're well enough to race, don't line up at the start.

- Don't let one particular rhythm lull you to sleep in a race. Practice breaking out of your rut and running faster when you need to. Fartleks are excellent training for this.

- Be fierce. Work to develop aggression whether you're training with your mates or digging deep to get up to the top of that impossibly muddy hill in a cross country. It opens up a dimension of the sport that makes it much more fun and rewarding.

- Tactically, make your move at the last possible moment that still suits your strengths. And when you make your move, be decisive and completely committed.

Chapter **13**

Reaching Your Peak

Getting it right on the day can be a mysterious process. Sometimes you feel great leading up to a race—fit, lean, and strong—but when race day comes, you're sluggish and never really get going. Other times you bruise your heel, curtail your training—and win the National Cross Country Championship, leaving Olympians puffing in your wake.

No one gets it bang-on every time. It's not possible: Some days are just better than others. But there are ways you can try to create the conditions necessary to get it right on the day and give yourself the best possible chance of turning in a peak performance when it matters most.

The idea, of course, is to find a way to take full advantage of all the physical training you've put in and all the mental toughness you've built up. Doing that involves tapering before the race, which is an art in itself because you want to leave yourself rested but not sluggish. More on that in a bit.

But beyond that, peaking involves focusing on the special event you're targeting, not as just another race but as one that's more important than all the others. It requires a long-term plan that allows you to fit in all the different kinds of training you're going to need to run the race of your life on that particular day.

PERIODISATION

The art of peaking for the big race you're really aiming for begins many months in advance, and involves periodisation—training differently during different periods of time, in progressive steps toward full readiness to race your best on the day in question.

Periodisation is about helping you surprise yourself and perform out of your skin at certain times of the year. To enable yourself to do that, you've got to progressively develop and adjust your training as you build up towards the big day. Train the same, race the same, they say. So, to fit all the building blocks of training in and run better than ever, you really need to plan and periodise your training.

Besides, training exactly the same way all year round would be boring. You'd avoid the troughs but you'd also avoid the peaks. You'd get stuck in a rut, you'd wind up mentally flat, and the fun—the feel-good factor—would be lost. Without that, what's the point?

To run your best, you're going to need a solid endurance base, a period of fairly intense quality training, some specific race preparation, and then, during the competition season, a flexible training regime that allows you to prepare for races—and recover from them—without overtiring yourself. And just as you can't address all your weekly training aims in a single run, neither can you focus on every element you'll need to race well in the course of a single month.

Periodisation does not imply radical changes from one block of training to the next. By and large, your basic pattern of training will remain the same throughout the year. In most phases, you'll still do your four or five key sessions a week: a long run, a fartlek, some sort of repetitions whether on hills or on the flat, and at least one steady recovery run. And rather than shifting abruptly from one kind of training to another, each phase should merge quite nicely into the next.

What we're looking for in periodisation is a change of emphasis. At certain times of the year, your long runs will be much longer than at other times. In certain training periods your interval training will be more intense that at others. At other times of the year, you'll want to fit more recovery runs into your training between hard and demanding races.

Periodisation involves dividing your training into six distinct phases throughout the year, each lasting several weeks. Each phase will involve a different workload and a different mental approach.

Starting after your last major race of the season, table 13.1 shows what your plan might look like.

Table 13.1   Six Distinct Phases Make Up a Typical Plan for a Periodised Year

Months	Duration (weeks)	Phase	Intensity	Mileage
Oct.	4	Active rest	Very low	Low-medium
Nov.-Dec.	4-6	Basic conditioning	Low-medium	Medium-high
Dec.-Feb.	8-10	Endurance base	Medium-high	High-very high
Mar.-Apr.	6-8	Quality training	High-very high	Medium-high
Apr.-May	4-6	Race preparation	Medium-high	Medium
June-Sept.	10-14	Competition phase	Medium-high	Low-medium

There is plenty of scope for flexibility, depending on illness, injuries, and how your training is going. And quite possibly you'll make adjustments to this basic plan to allow yourself both a winter and a summer competition phase. But it is very important to have a plan that avoids aimless, uniform training throughout the year.

In practice, instead of planning forward from a start point, you will want to construct your plan by working back from the date of your target race. See how many months you have and, if need be, shrink the different phases to fit the available time.

But if you don't yet know the exact date of the race, you still probably know that you want to be racing from June to August or September, so you can at least plan your build-up towards this competition phase.

Let's take each of these phases in turn.

The *active rest* phase is just as it sounds. Presumably, you've raced quite a lot over the summer. You're tired, physically and mentally. You need a break. But you don't want to turn into a blob. So stay active in a relaxed and unstructured way, without putting any pressure on yourself. Just get off the sofa a little bit in whatever way you fancy.

You might swim, take a beach holiday, or do some walking. A hike in the mountains would be great. Some biking could be good, too, if it appeals to you. You'll probably still be doing a little running, but you won't go far and you won't run hard. And remember to rest mentally: There's no schedule, no goal of X number of miles per week. If you don't feel like running, take the day off. But if it's a nice day and you just can't resist, well, go ahead, do something gentle. And don't time yourself, for heaven's sake—just enjoy the day.

At the end of that period, you should feel rested and fresh—you've ticked over nicely, kept the blood circulating, rediscovered your desire, and now you're ready to move to something a little more vigorous.

Basic conditioning involves building your overall strength and making yourself a more resilient athlete. Let's face it, runners are quite strong in certain ways, but in other ways they're sort of fragile. When they do something that doesn't involve running, whether it's lifting or some other activity, they tend to feel it.

Basic conditioning is a chance to address those weaknesses. An ideal way to do this is to incorporate some gym work and circuit training, where you work your way round a circuit of different exercises—including press-ups, curls, sit-ups, dips, star jumps, squat thrusts, dorsal raises, and so on. There are many more. You might spend 30 seconds on each exercise followed by a 30-second rest, and go round the circuit three times.

You'll also start to bring your mileage up a bit during this phase, though without the high intensity you'll work into later.

I have to confess that I didn't do this sort of overall basic conditioning often enough. I did a bit when I was in the Air Force, perhaps, but the only time I really did it properly was after tearing ankle ligaments and having my ankle in plaster for three weeks. From being unable to walk, I embarked on an intensive remedial therapy and strengthening program.

I remember thinking, 'Wow, I've only had six weeks here and I haven't been able to run at all, but I feel *very* strong! We should do six weeks of this every year, even when we're not injured!'

A few weeks later I was back running well enough to be selected for the England Cross Country team for the world championships. It was amazing after having been resigned to writing off the season following the injury only three months earlier. I remember vowing to include this sort of training every winter, but moving around with RAF postings did not always allow it. But certainly it was a lesson learned.

Concentrate on all-round strength and resilience in this period of your training—core and upper body strength, in today's parlance. You'll find that, after building up this strength and resilience, you'll be able to cope with the training better—especially cross country running, where you're slipping and sliding and stumbling a bit. And you feel less stiff afterwards. So I'd really recommend it.

Having stepped up your mileage and worked on your strength and resilience, you're now ready to build the *endurance base* that will be critical to racing well. Here you'll be putting in quite a lot of miles, working on up to very high mileage. That will mean different things to different people; we're talking about whatever high means to *you*, based on what you've done in the past. But whatever the mileage, make sure you run at different speeds and, above all else, avoid plodding.

The important thing about these first three phases—active rest, basic conditioning, and endurance base—is this: Your approach should not be that you're desperately seeking top fitness. Don't feel, 'I've got to do more, I've got to do more'. Don't worry if your reps are two seconds slower than last week. Maybe it was windy; maybe you were tired.

You're just getting into a routine. Sometimes you may be running hard. But there are very few eyeballs-out sessions. You're not frantically chasing fitness. Instead, to use a phrase my coach Harry Wilson used a lot, 'You're letting the fitness come to you.' You're just doing the sessions. You're building.

That's the whole basis of periodisation—building. And in these early phases, you're getting fit enough to train hard, which is half the battle.

There's something else that bears repetition at this point: Whatever phase you're in, your main aim is to be fit enough to train tomorrow. So you shouldn't think of any of this as rigid. It's not set in stone. It's important not to arrive at the next stage, which will be quality training, super-fit but injured. That's no good at all. Just because you think you're supposed to be doing very high mileage, don't push it if you've got a worrisome niggle. No training session is worth setting yourself back that way.

Now, strengthened by the basic conditioning and that good chunk of high mileage, you're ready to go out, work very hard, and reach for fitness.

In the *quality training* phase, your repeats—your track work, your hill work, and your fartleks—will be more intense than at any other point in your program. You're going to really work on your speed, your changes of pace, and your speed endurance: all the things you need in order to race your best.

While the previous phases will constitute good preparation for any runner, here your training gets more specific depending on the event you're training for.

I've talked about the different kinds of speedwork in chapter 10. But generally speaking, runners gearing for events such as the 1,500 metres might do very fast repetitions, but not so many of them—and with long rests in between, so they can keep practicing that flat-out speed. Those gearing toward longer events, such as the 10,000, will do the reps slightly slower, but will run more of them, and without so much rest in between, so they enhance their speed endurance.

As an illustration, a top-class 1,500-metre runner might do 10 times 400 metres, each one in 56 or 57 seconds, perhaps with three minutes rest in between. But a runner aiming for the 5,000 or the 10,000 might run them in 62 or 63 seconds—but do 15 of them, maybe with only two-minute rests.

There would be a similar difference in how they would do 200-metre repeats, as well. The 1,500-metre runner might run them in 24 or 25 seconds, which is really very fast. He might run 10 of them and, since he's quite interested in true speed, he'd give himself long rests—as much as he needs in order to maintain that speed.

The runner aiming for a longer race might do more than 10. But he might be running them in 29 or 30 seconds each. And since he is quite interested in speed endurance—running fast while he's tired—he might group them into sets of three or four, with only 30-second recoveries, taking longer rests only between sets.

It is up to each runner to determine how to adapt these principles to fit his or her goals, fitness, and lifestyle. The important thing is not how many seconds a top athlete runs the repeats in. It's that your repeats, unless you're intentionally varying your pace, should all be run in approximately the same time, to within a second or two. This will be very hard, since this is the quality phase of training. But by digging deep, you should be able to run the final rep just as fast as the first one. Slowing down is not something you want to practice.

Having worked that intensely while still putting in fairly high mileage will have made you very fit. It has not, however, made you ready to race: You can't race your best when you're tired from putting in so much hard work.

What you need is a four- to six-week *race preparation* phase. You're still going to train quite intensely—after all, you want to keep your feet quick and retain your ability to cope with being out of breath. But in this phase, you may want to work more on tactics, pace judgment, and changes of pace. You'll want to focus on sessions that re-create the feelings you experience at crucial parts of a race: You might take the lead in your training group, when your ability to judge pace will be very important. You might run in a group and practice being able to run relaxed despite being closely boxed in. You'll also want to work on changing pace—which is not necessarily something you'll do only at the end of a race—and on sprint finishes. And practice these things not once, as in a race, but many times in the same session.

These sessions should give you a good indication of your strengths and weaknesses, and therefore the best tactics to use in a race. You don't want to just go into a race and see what happens. You need to be better prepared than that, and to have a more positive approach.

And during this race preparation phase, you'll want to ease down the mileage somewhat and perhaps do just one or two very high intensity sessions each week. You want to give your body a chance to absorb all your training and be fresh and ready for each of those intense sessions.

The *competition phase* poses a dilemma, especially if you plan a long racing season. The challenge is staying in top condition without making yourself too tired to race at your absolute best. Looking back, this is not something I always did to perfection. When your training is going well, it's so tempting to just keep it going. You feel great. You're in a routine. You like it. And those big weekly mileage numbers give you confidence.

But even though you feel great, you may find in those last couple of laps of a race—or the final mile of your 10K—that you feel more tired than you ought to feel. Maybe you think, 'Well, that was just a bad run.' Worse still are those races where you already feel tired just warming up beforehand!

I sometimes look back at my training diary and think, 'Wow, what on earth was I playing at, trying to run fast on the track after another 86-mile week?' I know I couldn't ease down for a race every week, and it was all good preparation for the main aims of the season, big 5,000s and 10,000s. But looking back at it, it probably would have been much cleverer to have just done 45-60 miles a week at that stage of the season.

If I had it to do over again, I'd probably do it differently. But it can be hard to hold yourself back when you're going well, and there are some benefits in keeping to your routine. You really need a coach to tell you to ease off—and that is perhaps the greatest art in coaching, judging when and how to do this.

My recommendation is to work hard and get in some good quality work during the competition season. But don't overdo the mileage and make sure you ease down sufficiently, and not just before your major races.

So periodisation is a critical element of your yearly training cycle. Following this sort of plan can bring you to the competition phase in the best possible shape.

PEAKING

But peaking for a particular race, perhaps the most important race of the year, on a particular day—this is not so simple. Of course it will involve tapering down, but it's not as straightforward as just doing less, or even nothing, for the final few days. It is a very individual thing, and to get it right, you really need to be tuned in to your physical and mental state.

What works best will be different for different people—and even different for the same person on different days. Even when you've found what works for you, you can't re-create it every time.

A race is a performance, and your mental preparation for it should in some ways be similar to preparing for other performances, like a concert, a play, or an exam. The answer is *not* to do nothing in the last few days, but neither should you do too much.

Over time, you'll find that some build-ups work better for you than others. It's important to keep a training diary so that when you race poorly—or, more happily, produce a performance beyond any you've done before—you can look back and see what you did in the days leading up to the race. Don't trust your memory; write it down.

While individual runners vary in what brings out the best in them, there are some guidelines that should help everybody. Let's start with the physical side.

Why is it so difficult to time it right? A lot of everyday runners figure the thing to do is keep training as hard as they normally do until the Tuesday or Wednesday before a weekend race, at which point they stop any kind of training altogether.

I think that's a big mistake. You're likely to leave yourself feeling sluggish. Training less can lead to lethargy, often combined with overeating. You wind up training less, yet feeling worse. Often runners who take this approach have a bad race, then feel brilliant the following day, after the race has blown away the cobwebs.

‘ To avoid this pre-race lethargy, get your recovery in early. Start tapering down a good 10 days before the race, even taking two or three days off if you find you're over-tired. And pretend to yourself the race is one day earlier than it really is. ’

There are several indicators that would suggest you've been overtraining and need to take two or three days off: If your urine is dark, it's a sign you're dehydrated. Feeling thirsty all the time or sleeping poorly or feeling that you want to eat everything in sight including the tablecloth—these too can be indicators you've been training too hard. Not to mention, of course, just how you feel generally. If you go for an easy run and you feel like you're flying, that's the feeling you want. But if an easy run doesn't feel so easy, there's something wrong.

If there are 10 days to go before the race, you still have time to do something about it. On the other hand, if you're feeling like this only a couple of days before the race, you have a problem.

The other reason to get your rest in early is that you want to be fresh not just for race day, but *before* the final four- or five-day countdown. Often, people think these last few days are the time to do nothing. On the contrary, that's when you want to be on the up again, feeling lively, and keeping sharp by doing some easy running interspersed with some fast, hard efforts.

If you need to rest, don't tell yourself, I know I'm not recovered so I'll just go for an easy run today. Because you still might not feel recovered the next day, and decide to go for another easy run. And the same the day after, and the day after that. You can end up having a whole series of days where you're just doing something fairly easy—but still just hard enough to prevent you from recovering for the next day.

Well, you get all the way to Friday and you've only got two days before the race. What are you going to do if you *still* feel like that? Just take the day before the race off and hope you're OK? Carry on regardless? It's too late. You've run out of options. So if you find yourself that tired, don't try to run through it. Get some rest. And make that decision early, so you've got time to be on the up as the race draws near.

This is the reason for pretending the race is a day before it really is, and to attack it from that end as well. I would maintain that, if you feel good the day before a race, you're going to be *great* for the day of the race. But if you're not good the day before the race, you've still got an extra day in hand. It's just another little bit of insurance.

TAPERING

Once you know you have recovered and are feeling fresh, you want to get back to your normal training routine, but with certain key differences. Most of your running should feel easy, and any intervals you do should be shorter, still fast—but with more rest and not so intense.

You might keep your steady runs easy by setting your max heart rate to 145 and making sure not to cross that line. But in your interval sessions, don't be frightened of going quite fast at times, as long as you don't run too fast too many times. That way, there shouldn't be any risk of getting too tired.

At this stage, you're training more for feelings than for fitness: If the race is now less than a week away, you have to accept you are not going to get any fitter.

It's like an exam—you can't learn things at the last minute. Any training you do on Tuesday is not going to give you more endurance or make you any stronger by Saturday. Your aim in the last few days is to make yourself feel good—physically quick, lively, supple, and mentally excited and ready to go.

You want sessions that leave you excited and confident. Though your week might be easier in general, you'll still find that doing two times 1,200 metres, nearly flat out with a good five or six minutes rest in between, can be an excellent workout three or four days before a big race. A 1,500 metre runner might try to generate this exhilaration and confidence by running three times 600 metres fast, with five or six minutes rest between each one. And throughout this period, make sure to drink plenty of water so you're fully hydrated. Lining up at the start with a borderline case of dehydration just won't do.

So long as you've recovered and are feeling on the up, it can still be fine to train twice on the day before the race—especially if you've had a long journey. Do an easy jog in the morning and a bit of stretching. Then have a relaxing day. Go out again in the afternoon or evening for a jog of two miles or so, followed by a few strides—a few times 100 metres or so, running fast and powerfully, but not sprinting.

That would be just like your race-day warm-up—only you're also doing it the day before the race, just to keep yourself loose and ready. Almost like a dress rehearsal of the approaching performance.

I remember the first race I had as a kid where I felt perfectly prepared. It was the 1970 English National Youths Cross Country Championships, in Blackpool, on England's northwestern coast. Dave Bedford was there, too—still a junior but running in the senior event. Both of us had the good fortune at the time to be coached by Bob Parker.

I'd won all my races so far that winter, so I knew I was in great shape. And Bob tapered us down really well: It was an easier week, right from the Sunday beforehand. Then on the Wednesday we did a session that was probably really designed for Dave. He did three efforts of about 1,200 metres on the road, quite fast, with five or six minutes between. And I did two of them with him.

I'd never done anything like that before. And I thought, 'Blimey, that's a bit fast! But I'll do it anyway.' And I was flying around. And I felt very good afterwards—which I'm sure was the point. The cobwebs had been well and truly blown away, but the session was not long enough to leave me feeling tired for long.

We went for a massage on the Thursday at the local football club, to loosen the legs and get any stiffness out of the muscles. And I felt even better after that. Then on Friday morning, the day before the race, I did an easy run at school in the morning, in my PE lesson. In the evening, my dad drove us up to Southport, a lovely coastal resort just south of Blackpool. We arrived after dark, probably around eight.

And Dave—typical Dave—said, 'No, we're not going straight down to have a meal. We've got to go for a jog and loosen up after the journey.' So we went out for a couple of miles, and I felt much better. After that we had an excellent meal and, although I was nervous, I slept really well.

Come the next day, I ran absolutely brilliantly, even though I say it myself! I'd never before run anything like as fast. Unfortunately, I was tripped and fell shortly after the start. I was almost back on my feet when the next wave of runners knocked me back down, and then I was pretty much trampled by the galloping herd until they had all passed. So basically I started from the back of the field of 400 runners. But it didn't take long before I was back in my stride, and soon I was absolutely flying, charging through the field and working my way back up to the front. I did get as high as second place, but had nothing left for a sprint finish, eventually getting shunted back to 4th place. Outside the medals, but satisfying nevertheless. I was well pleased, and felt sure I would have won the race had I not fallen.

That was my first introduction to producing in a race something far better than I'd ever done in training. I learned from the build-up to that performance that as a race approaches, the *feeling's* the important thing. We still kept to a regular training routine, but the different sessions, the travelling, and the sense of excitement and anticipation were added feel-good factors. Nervous? Yes. Paralysed with fear? Absolutely not!

I learned, as well, that it was safe to run really fast just a couple of days before the race. In fact, I would say that three days before the race is the key day for your final hard session, and two days before is the important time to cut back on any socialising and ensure you get a good sleep. For some strange reason the night before the race is less important, and I have heard numerous stories of athletes partying, discoing, and not getting much sleep the night before the race, and then going out and running a blinder. Not that I am necessarily suggesting this as the best way to prepare!

And I also learned it was beneficial even to run twice the day before the race. I knew straightaway that, had I not run at all that Friday evening, I would not have felt so good for the race. Of course, that easy run didn't get me any fitter, but without it I would have felt heavier and more lethargic.

Of course, the way to make a regimen like that possible in the final week is to get your recovery in the week before. It just wouldn't work if you started this regimen already tired and jaded. Then, in the last few days, train not to gain more fitness, but just to feel good—quick, confident, loose, excited, and ready.

> ❛ As a big race approaches, train for feelings not for fitness.   ❜

Don't run a personal best in training on Wednesday only to put in a sub-par performance in Saturday's race. History is littered with the dreams of excellent athletes who ran spectacular times mid-week and left themselves flat for the race. Walter Wilkinson was one of Britain's premier middle-distance men in the 1960s and '70s, and once held the British record for the mile. But he was renowned for doing his best session on a Wednesday and then being not so good on race day at the weekend.

That's not what you want to do at all.

Sure, Dave and I ran those 1,200s quite fast three days before the National Cross Country Championships. But they weren't personal bests. We didn't crawl away from that session on our hands and knees. We left ourselves invigorated, not devastated.

Clearly it's difficult to judge how fast you should be running in the days leading up to a big race. I went out for a run with Bedford in 1973, the night before he set his world record in the 10,000. It was Thursday, and he was running in the AAA 10,000 metres—the English national championship—at Crystal Palace on the Friday night. I was running in the 5,000 on the Saturday. There were rumours he might go for a world record despite have just returned from an injury. And I think Dave, being Dave, had mentioned something of the kind to the press. That would get the crowd interested. The press liked it. And it worked well for him because it created a bit of pressure, which he generally thrived on.

Besides, he could afford to say that sort of thing. No one else in England was going to give him much of a race in those days. So if he missed the world record but still won by half a minute or so, it wouldn't be the end of the world.

Ideally this Thursday, two days before my race, and having done my final sharpening session of four times 800 metres the day before I should have just been going for an easy 20- or 30-minute run. And maybe Dave, since it was just one day before his race, just should have been doing an easy run, too, along with a few 100-metre strides.

But instead Bob Parker said, 'Why don't you and Dave just go for a steady run?' He was the coach so we went out for a steady run. We kept up quite a strong pace, running through the woods, talking all the way. All that chatting showed we were psyching ourselves up and getting excited about our upcoming races. We were going fast yet hardly breathing, and it felt great. That run—five or six miles at quite a good pace—had Dave buzzing. And the next day he went out and set the world record—27:30—defeating Tony Simmons by a full 49 seconds.

Arguably, Dave had done the wrong thing on that Thursday night before the race. But again, we're talking about art as well as science. That run certainly did Dave a power of good. At that stage you need to run for feelings, not according to some rigid plan. A few days before an important race, it can be very helpful to run quite fast, leaving yourself confident, keyed up, and excited. However although I enjoyed the run, I feel I made a mistake and should have gone for a shorter, slower run that evening.

PEAK CLEAN, DON'T CHEAT

This is a hard thing to say, but I'm sure I'm not alone in feeling disillusioned with my own sport—and with others, too—because of all the drugs being used to enhance performance. Sport is beset by one revelation after another, and I think most people now view exceptional performances with a mixture of scepticism and disbelief.

Peter Hildreth, a former international hurdler and athletics correspondent, who is sadly no longer with us, had an office full of press reports, drug cheats, and many other reports of questionable and suspicious performances. He suspected almost every athlete and almost every outstanding performance. Even if he was only half right, there are still an enormous number of drug cheats out there in all sports.

I'm not naive. Cheating is nothing new. In 388 B.C., a boxer named Eupolus bribed three of his opponents to take dives in the ancient Olympics. And even then, athletes took various potions to improve performance.

Right from the beginning of the Tour de France, more than 100 years ago, there was all kinds of cheating—people interfering with bikes, cutting brake cables, hitching lifts, and doing other unscrupulous things.

During the Cold War era, cheating was rampant, particularly among the East Germans, whose drug programs even blurred the distinction between the sexes. The Finnish runner Lasse Viren was widely believed to have used blood doping: freezing blood, then returning it to the body later to increase the red cell count and improve aerobic capacity. It wasn't illegal at the time—it is now—but people still considered it cheating, ethically. Viren has never acknowledged blood doping. But he used to do almost nothing of note for four years, after which he'd emerge head and shoulders above any other runner in the world—winning both the 5,000 and the 10,000 in two different Olympics. He put it down to 'reindeer milk.'

But the Brits? We were always the champions of fair play. And in my view that is the rock on which all sport should be based. So, yes, if you like, I have to admit it. I'm British, and maybe I *am* naive.

I never believed anybody I was running against was cheating. We were led to believe that steroids and the like were beneficial to throwers and sprinters but not distance runners. But it has subsequently been revealed that there were indeed cheats competing in my races, and that leaves a bitter taste in my mouth.

I finished fifth in the 10,000 in the European Championships in Athens in 1982. Not bad—except that three of the four people who beat me were subsequently tainted. The guy who won the race, an Italian runner named Alberto Cova, later admitted blood doping—including, according to his coach, in that race. The silver medallist, Werner Schildhauer, was East German, and we know what their athletics program was like. And the bronze medallist, Martti Vainio of Finland, was caught using steroids at the Olympics two years later and disqualified.

On the one hand, I feel proud of what I accomplished and how I did it. I never took anything remotely shady. I would hate to have won any medal and constantly have at the back of my mind that I'd done it by cheating. The medal would have been a lie.

But I still feel cheated. Cheated not only by those athletes, but also by the system that allowed this to take place and, worse still, even condoned it and protected the cheats. Even with all the high-profile testing today, I believe the cheats are usually one or two steps ahead of the testers. But even when the testers catch up with them, they often get off on a technicality, or at worst are only handed temporary bans and then allowed back into the sport. What sort of deterrent is that? In my view, athletes caught cheating should be banned from all sports for life.

No wonder I've become increasingly disillusioned with international and professional sport and a bit bitter and twisted in my old age.

It's not only the top guys who cheat, and that's the reason I'm talking about it here. Everyday athletes do it, too. I know a German mountain biker who lived in California for quite a while. Not a top athlete, just a good semi-pro. And he was quite up-front in admitting he used to take human growth hormone. 'Great stuff', he said. 'It's normal out there in California. Helps keep you looking young, too. I'd still take it today if I could afford it'.

> **Run clean. Don't resort to taking performance-enhancing drugs. It's cheating, and it defeats the purpose of sport.**

The ideal of sport is supposed to be pure: honest competition and fair play. But sometimes it seems that who wins is determined not by who's the better athlete but by who's got more money or who's got the better chemist. It's not just man against man. I guess it's always been human nature to cheat, and that's a little dispiriting in itself. To my mind the essence of sport is a healthy mind in a healthy body. It's not win at all costs.

But the thing that really gets me down is this: Far from being suspicious of the possibility of producing a superhuman performance, I am the *first* to believe in the possibility of sudden breakthroughs. I know for certain that you can have a one-off, blimey performance where everything goes just right.

That's what we're all training for. That's what the advice in this book is all about—there's more to performance than just science. The psychological bit, the peaking, the hunger, and the fierceness can all combine to produce amazing performances. My performance at the National was probably one of them. Dave Moorcroft's world record in the 5,000 was another—a great time but considerably faster than any he ran before or after.

That kind of breakthrough is what I want for *you*. It's something I believe in. As I said right at the start of this book, it's the Holy Grail we're all seeking. So it kind of breaks my heart to find that, whenever I read about a top runner posting a time far faster than he's ever done before, I feel suspicious. I can't be sure whether to believe it. The profusion of drugs in sport has made me cynical.

RACING, BUT NOT OVERRACING, HELPS YOU REACH YOUR PEAK

A lot of running clubs these days put pressure on members to race week in and week out. Over time one race becomes pretty much like another and you go a bit flat: Your chances of producing an exceptional performance in the race that means most to you are diminished.

I certainly succumbed to that a bit myself. There was pressure on me to race sometimes and, besides, I *liked* to race. I definitely raced too much for my own good.

Take the World Cross Country Championships in 1981. I was racing every week in the lead-up to that race. I ran the RAF Championships midweek, and that weekend I ran a fast five-mile road race. The following week, I ran the Inter-Services Cross Country Championship, where I bruised my heel so badly. A week later, I won the English National Cross Country Championship. The next week, I won a tough six-mile cross country race for the Combined Services. And the following week, I won another six-mile road race.

And the week after that was the World Cross Country Championship. My seventh race in just over six weeks. It was not very clever.

Looking back on it, I didn't really focus on the World Cross Country Championships as I should have done. For one thing, I couldn't look past the National, because if I didn't run well there I wouldn't make it to the World Cross at all.

And in retrospect, my coach, Harry Wilson, didn't quite focus my mind the way he could have done. I think maybe, straight after the National, he could have taken me aside and said, 'Two minutes against a field like that is absolutely incredible. You're in *such* good form. You know, you can *win* this World Cross. You've got three weeks to go. There's no one in the world who can beat you right now. No more races until then.'

If he had, I might have been more focused. But peaking does involve a degree of luck, and who is to say I might have done better? That's just the way things happen. You only get one bite at the cherry. You can't look back and point fingers. Of course I knew I was in good shape. I know this sounds a bit stupid, but at the time I thought my National was just a good run. I really didn't quite realize how good it was. Perhaps I was just too happy-go-lucky. But there again, if you try too hard, your performance often goes down.

Anyway, maybe because I had to go back to work, maybe because of those two intervening races, I arrived in Madrid for the World Cross without the focus I might have wished.

In the event, it turned out to be a funny race. The course, if I remember right, was four laps, each a bit over a mile and a half. And halfway into the race, a group of Ethiopians took off like rabbits, opening up a huge gap on the rest of us. I thought, 'Either I'm running badly or those guys are fantastic.' I was running with the Australian Rob de Castella, who would set the world best in the marathon later that year. And I remember saying to him, 'Either those guys are in a different league to us, or they've miscounted the laps!'

Well, I was right. They had. Amazingly, they'd taken off too soon. And with a lap still to be run, they were trying to move over into the finishing funnel, and actually stopped when they were level with the finish line.

Suddenly the rest of us were right back in the fight. And then, bad luck, I came down with severe intestinal distress. Had that not happened, I still might have won the race. But as it was, I finished fourth, four seconds out of the medals and eight seconds behind the winner, the American runner Craig Virgin.

But that's racing. There are always what-ifs. You can think about what would have happened if I hadn't had stomach trouble on the last lap. But then you can also speculate that, had the Ethiopians not miscounted the laps, more of them would have beaten me. (One of them, Mohamed Kedir, survived the mistake to finish second.)

But I do regret not focusing more on that race in advance and skipping at least one of the two races I ran in the two weeks leading up to it. With more rest, less travelling and better focus, and had my guts not let me down, I might very well have won that race—which was, back then, the premier distance event in the world.

Your best bet is not to repeat my mistake. Don't over-race. Key in on the important races, sacrificing others if they detract from your preparations for the big one.

EXPECT MIRACLES

When you line up for a race, do you just *hope* to do well? Would you be pleased merely to run as well as you usually do in training? Or do you genuinely *expect* to do well. And are you looking for something extra, something beyond what you normally do?

Of course, the answers to these questions may well depend on the importance of the race and the standard of the opposition. But they will also reflect a much more basic attitude toward racing—and, crucially, how susceptible you are to peaking mentally and being able to rise to the occasion.

Let's put it another way. How prepared would you be to set off at a pace that you had never managed to maintain before? Would you think of starting so fast as foolhardy, as throwing caution to the wind? Or could you throw off your shackles and accept that—by reaching this higher mental plane—you can *expect* this faster pace to now feel comfortable enough to maintain?

Some athletes consider training a proving ground. They think you have to have done something in training first before you can expect to produce the same performance in a race. But others have the attitude that training is merely preparation, and that other factors beyond just fitness can be harnessed that enable people to produce performances far in excess of their normal ability or current fitness level.

The difference between these two approaches has a lot to do with confidence and self-belief, and with one's ability to let the power of the mind take over in certain situations. One approach restricts you; the other opens new horizons.

I remember one performance in 1982 that showed me not only the value of listening to your body, rather than following a rigid schedule, but also the power of the mind.

I'd had a good year in 1981. In addition to winning the National, at the end of the year I set personal bests for the 5,000 metres—13:15—and the 10,000—27:47. So I was *expecting* great things in 1982.

But the year posed a significant challenge, too: I was going to have a big 10,000-metre race virtually every month from May through October—an important race once a month for six months in a row.

I won the first of those races, the UK Championship in May, by a wide margin. The next race was the Bislett Games in Oslo, in June. The top runners in the world would be there, including the Kenyan Henry Rono, who held the world record at 27:22, so I needed to be in top form.

But it wasn't the most important race of the year. I was really aiming for the European Championships in September, and the Commonwealth games in October. But to get selected to these, I of course had to do the AAA Championship in July. So I continued to train very hard. I've got a long season, I thought. It's not time to be peaking yet.

But all that hard training, as well as over-racing and the usual hassles at work, were taking their toll.

And one Saturday morning, just a week before the Bislett Games, things unravelled. I was totally exhausted. I felt so bad I just quit my run—something I never do—after three or four miles. 'I've overcooked it', I thought. I just can't carry on. I must have a rest. And it's too late to put things right before next week: I've already screwed up the race in Oslo.

"I will always listen to my coaches," the Ethiopian champion Haile Gebreselassie told the Guardian newspaper in 2002. "But first I listen to my body. If what they tell me suits my body, great. If my body doesn't feel good with what they say, then always my body comes first."

I'm not sure I had much choice. My body was pretty insistent on what it needed.

Some friends from London were staying with us up at Harrogate that weekend. Having given up on my run, I went with them to Bettys Café Tea Rooms. And ate. Then we went out for a walk on the moors and ended up in a nice pub. And ate some more. After that, we walked a bit more, then went into a place that served an unbelievable Yorkshire tea. We ate again—not just tea and cake, but ham salad, potatoes, bread, and then jam, and then cakes, and then apple pie, and who knows what else. I felt starved. And it felt *great* to switch off from my rigorous training regimen and just live a bit more normally.

The next day, naturally, I felt very heavy and not good at all. There were only six days to go before the race. If I hadn't buggered it up by overtraining, surely I had buggered it up now by overeating. Still, I did a bit of training early that week

Mark Shearman, Athletics Images

Henry Rono—world record holder for 3K, 5K, 10K, and 3K steeplechase—setting a UK All-Comers record of 13:12 for 5K at Crystal Palace in 1981, ahead of Julian Goater.

and started to get back somewhat to my normal build-up for a big race—doing some short sharp sessions, trying to feel light on my feet and able to cope with being out of breath, an ability you need in a race.

We were leaving for Oslo on Friday. Thursday evening, I did another session, probably two times a mile, hard. I felt better than I had at the weekend, but that's not saying much. I still felt heavy and out of breath—not very good at all. I was expecting a mediocre time in Oslo. 'No way', I thought, 'would I get under 28:00.'

But the ambience in Oslo was fantastic. I had a run round the lake with Dave Moorcroft and Steve Ovett and some of the other guys, nice and easy—probably easier than if I'd gone out on my own, so that was good. (Luckily, Bedford wasn't there!) And then we did five or six times 100 metres, but instead of taking the usual 15 or 20 seconds rest, we just had nice, leisurely walks back to the start. It was great: I felt nice and loose and rangy.

After that, we went to the organisers' house for the traditional pre-Bislett strawberry party, and all the other athletes were there—pole vaulters, hurdlers, and sprinters: world class stars in every event. The atmosphere was building up nicely to the race. It was going to be a celebration, a chance to be on the stage and show what you could do.

That's what made me think a lot about how, the closer you get to the race, the more your preparation should be about feelings. You're not looking for more fitness. You want a mixture of excitement and perhaps just a little nervous apprehension.

The next day, I lined up against the best runners in the world, including Rono; the American Alberto Salazar, who's now coaching the British runner Mo Farah with such success; and Carlos Lopes of Portugal, a future Olympic gold medallist in the marathon. Rono, as I've said, was the current world record holder in the 10,000. Salazar was in the middle of a run of three successive victories in the New York City Marathon, and Lopes would go on to break the world marathon record.

There was a pacemaker, and round we went at world record pace. There was a big crowd and it carried us along, clapping and stamping in time with our rhythm. I was just ticking the laps off, feeling nice and light. It felt like surfing: I was just telling myself, don't fall off. I had no time to think about the speed. All I had to do was tuck in and hang on.

Unfortunately, I lost concentration and had a couple of bad laps near the end, and I was not in any danger of winning the race. But it was very fast. Lopes won in 27:24, just missing the world record. Salazar finished second, in an American record and a lifetime personal best. Next came the Belgian runner Alex Hagelsteens, also running a lifetime personal best and a Belgian record, followed by Rono.

And fifth was me, in a time of 27:34, which would turn out to be my lifetime best, as well—but regrettably four seconds outside the British record held by Brendan Foster, and the Shaftesbury Harriers' club record and previous world record, held by Dave Bedford.

Depending on how you looked at it, it had in the end been a great race for me, despite the troubles of the previous weekend. Even though I was overtired, I'd had time to recover the situation to some extent. I'd listened to my body—just in time! I'd trained for feelings not for fitness. And, perhaps most importantly, by the time of the race, I was excited, keyed up, and I *expected* something great.

On the other hand, it's possible that, had I not overtrained and overeaten, and had I instead got my preparations right that day, I was fit enough to have broken the world record myself.

Either way, here's the key. Expect great things of yourself. Whether you call it psyching yourself up, positive thinking or just mental preparation, this process is a crucial part of peaking. It's where the art comes in, rather than the science. This thinking plays a major role in the preparation and performance of elite sportsmen and women.

‘ **Believe in the possibilities. Believe in yourself. Expect miracles.** ’

It may be that few everyday runners recognise the power of the mind sufficiently to include it in their preparation. But I urge you to think about it. Expect miracles. If you do, they may well happen.

And on a particular day when the conditions are right and your expectations are high, you'll do something far, far better than you've ever done in training—maybe much better, even, than in any previous race. You'll have dug deep, found that you were capable of much more than you believed possible, and run to your true capabilities.

And that feeling is the Holy Grail, the goal toward which we all strive—and the ultimate feel-good factor.

KEY POINTS TO REMEMBER

- Focus on an important race months in advance and use other races to help you build up to the important one. Don't overrace.
- Develop a long-term plan using periodisation to focus in turn on different types of training as building blocks toward the peak fitness you want for that most important race.
- When you think about tapering for the big race, get your recovery in early. And pretend the race is one day earlier than it really is.
- Keep pretty much to your routine: Reduce the intensity of your training but not necessarily the number of sessions. And stay hydrated.
- In the days leading up to a race, train for feelings, not for extra fitness.
- The power of the mind can help you achieve performances far better than you've achieved in training. So believe in yourself, and expect miracles.

APPENDIX

This appendix contains sample training schedules for beginners, intermediates, good club runners, advanced club runners, and those training for a marathon or half marathon.

Training Schedule A: 10-15 Miles Per Week

A SAMPLE BASIC TRAINING SCHEDULE FOR COMPLETE BEGINNERS					
Day	Duration	Intensity	Terrain	Description	Mileage
1	20 min	Easy	Flat	Steady run	2-3
2	Rest day				
3	30 min	Varied	Undulating	Fartlek session	3-4
4	Rest day				
5	20 min	Moderate	Hilly	Steady run	2-3
6	Rest day				
7	30-40 min	Easy	Undulating	Steady run	3-5
NOTE: STOP, WALK, AND STRETCH WHENEVER YOU FEEL YOU NEED TO.					

Training Schedule B: 20-25 Miles Per Week

A SAMPLE BASIC TRAINING SCHEDULE FOR INTERMEDIATES WHO ARE COMFORTABLE WITH SCHEDULE A.					
Day	Duration	Intensity	Terrain	Description	Mileage
1	30 min	Easy	Undulating	Steady run	3-4
2	30-40 min	Moderate/hard	Undulating	Fartlek session	4-5
3	Rest day				
4	40-50 min	Moderate/hard	Flat/ undulating	Repetition/interval session • 10 x 1 min with 2 min jog recoveries • or pyramid 3, 2, 1, 1, 2, 3 min. Jog recoveries the same as previous effort	4-5
5	20 min	Easy	Flat	Recovery run	2-3
6	50-60 min	Easy/moderate	Undulating	Long, steady, continuous run	7-8
7	Rest day				
NOTE: TWO REST DAYS.					

Training Schedule C: 43-50 Miles Per Week

A SAMPLE BASIC TRAINING SCHEDULE FOR GOOD CLUB RUNNERS					
Day	Duration	Intensity	Terrain	Description	Mileage
1:AM	20 min	Easy	Flat	Recovery run	3
1:PM	30 min	Moderate	Undulating	Steady run	4-5
2	10 min warmup; 30 min run; 5 min warmdown	Moderate/hard	Undulating	Fartlek: 10-12 efforts 30 sec-3min each	7
3	45-60 min	Moderate	Undulating	Steady run	6-8
4:AM	20 min	Easy	Flat	Recovery run	3
4:PM	10 min warmup; 20 min run; 10 min warmdown	Hard	Flat	Fast sustained threshold run (20 min)	6-7
5	Rest day. Or easy 3-mile run. Or walk. Or swim.				
6	45 min	Hard	Hilly	Hill session • 12 x 30 sec • or 6 x 90 sec • or 4 sets of 1 x 90, 2 x 30 sec • or race	6-7
7	60-75 min	Easy/moderate	Undulating	Steady run	8-10
NOTE: TAKE ONE DAY OFF FOR REST.					

Training Schedule D: 70-78 Miles Per Week

Day	Duration	Intensity	Terrain	Description	Mileage
A SAMPLE BASIC TRAINING SCHEDULE FOR ADVANCED CLUB RUNNERS					
1:AM	30 min	Easy	Undulating	Steady run	5
1:PM	50 min	Hard	Hilly	Hill session • 12 x 45 sec • or 8 x 90 sec • or 6 sets (1 x 90 sec, 1 x 30 sec)	7
2:AM	30 min	Easy	Flat: grass, road, or track	Steady run	5
2:PM	50 min	Hard	Flat: road or track	Long reps • 5 x 1 mile (4 min rests) • or 6 x 800 metres (3 min rests) • or 4 sets of 4 x 400 metres (1 min rests) with 3 min between sets	8
3	60 min	Moderate	Undulating	Steady run	8-10
4:AM	30 min	Easy	Undulating	Steady run	5
4:PM	10 min warmup; 20 min run; 10 min warmdown	Hard	Flat	Fast sustained threshold run (20 min)	6-8
5:AM	20 min	Easy	Flat	Recovery run	3
5:PM	30 min	Easy	Undulating	Steady run	5
6	10 min warmup; 40 min run; 5 min warmdown	Hard	Undulating	Fartlek • 10-12 efforts 30 sec-3 min each • or race	7-9
7	75-90 min	Moderate	Undulating	Steady run	11-13

Training Schedule E: 77-83 miles Per Week

A SAMPLE BASIC TRAINING SCHEDULE FOR MARATHON OR HALF MARATHON COMPETITORS					
Day	**Duration**	**Intensity**	**Terrain**	**Description**	**Mileage**
1:AM	30 min	Easy	Undulating	Steady run	4
1:PM	60 min	Hard	Hilly	Hill session • 16 x 1 min; • or 8 x 2 min • or 6 sets (1 x 90 sec, 1 x 30)	8
2:AM	30 min	Easy	Flat	Recovery run	4
2:PM	50 min	Moderate/hard	Flat: road	Pyramid session • 5, 4, 3, 2, 1, 2, 3, 4, 5 min efforts • Recovery half previous effort time down pyramid • Half time of next effort up the pyramid	8
3:AM	30 min	Easy	Flat	Steady run	4
3:PM	60 min	Moderate	Undulating	Fartlek	8
4:AM	30 min	Easy	Flat	Steady run	4
4:PM	10 min warmup; 60 min run; 10 min warmdown	Hard	Flat: grass, road, or track	Long reps • 4 x 2 miles with 4 min recoveries • or 20 x 400 metres with 1 min rests • or 4 sets of 3 x 800 metres with 2 min rests and 3 min between sets	10
5:AM	20 min	Easy	Flat	Recovery run	3
5:PM	30 min	Easy	Undulating	Steady run	4
6	10 min warmup; 40 min run; 10 min warmdown	Hard	Undulating	Fartlek • 10-12 efforts between 30 sec-3min • or race.	8-9
7	90-120 min	Moderate	Undulating	Steady run	12-17
NOTE: KEEP THE SAME BALANCE OF SESSIONS EVEN IF YOU ARE NOT ABLE TO DO AS MUCH AS 70 MILES PER WEEK. JUST REDUCE THE DISTANCES AND NUMBER OF REPS ACCORDINGLY.					

INDEX

Note: The italicized *t* following page numbers refers to tables.

ABOUT THE AUTHORS

Julian Goater is a former world-class runner. He has competed in numerous championships, including the World Championships, the Commonwealth Games, European Championships, and World Cross Country Championships. His times for 5,000 and 10,000 metres remain among the fastest ever by a British athlete.

Since retiring from international running, Julian has been coaching runners of all abilities. His athletes continue to achieve remarkable results by improving their running technique and training methods. Julian has been active in road running, cross country running, duathlon, and triathlon. He has won gold twice in his age group at the World Duathlon Championships, and has also won the British Triathlon in his age group. He lives in Surrey with his wife, Sue.

Don Melvin is an author, journalist, and lifelong fun runner. His assignments have included coverage of the Olympic Games in Atlanta and Athens. He has also reported on international political and social topics. Don is an editor and correspondent for the Associated Press and has published, under another name, numerous novels for children. A native Vermonter, he now lives in Brussels with his wife, Rodica.

You'll find other outstanding running resources at

www.HumanKinetics.com/running

In the U.S. call 1-800-747-4457

Australia 08 8372 0999 • Canada 1-800-465-7301
Europe +44 (0) 113 255 5665 • New Zealand 0800 222 062

HUMAN KINETICS
The Premier Publisher for Sports & Fitness
P.O. Box 5076 • Champaign, IL 61825-5076 USA

eBook
available at
HumanKinetics.com